北京大学政府和社会资本合作（PPP）研究中心　著

北京大学
中国PPP指数报告
（中英双语版）

北京大学出版社

图书在版编目(CIP)数据

北京大学中国PPP指数报告:汉、英/北京大学政府和社会资本合作(PPP)研究中心著.—北京:北京大学出版社,2020.7

ISBN 978-7-301-31450-0

Ⅰ.①北… Ⅱ.①北… Ⅲ.①政府投资—合作—社会资本—研究报告—中国—汉、英 Ⅳ.①F832.48②F124.7

中国版本图书馆CIP数据核字(2020)第125869号

书　　　名	北京大学中国PPP指数报告(中英双语版) BEIJINGDAXUE ZHONGGUO PPP ZHISHU BAOGAO(ZHONGYINGSHUANGYU BAN)
著作责任者	北京大学政府和社会资本合作(PPP)研究中心　著
责任编辑	兰　慧
标准书号	ISBN 978-7-301-31450-0
出版发行	北京大学出版社
地　　　址	北京市海淀区成府路205号　100871
网　　　址	http://www.pup.cn
微信公众号	北京大学经管书苑(pupembook)
电子信箱	em@pup.cn
电　　　话	邮购部 010-62752015　发行部 010-62750672 编辑部 010-62752926
印刷者	天津中印联印务有限公司
经销者	新华书店 787毫米×1092毫米　16开本　20.5印张　304千字 2020年7月第1版　2020年7月第1次印刷
定　　　价	75.00元

未经许可,不得以任何方式复制或抄袭本书之部分或全部内容。
版权所有,侵权必究
举报电话:010-62752024　电子信箱:fd@pup.pku.edu.cn
图书如有印装质量问题,请与出版部联系,电话:010-62756370

主　　编：孙祁祥

执行主编：王一鸣

编 写 组：王立夫　董婧延　梁　月　刘蔚绮

　　　　　邵锐成　张奇琦　朱　彤

内容提要

2014年以来，按照党中央、国务院的决策部署，财政部等部门在公共服务领域推广PPP改革，建立了法律、政策、指南、合同、标准的"五位一体"制度体系，推动中国的PPP发展迈入了系统化的新阶段。

与此同时，各个省份的PPP发展并不均衡。为全面、系统管理PPP相关项目信息，财政部建立了"全国PPP综合信息平台"，其中项目信息库分管理库和储备项目库两部分。根据信息库中的数据，截至2017年年底，管理库项目数前三名为山东（692）、河南（646）、湖南（528），三者占入库总数量的26.1%；管理库投资额前三名为贵州（8 453亿元）、湖南（8 251亿元）、河南（7 870亿元），三者占入库项目总投资额的22%。各个省份的PPP数量、总投资额情况及发展状况都各不相同。①

为了能够全面客观地评价全国PPP发展情况，本书试着从宏观的角度出发，构建了一套能够反映各个省份PPP发展情况的指数。该指数力争达到以下四个目的：一是衡量当地政府保障水平，以期当地政府能够为PPP项目的运行提供更好的保障，二是反映PPP市场整体的运行状态，引导社会资金进入，给机构投资者提供参考；三是规范参与PPP市场的社会参与方的行为，使得PPP市场健康有序地运行；四是通过PPP发展空间评估

---

① 由于统计口径的原因，本书的数据统计范围仅包括中国内地（大陆），不包括中国香港地区、澳门地区和台湾地区。数据截止日期为2017年12月31日，以下同。

不同省份的发展机会。

我们经计算得到 31 个省份的 2017 年度 PPP 指数得分，按照 PPP 指数得分高低将 31 个省份划分成三个方阵：第一方阵有北京、广东、河南、江苏、山东、浙江；第二方阵有安徽、福建、贵州、海南、河北、湖北、湖南、江西、陕西、上海、四川、新疆、云南；第三方阵有重庆、甘肃、广西、黑龙江、吉林、辽宁、内蒙古、宁夏、青海、山西、天津、西藏。每个方阵内的省份先后按照字母顺序排列，与得分高低无关。

我们以 31 个省份的常住人口数量和 GDP 乘积为权重，综合考虑经济和人口因素，对不同省份 PPP 指数得分加权平均，计算得到 2017 年度全国相应的指数得分，其中 PPP 总体指数得分为 73.62 分，政府保障指数得分为 76.93 分，社会参与指数得分为 64.02 分，项目运行指数得分为 78.33 分。

通过对各个省份 PPP 指数的分析，我们得出以下六个方面的结论：

第一，从各个省份 PPP 指数排名得分情况来看，华中地区和华东地区排名较前，西北地区和东北地区排名较后。PPP 指数排名第 1 的省份比排名倒数第 1 的省份得分高出 21.94 分，80% 左右的省份 PPP 指数得分集中在 64.19 分和 75.60 分之间。

华中地区（73.33）和华东地区（72.94）的 PPP 指数得分超过 70 分，华南地区（69.09）、西南地区（69.04）和华北地区（68.63）的得分相近，西北地区和东北地区得分最低。

第二，从各个省份的政府保障工作指数得分情况来看，华东地区政府保障工作最好。其中最优秀的北京是唯一一个 90 分以上的省级行政区，得分超出倒数第 1 名 39.54 分。80 分至 90 分的有山东、江苏、广东和福建，70 分至 80 分的有 16 个省份，剩余 10 个省份的政府保障指数得分在 70 分以下。

华东地区的政府保障指数得分（79.84）高出排名第 2 的华南地区 6.23 分，这主要得力于山东、江苏、福建和浙江排名非常靠前，分别排第

2、3、5、6名。华南、华中、华北、西南和西北地区的政府保障得分相近，在73.18分和71.24分之间。

第三，现阶段PPP行业社会参与程度普遍较低，西北地区社会参与程度最低。除北京、广东、浙江、江苏等9个省份表现较好以外，新疆、福建、吉林等22个省份的社会参与指数均低于60分。①

华东、华中、华南和华北地区得分在61.22分和59.92分之间，其中华东地区社会参与程度最高，西北地区的社会参与得分最低，为51.06分。

第四，中西部省份项目整体运行指数高于东部发达地区，华中地区项目运行最佳。河南、新疆、贵州、四川、安徽等中西部省份项目运行指数排名比较靠前，分别排第1、3、4、5、6名，经济相对发达的四大直辖市排名则靠后，排在倒数后5名。

华中地区项目运行指数得分为82.87分，比第2名华东地区高5.99分。华中地区是唯一一个超过80分的地区，这主要是由于该地区的河南、湖北、湖南的排名比较靠前，分别排第1、8、9名，其他地区的得分在70.15分和76.88分之间。

第五，各个省份PPP发展程度差别很大，其中华东地区和华中地区PPP发展程度较高。山东、安徽比重庆、天津的PPP发展程度得分高出25分以上。

华东地区和华中地区的PPP发展程度得分分别为67.45分和66.62分，其余地区的PPP发展程度得分集中在58.03分和61.35分之间。

第六，各个省份的PPP发展空间差别很大，经济相对落后地区发展空间较大。PPP发展空间得分最高的贵州比最低的北京高出40分。经济欠发达省份基础设施相对比较欠缺，需要引进社会资本来参与建设。西南地区和华中地区的PPP发展空间最大，得分分别为55.46分和55.25分，华北地区的PPP发展空间最小，仅得38.46分。

---

① 本书中的"社会参与程度"是指注册地企业在全国PPP市场的项目参与情况。

根据 PPP 指数的分析结果，本书提出三个方面的政策建议。首先，在政府保障领域：从宏观和微观两个方面促进中部地区和北部地区省份的 PPP 发展；建立健全 PPP 相关的法律法规，提升法治水平；各地政府需要进一步提升 PPP 引导基金规模与项目规模的匹配度；完善 PPP 引导基金内部结构设计、防控风险，促进区域间平衡发展；需要进一步规范办事流程，提高办事效率，提升政府透明度，强化政府公信力。其次，在社会参与领域：降低融资成本，提高社会资本总体参与度和民营企业、港澳台企业及外资企业参与度；建立健全规范社会资本退出方式的法律法规，完善中国 PPP 市场建设。最后，在项目运行领域：优化资源配置，加强规范管理，保障 PPP 项目收益，防范收益不足风险；重视风险识别分配机制，加强风险防控。

尽管我们在撰写过程中，力求科学、全面、客观地构建北京大学中国 PPP 指数，但囿于中国 PPP 行业发展现状的复杂性和多样性，加之部分最新数据获取比较困难，本书作为阶段性研究成果难免有不足之处，恳请广大读者批评指正。

目录 contents

第一章　北京大学中国 PPP 指数的构建 ················· 001
　一、北京大学中国 PPP 指数编制背景 ················· 001
　二、北京大学中国 PPP 指数说明 ················· 002
　三、指标计算的原则和方法 ················· 002

第二章　北京大学中国 PPP 指数总体评价 ················· 006
　一、中国 PPP 市场各省份排名 ················· 007
　二、中国 PPP 市场不同地区排名 ················· 011

第三章　北京大学中国 PPP 指数分项评价 ················· 014
　一、政府保障指数排名 ················· 014
　二、社会参与指数排名 ················· 036
　三、项目运行指数排名 ················· 067

第四章　政策建议 ················· 115
　一、政府保障领域 ················· 115
　二、社会参与领域 ················· 118

三、项目运行领域 …………………………………………… 120

第五章　北京大学中国 PPP 指数应用 ……………………… 127
　一、PPP 指数 …………………………………………………… 127
　二、政府保障指数 ……………………………………………… 127
　三、社会参与指数 ……………………………………………… 128
　四、项目运行指数 ……………………………………………… 129

附录　北京大学中国 PPP 指数计算说明 …………………… 131
　一、北京大学中国 PPP 指数指标的确定 …………………… 131
　二、北京大学中国 PPP 指数的构建步骤 …………………… 132
　三、对原始数据的处理 ………………………………………… 133
　四、北京大学中国 PPP 指数的计算 ………………………… 133

后　记 …………………………………………………………… 135

图 目 录

图 1.1　北京大学中国 PPP 指数指标体系框架 ……………………… 003

图 2.1　北京大学中国 PPP 指数指标体系框架 ……………………… 008

图 2.2　北京大学中国 PPP 指数权重分布 …………………………… 008

图 2.3　2017 年度不同地区 PPP 指数和分项指数得分及排名 ……… 013

图 3.1　政府保障指数指标体系框架 ………………………………… 015

图 3.2　2017 年度各个省份政府保障指数得分及排名 ……………… 017

图 3.3　2017 年度不同地区政府保障指数得分及排名 ……………… 018

图 3.4　政府财政保障指标体系框架 ………………………………… 020

图 3.5　2017 年度各个省份政府财政保障得分及排名 ……………… 023

图 3.6　2017 年度不同地区政府财政保障得分及排名 ……………… 024

图 3.7　2017 年度各个省份政府服务保障得分及排名 ……………… 026

图 3.8　2017 年度不同地区政府服务保障得分及排名 ……………… 027

图 3.9　2017 年度不同地区政府法律政策保障得分及排名 ………… 029

图 3.10　2017 年度不同地区政府金融保障得分及排名 …………… 032

图 3.11　2017 年度不同地区政府公信力指数得分及排名 ………… 036

图 3.12　社会参与指数指标体系框架 ……………………………… 038

图 3.13　2017 年度各个省份社会参与指数得分及排名 …………… 039

图 3.14　2017 年度不同地区社会参与指数得分及排名 …………… 040

图 3.15	PPP 企业参与程度指标体系框架	043
图 3.16	2017 年度各个省份 PPP 企业参与程度得分及排名	045
图 3.17	2017 年度不同地区 PPP 企业参与程度得分及排名	046
图 3.18	2017 年度不同地区企业信誉水平得分及排名	048
图 3.19	社会资本融资指标体系框架	049
图 3.20	2017 年度各个省份社会资本融资得分及排名	051
图 3.21	2017 年度不同地区社会资本融资得分及排名	053
图 3.22	金融服务指标体系框架	054
图 3.23	2017 年度各个省份金融服务得分及排名	055
图 3.24	2017 年度不同地区金融服务得分及排名	057
图 3.25	法律服务指标体系框架	058
图 3.26	2017 年度各个省份法律服务得分及排名	059
图 3.27	2017 年度不同地区法律服务得分及排名	060
图 3.28	咨询服务指标体系框架	062
图 3.29	2017 年度各个省份咨询服务得分及排名	063
图 3.30	2017 年度不同地区咨询服务得分及排名	066
图 3.31	PPP 项目运行指数指标体系框架	067
图 3.32	2017 年度各个省份项目运行指数得分及排名	069
图 3.33	2017 年度不同地区项目运行指数得分及排名	071
图 3.34	PPP 发展程度指标体系框架	073
图 3.35	2017 年度各个省份 PPP 发展程度得分及排名	074
图 3.36	2017 年度不同地区 PPP 发展程度得分及排名	075
图 3.37	2017 年度各个省份 PPP 发展规模得分及排名	078
图 3.38	2017 年度不同地区 PPP 发展规模得分及排名	079
图 3.39	2017 年度各个省份 PPP 项目分布得分及排名	082
图 3.40	2017 年度不同地区 PPP 项目分布得分及排名	083
图 3.41	2017 年度各个省份 PPP 工作进展得分及排名	086

图目录

图 3.42　2017 年度不同地区 PPP 工作进展得分及排名 …………… 086
图 3.43　2017 年度各个省份 PPP 规范化程度得分及排名 ………… 090
图 3.44　2017 年度不同地区 PPP 规范化程度得分及排名 ………… 091
图 3.45　2017 年度各个省份 PPP 透明化程度得分及排名 ………… 095
图 3.46　2017 年度不同地区 PPP 透明化程度得分及排名 ………… 096
图 3.47　PPP 风险收益指标体系框架 …………………………………… 101
图 3.48　2017 年度各个省份 PPP 风险收益得分及排名 …………… 104
图 3.49　2017 年度不同地区 PPP 风险收益得分及排名 …………… 106
图 3.50　PPP 发展空间指标体系框架 …………………………………… 107
图 3.51　2017 年度各个省份 PPP 发展空间得分及排名 …………… 111
图 3.52　2017 年度不同地区 PPP 发展空间得分及排名 …………… 113

表 目 录

表 1.1　权重值层次分析法比较 ………………………………………… 005
表 2.1　2017 年度各个省份 PPP 指数和分项指数得分 ………………… 009
表 2.2　中国七大地理地区划分 ………………………………………… 012
表 2.3　2017 年度不同地区 PPP 指数和分项指数得分及排名 ………… 012
表 3.1　2017 年度各个省份政府保障指数得分及排名 ………………… 016
表 3.2　2017 年度不同地区政府保障指数得分及排名 ………………… 018
表 3.3　政府财政保障指标体系构成 …………………………………… 021
表 3.4　2017 年度各个省份政府财政保障得分及排名 ………………… 022
表 3.5　2017 年度不同地区政府财政保障得分及排名 ………………… 023
表 3.6　政府服务保障指标体系构成 …………………………………… 025
表 3.7　2017 年度各个省份政府服务保障得分及排名 ………………… 025
表 3.8　2017 年度不同地区政府服务保障得分及排名 ………………… 027
表 3.9　政府法律政策保障指标体系构成 ……………………………… 028
表 3.10　2017 年度不同地区政府法律政策保障得分及排名 ………… 029
表 3.11　政府金融保障指标体系构成 ………………………………… 031
表 3.12　2017 年度不同地区政府金融保障得分及排名 ……………… 031
表 3.13　政府公信力指数指标体系构成 ……………………………… 033
表 3.14　2017 年度不同地区政府公信力指数得分及排名 …………… 034

表 3.15	2017 年度各个省份社会参与指数得分及排名	039
表 3.16	2017 年度不同地区社会参与指数得分及排名	040
表 3.17	PPP 企业参与程度指标体系构成	042
表 3.18	2017 年度各个省份 PPP 企业参与程度得分及排名	044
表 3.19	2017 年度不同地区 PPP 企业参与程度得分及排名	045
表 3.20	企业信誉水平指标体系构成	047
表 3.21	2017 年度不同地区企业信誉水平得分及排名	047
表 3.22	社会资本融资指标体系构成	049
表 3.23	2017 年度各个省份社会资本融资得分及排名	050
表 3.24	2017 年度不同地区社会资本融资得分及排名	052
表 3.25	金融服务指标体系构成	054
表 3.26	2017 年度各个省份金融服务得分及排名	055
表 3.27	2017 年度不同地区金融服务得分及排名	056
表 3.28	法律服务指标体系构成	058
表 3.29	2017 年度各个省份法律服务得分及排名	058
表 3.30	2017 年度不同地区法律服务得分及排名	060
表 3.31	咨询服务指标体系构成	062
表 3.32	2017 年度各个省份咨询服务得分及排名	064
表 3.33	2017 年度不同地区咨询服务得分及排名	065
表 3.34	2017 年度各个省份项目运行指数得分及排名	068
表 3.35	2017 年度不同地区项目运行指数得分及排名	071
表 3.36	2017 年度各个省份 PPP 发展程度得分及排名	073
表 3.37	2017 年度不同地区 PPP 发展程度得分及排名	075
表 3.38	PPP 发展规模指标体系构成	077
表 3.39	2017 年度各个省份 PPP 发展规模得分及排名	078
表 3.40	2017 年度不同地区 PPP 发展规模得分及排名	079
表 3.41	PPP 项目分布指标体系构成	081

表 3.42　2017 年度各个省份 PPP 项目分布得分及排名 ………… 081
表 3.43　2017 年度不同地区 PPP 项目分布得分及排名 ………… 083
表 3.44　PPP 工作进展指标体系构成 …………………………… 084
表 3.45　2017 年度各个省份 PPP 工作进展得分及排名 ………… 085
表 3.46　2017 年度不同地区 PPP 工作进展得分及排名 ………… 086
表 3.47　PPP 规范化程度指标体系构成 ………………………… 088
表 3.48　2017 年度各个省份 PPP 规范化程度得分及排名 ……… 090
表 3.49　2017 年度不同地区 PPP 规范化程度得分及排名 ……… 091
表 3.50　PPP 透明化程度指标体系构成 ………………………… 093
表 3.51　2017 年度各个省份 PPP 透明化程度得分及排名 ……… 094
表 3.52　2017 年度不同地区 PPP 透明化程度得分及排名 ……… 095
表 3.53　PPP 执行情况指标体系构成 …………………………… 097
表 3.54　PPP 移交情况指标体系构成 …………………………… 099
表 3.55　PPP 风险收益指标体系构成 …………………………… 101
表 3.56　2017 年度各个省份 PPP 风险收益得分及排名 ………… 103
表 3.57　2017 年度不同地区 PPP 风险收益得分及排名 ………… 105
表 3.58　PPP 发展空间指标体系构成 …………………………… 108
表 3.59　2017 年度各个省份 PPP 发展空间得分及排名 ………… 110
表 3.60　2017 年度不同地区 PPP 发展空间得分及排名 ………… 112

第一章 北京大学中国PPP指数的构建

一、北京大学中国PPP指数编制背景

《财政部关于推广运用政府和社会资本合作模式有关问题的通知》(财金〔2014〕76号)中给出政府和社会资本合作(PPP)的确切定义:"政府和社会资本合作模式是在基础设施及公共服务领域建立的一种长期合作关系。通常模式是由社会资本承担设计、建设、运营、维护基础设施的大部分工作,并通过'使用者付费'及必要的'政府付费'获得合理投资回报;政府部门负责基础设施及公共服务价格和质量监管,以保证公共利益最大化。"

2013年中国共产党第十八届三中全会通过的《中共中央关于全面深化改革若干重大问题的决定》指出,要发挥市场在资源配置中的决定性作用。2014年以来,财政部和国家发展改革委等不断推出鼓励PPP的新政,PPP进入了发展的新阶段。财政部政府和社会资本合作(PPP)中心主任焦小平在2018年第四届中国PPP融资论坛上指出:PPP改革是一项推进国家治理现代化的体制机制变革,5年改革成效显著;只有规范发展、严控风险,PPP事业才能行稳致远;要积极规范推进,加大多样化多层次高质量公共服务供给。

截至 2017 年 12 月末，全国 PPP 综合信息平台项目库共收录 PPP 项目 14 424 个，总投资额 18.2 万亿元；其中，处于准备、采购、执行和移交阶段的项目共 7 137 个，投资额 10.8 万亿元，覆盖 31 个省份及新疆生产建设兵团，包含 19 个行业领域。

我们从宏观的角度出发，构建一个能够反映市场情况的 PPP 指数。该指数力求达到以下四个目的：一是衡量当地政府保障水平，以期当地政府能够为 PPP 项目的运行提供更好的保障；二是反映 PPP 市场整体的运行状态，引导社会资金进入，给机构投资者提供参考；三是规范参与 PPP 市场的社会参与方的行为，使得 PPP 市场健康有序地运行；四是通过 PPP 发展空间评估不同省份的发展机会。

二、北京大学中国 PPP 指数说明

PPP 是 Public-Private Partnership 的简写，我们将从资本需求方（Public）、资金供给方（Private）及双方达成的项目（Partnership）这三个方面分别建立相应的指数，指数结构具体如图 1.1 所示。

三、指标计算的原则和方法

北京大学中国 PPP 指数的计算是基于截至 2017 年年底的数据，这些数据主要来源于财政部 PPP 中心，部分数据来源于各省国民经济和社会发展统计公报、国家统计局和 Wind 数据库等。

北京大学中国 PPP 指数指标体系的设计遵循以下原则：

第一，系统性。强调北京大学中国 PPP 指数的每个指标都应反映中国 PPP 市场的主要特征，尽可能从多角度全面反映中国各个省份 PPP 市场的发展现状。未来指数研究将具有一定延展性，更大程度依据社会反馈的意见和建议进行修正、补充和完善。

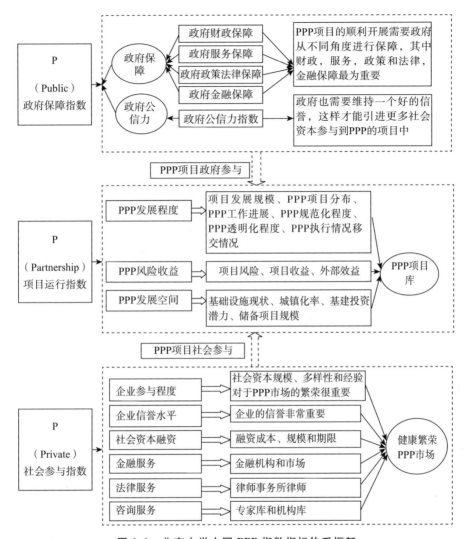

图 1.1　北京大学中国 PPP 指数指标体系框架

第二，客观性。强调对数据的科学处理，辅之以权重体系进行计算，避免指数的灰色性、模糊性和不可追溯性，力求分析方法客观、分析结果可复制。

第三，科学性。北京大学中国 PPP 指数指标体系的设计经多次专家、教授意见征集和专家教授委员会座谈确定，各指标间具有互补性，且相关性较低，避免了遗漏空缺，同时避免特征上交叉重叠。各指标相辅相成，综合涵盖 PPP 市场发展的各个方面。指标具有代表性和可比性，相差悬殊的指标不在同一类别比较。

第四，可操作性。北京大学中国 PPP 指数指标充分考虑数据来源的稳定性、数据的连续性和规范性及口径统一等原则，使评价指标含义明确，数据易于计算比较。

第五，可比性。北京大学中国 PPP 指数的设计需要对各个省份的 PPP 发展进行截面比较，即指标体系应具有可比性。

北京大学中国 PPP 指数以系统性、客观性、科学性、可操作性和可比性为基本原则，采用主观评价和客观评价相结合的评价体系，综合分析各个省份 PPP 市场发展现状。本书分析基于宏观经济的相关理论，综合运用专家法和层次分析法（Analytic Hierarchy Process）对各个省份的 PPP 市场进行分析研究。

北京大学中国 PPP 指数指标体系属于客观指标体系，该指标体系包括政府保障、社会参与、项目运行三个一级指标，分别从三个不同维度全面衡量各个省份 PPP 的发展情况。

我们在确立指标体系的基础上，进而确定各指标的权重，按照权重将各子指标进行线性加权，最终加总构成整体的北京大学中国 PPP 指数。指标权重的设定对北京大学中国 PPP 指数的最终结果具有重要影响。目前学术界有客观赋权法和主观赋权法两大类权重设定方法。客观赋权法依赖各指标的原始数据，在一定的统计标准下计算原始数据的指标权重。该方法完全不依赖于人的主观判断，因而具有较强的客观性，但其缺陷是忽略了指标的具体经济意义分析。从方法论的角度看，该方法完全依赖历史数据，其本质上体现的是历史的、后看的信息价值，而无法契合 PPP 发展的前瞻性特征。因此，为更好地满足促进 PPP 发展的导向性需求，本书以主观赋权的专家法为主，并辅之以层次分析法最终确定指标权重。具体而言，专家法通过业内专家座谈研讨方式，根据每位专家出具的权重意见及其理由，综合整理构建权重体系；权重值层次分析法如表 1.1 所示，采用两两比较的方法判断重要性不同的指标的权重值，即比较判断各指标间的相对重要性，最后综合给出各指标的权重。

表1.1 权重值层次分析法比较

指标对比	权重值比较
同等重要	相同
较强重要	较大
非常重要	最大

第二章　北京大学中国 PPP 指数总体评价

　　PPP 模式强调政府与社会资本合作，以及社会资本对项目的经营，因而具有以下优势：一是依靠利益共享和风险共担的伙伴关系，有效降低项目的整体成本，达到更高的经济效益，实现物有所值；二是 PPP 项目完工所需时间显著低于传统模式项目，具有更高的时间效率；三是 PPP 项目融资更多的是由社会资本完成，因而缓解了政府财政压力，可以增加更多的基础设施项目投资；四是社会资本在相关领域具有丰富的经验和技术，可以使得基础设施和公共服务的品质得到改善。

　　PPP 能够提高经济效益和时间效益，提供更多、更优质的公共服务。但是当前中国的 PPP 市场出现的一系列问题，使 PPP 难以发挥其应有的作用。对此财政部发布《关于进一步加强政府和社会资本合作（PPP）示范项目规范管理的通知》（财金〔2018〕54 号），并根据核查中存在的问题，对 173 个示范项目分类进行处置，以加强项目规范管理，切实强化信息公开，更好地接受社会监督。

　　在财政部 PPP 中心的指导下，我们针对 PPP 发展过程中出现的不同问题遴选相应指标，构建北京大学中国 PPP 指数，用定量的方法度量中国各个省份的 PPP 市场健康程度，并对各个省份的得分进行排序，为投资者投资提供参考，引导中国 PPP 市场健康发展。

一、中国 PPP 市场各省份排名

北京大学中国 PPP 指数旨在衡量中国各省份 PPP 市场发展的情况，以期为社会各界提供一项参考指标。一个地区的分数越高，说明该地区 PPP 发展越健康。我们的研究以省为对象，主要因为本指数属于宏观指数，意在刻画各个省份的 PPP 市场发展情况，而不是度量不同地级市的 PPP 营商环境。

北京大学中国 PPP 指数由三个一级指标构成，分别是政府保障指数、社会参与指数和项目运行指数，从三个角度刻画 PPP 市场运行状态：政府保障指数越高，说明政府在 PPP 保障上做得越好；社会参与指数越高，说明社会资本参与 PPP 越活跃，社会中金融服务、法律服务和咨询服务做得越好；项目运行指数越高，说明项目的运行质量和发展空间越大。

此外，指数的每个一级指标由多个二级指标构成：政府保障指数由政府财政保障、政府服务保障、政府法律政策保障、政府金融保障、政府公信力指数五个指标构成；社会参与指数由企业参与程度、企业信誉水平、社会资本融资、金融服务、法律服务、咨询服务六个指标构成；项目运行指数由 PPP 发展程度、PPP 风险收益、PPP 发展空间三个指标构成。北京大学中国 PPP 指数指标体系如图 2.1 所示。

在构建指数的过程中，利用专家法，三个一级指标所占权重（见图 2.2）分别是：政府保障指数占 30%，社会参与指数占 30%，项目运行指数占 40%。

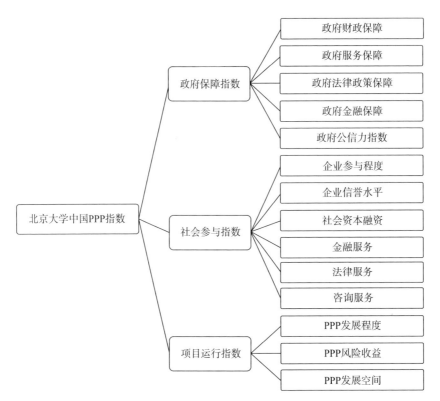

图 2.1　北京大学中国 PPP 指数指标体系框架

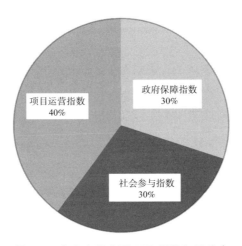

图 2.2　北京大学中国 PPP 指数权重分布

根据搜集的数据，我们计算得到北京、天津、河北等 31 个省份的北京大学中国 PPP 指数（以下简称"PPP 指数"）。为便于使用，PPP 指数及其三个一级指数都有 20 分的基本分，即在原始分的基础上加上 20 分。三级指数和四级指数均不加分。

31 个省份按照 PPP 指数得分高低被分成三个方阵（见表 2.1）：

第一方阵：北京、广东、河南、江苏、山东、浙江。

第二方阵：安徽、福建、贵州、海南、河北、湖北、湖南、江西、陕西、上海、四川、新疆、云南。

第三方阵：重庆、甘肃、广西、黑龙江、吉林、辽宁、内蒙古、宁夏、青海、山西、天津、西藏。

表 2.1　2017 年度各个省份 PPP 指数和分项指数得分

方阵	省份名称	政府保障指数	社会参与指数	项目运行指数
第一方阵	北京	93.84	90.42	62.65
	广东	80.33	73.35	73.75
	河南	71.80	64.23	86.89
	江苏	80.99	67.60	75.60
	山东	85.36	65.70	86.55
	浙江	79.79	67.75	76.21
第二方阵	安徽	76.24	54.36	82.71
	福建	80.23	59.25	77.32
	贵州	72.93	56.38	83.94
	海南	76.66	54.72	71.01
	河北	65.79	56.98	79.84
	湖北	74.49	60.03	80.89
	湖南	72.97	58.27	80.83
	江西	77.31	51.45	73.17
	陕西	69.71	51.51	77.00

（续表）

方阵	省份名称	政府保障指数	社会参与指数	项目运行指数
	上海	75.91	62.43	66.57
	四川	73.50	61.72	82.86
	新疆	74.38	59.40	84.84
	云南	78.06	55.63	82.27
第三方阵	重庆	78.99	56.27	63.42
	甘肃	73.67	50.52	68.03
	广西	62.54	54.15	72.12
	黑龙江	68.87	53.88	71.30
	吉林	63.58	58.34	75.37
	辽宁	54.30	55.33	63.77
	内蒙古	64.57	52.27	79.03
	宁夏	73.90	46.23	70.39
	青海	64.54	47.65	69.68
	山西	69.02	52.68	74.83
	天津	70.59	47.26	63.94
	西藏	60.07	46.14	70.73

注：每个方阵内的不同省份是按照拼音首字母英文顺序进行排序的，与PPP指数得分大小无关。

如表2.1所示，全国各省份中，北京排在第一方阵。这主要得力于北京的政府保障指数得分和社会参与指数得分都非常高，分别为93.84分和90.42分。但不足之处在于项目运行指数得分62.65分排在非常靠后的位置，对北京的总得分造成了非常不利的影响。

华东地区的山东也排在第一方阵。这主要源于其政府保障指数得分与项目运行指数得分很高，分别为85.36分和86.55分；社会参与指数得分为65.70分，也是一个较好的成绩。这一结果说明山东在本次测评的三个整体维度中均表现较好，且水准较为平均。此外，同属华东地区的省份，例如江苏和浙江排名也较高，也都排在第一方阵。

新疆排在第二方阵。这主要源于其项目运行指数得分较高，为 84.84 分，说明新疆拥有较好的项目运行能力；政府保障指数得分与社会参与指数得分也不低，分别为 74.38 分和 59.40 分。此外，贵州也排在第二方阵，主要也是源于其项目运行指数得分较高，为 83.94 分。

除北京之外的其他三个直辖市中，上海排在第二方阵，重庆和天津排在第三方阵，排名都不是很靠前。各个直辖市的项目运行指数得分都偏低，上海为 66.57 分，天津为 63.94 分，重庆为 63.42 分，北京则为 62.65 分，均对各市的 PPP 指数排名起到了程度不一的负面影响。此外，上海的政府保障指数得分与社会参与指数得分中等偏上，分别为 75.91 分和 62.43 分；重庆的情况也类似，政府保障指数得分与社会参与指数得分分别为 78.99 分与 56.27 分；天津二者得分都偏低，分别为 70.59 分与 47.26 分。

二、中国 PPP 市场不同地区排名

第一小节中分析了中国 31 个省份的 PPP 指数得分及排名，但是由于省份数量较多，不太容易看出不同地区 PPP 发展的差异。因此，我们根据不同省份的地理位置进行分类，求每一个区域的平均值，以进行地区间比较。

常见的分类方法一般有两种：一种是分为东部、中部和西部；另一种是分为华东、华南、华中等七大地理地区。我们通过走访 PPP 领域的相关专家发现，按照第二种方法进行分类，能够反映更多的相关信息，并且在同一个地理地区内的省份之间存在更高程度的相似性。因而我们采用第二种分类方法，详细分类如表 2.2 所示。

表 2.2　中国七大地理地区划分

序号	地区	包含省份
1	华东地区	上海、江苏、浙江、安徽、福建、江西、山东、台湾
2	华南地区	广东、广西、海南、香港、澳门
3	华中地区	河南、湖北、湖南
4	华北地区	北京、天津、山西、河北、内蒙古
5	西南地区	四川、贵州、云南、重庆、西藏
6	西北地区	陕西、甘肃、青海、宁夏、新疆
7	东北地区	黑龙江、吉林、辽宁

本报告选取不同的地理地区，以地区内各省份的平均得分作为该地理地区的得分，并进行排名，具体如表 2.3 和图 2.3 所示。

表 2.3　2017 年度不同地区 PPP 指数和分项指数得分及排名

序号	地区	PPP 指数		政府保障指数		社会参与指数		项目运行指数	
		得分	排名	得分	排名	得分	排名	得分	排名
1	华中	73.33	1	73.08	3	60.84	2	82.87	1
2	华东	72.94	2	79.41	1	61.22	1	76.88	2
3	华南	69.09	3	73.18	2	60.74	3	72.29	5
4	西南	69.04	4	72.71	5	55.23	6	76.64	3
5	华北	68.63	5	72.76	4	59.92	4	72.06	6
6	西北	66.29	6	71.24	6	51.06	7	73.99	4
7	东北	63.49	7	62.25	7	55.85	5	70.15	7

华中地区的 PPP 指数得分排名第 1，主要源于社会参与指数和项目运行指数排名相对较好，分别为第 2 名和第 1 名；政府保障指数排名相对居中，为第 3 名。

华东地区的 PPP 指数得分排名第 2，主要源于政府保障指数、社会参与指数和项目运行指数排名均相对靠前，分别为第 1 名、第 1 名和第 2 名。

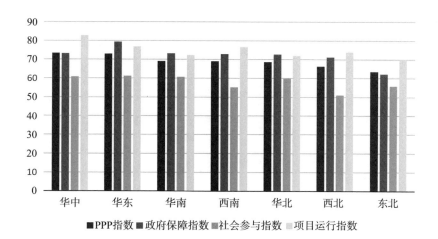

图 2.3 2017 年度不同地区 PPP 指数和分项指数得分及排名

华南地区的 PPP 指数得分排名第 3，其中，政府保障指数排名靠前，为第 2 名；社会参与指数排名相对居中，为第 3 名；项目运行指数排名靠后，为第 5 名，对华南地区的 PPP 指数得分呈现相对不利的影响。

西南地区的 PPP 指数得分排名第 4，其中，项目运行指数排名居中，为第 3 名；政府保障指数和社会参与指数排名靠后，分别为第 5 名和第 6 名。

华北地区的 PPP 指数得分排名第 5，其中，政府保障指数和社会参与指数排名相对居中，均为第 4 名；项目运行指数排名相对靠后，为第 6 名。

西北地区的 PPP 指数得分排名第 6，主要源于政府保障指数和社会参与指数排名相对靠后，分别为第 6 名和第 7 名；项目运行指数为第 4 名，对西北地区的 PPP 指数得分呈现中性的影响。

东北地区的 PPP 指数得分排名第 7，主要源于政府保障指数、社会参与指数和项目运行指数排名均相对靠后，分别为第 7 名、第 5 名和第 7 名。

第三章 北京大学中国 PPP 指数分项评价

这一章主要从政府保障指数、社会参与指数和项目运行指数三个一级指标及其指标下的二级、三级指标进行分析。

一、政府保障指数排名

(一) 政府保障指数总体评价

政府保障指数主要从多个维度衡量地方政府对 PPP 项目保障的能力。政府方作为 PPP 项目中的主导方，同时也是该领域法律法规的制定者与项目咨询融资等服务的提供者，对 PPP 项目能否合理运行起到至关重要的作用。当地政府对 PPP 的保障程度越高，该地 PPP 的发展环境就越好，社会参与者的利益也可以得到最大限度的保障。

2016 年 5 月 28 日，财政部、国家发展改革委联合下发《关于进一步共同做好政府和社会资本合作（PPP）有关工作的通知》（财金〔2016〕32 号），要求各地进一步加强部门间的协调配合，形成政策合力，积极推动政府和社会资本合作顺利实施。

政府保障指数主要从政府财政保障、政府服务保障、政策法律政策保障、政府金融保障及政府公信力指数五个方面构建，充分体现出当地政府在发展 PPP 项目方面的"硬实力"与"软实力"。"硬实力"主要指当地的经济发展水平与未来上升空间;"软实力"主要指政府对 PPP 项目采取的政策保障与优惠、政府信誉等。前者反映了当地财政资金的充裕程度,后者则体现出当地政府对 PPP 的重视程度,以及提供更加完善的服务与保障的决心,二者都是社会资本参与投资的重要考量。政府保障指数的指标体系框架如图 3.1 所示。

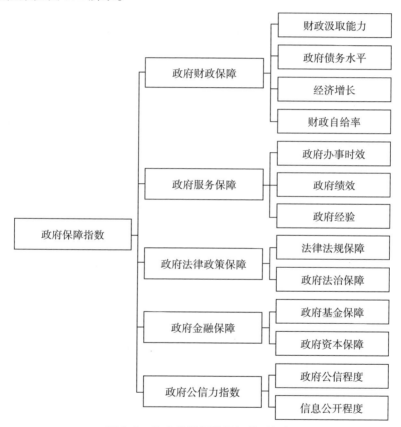

图 3.1　政府保障指数指标体系框架

地方政府在考虑是否通过 PPP 项目吸引社会资本入驻时,建议从以下四个方面进行考虑:(1) 加快发展经济,增加财政收入,减少负债;(2) 完善 PPP 有关的法律法规,让 PPP 项目开展中的一举一动尽量"有法可依";(3) 增加和提高融资服务的数量与质量,解决社会资本在项目开展中遇到的融资困难等问题;(4)减少违规腐败现象的发生,加强政府公信力建设。唯有如此,政府才可选择更优质适宜的PPP项目,并为项目顺利落地完工提供保障,使本地的PPP发展环境更加适宜,达到政府方与社会资本方的互利共赢。

我们根据搜集的数据,计算得到31个省份的政府保障指数得分,并根据政府保障指数得分进行排名,具体如表3.1和图3.2所示。

表 3.1　2017 年度各个省份政府保障指数得分及排名

省份	得分	排名	所属地区	省份	得分	排名	所属地区
北京	93.84	1	华北	四川	73.50	17	西南
山东	85.36	2	华东	湖南	72.97	18	华中
江苏	80.99	3	华东	贵州	72.93	19	西南
广东	80.33	4	华南	河南	71.80	20	华中
福建	80.23	5	华东	天津	70.59	21	华北
浙江	79.79	6	华东	陕西	69.71	22	西北
重庆	78.99	7	西南	山西	69.02	23	华北
云南	78.06	8	西南	黑龙江	68.87	24	东北
江西	77.31	9	华东	河北	65.79	25	华北
海南	76.66	10	华南	内蒙古	64.57	26	华北
安徽	76.24	11	华东	青海	64.54	27	西北
上海	75.91	12	华东	吉林	63.58	28	东北
湖北	74.49	13	华中	广西	62.54	29	华南
新疆	74.38	14	西北	西藏	60.07	30	西南
宁夏	73.90	15	西北	辽宁	54.30	31	东北
甘肃	73.67	16	西北				

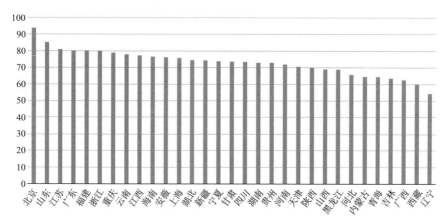

图 3.2 2017 年度各个省份政府保障指数得分及排名

位于华北地区的北京政府保障指数得分为 93.84 分，排名第 1。北京作为首都，各项二级指标得分都名列前茅，说明北京在本次指数测评的五个维度中都做得可圈可点，其中政府财政保障、政府金融保障、政府公信力指数排名都属顶尖，分别为第 1 名、第 2 名、第 2 名；政府服务保障、政府法律政策保障排名较为靠后，分别为第 8 名和第 6 名，略微拖累了北京的整体排名，说明北京在服务提供及相关法律法规制定方面还有可以进步的空间。

此外，位于华东地区的山东政府保障指数得分也非常高，为 85.36 分，排名第 2。山东各项二级指标排名都较为靠前，尤其是政府法律政策保障，排在第 2 名；政府财政保障、政府服务保障和政府金融保障均排在第 6 名，政府公信力指数排在第 8 名。

位于西北地区的新疆得分为 74.38 分，排名第 14，这也是一个不错的成绩，原因是新疆政府服务保障和政府金融保障的排名较为靠前，分别为第 3 名和第 4 名，而政府财政保障、政府法律政策保障、政府公信力指数的排名都较为靠后，分别为第 22 名、第 30 名和第 25 名，拖累了新疆的整体排名。

直辖市中排名最为靠后的天津得分为 70.59 分，排名第 21。天津各项二级指标排名均比较中庸，政府金融保障、政府公信力指数的排名在中游靠前，分别为第 12 名、第 11 名；政府财政保障、政府服务保障和政府法律政策保障的排名分别为第20名、第24名和第19名。

如前文所述，中国一般可以分为七大地理地区，同一个地理地区的省份之间存在一定的相似性，因而本书选取不同的地理地区作为整体，统计其平均得分，并进行排名，具体如表3.2和图3.3所示。

表3.2　2017年度不同地区政府保障指数得分及排名

排名	地区	本书涉及省份	平均得分
1	华东地区	上海、江苏、浙江、安徽、福建、江西、山东	79.41
2	华南地区	广东、广西、海南	73.18
3	华中地区	河南、湖北、湖南	73.08
4	华北地区	北京、天津、山西、河北、内蒙古	72.76
5	西南地区	四川、贵州、云南、重庆、西藏	72.71
6	西北地区	陕西、甘肃、青海、宁夏、新疆	71.24
7	东北地区	黑龙江、吉林、辽宁	62.25

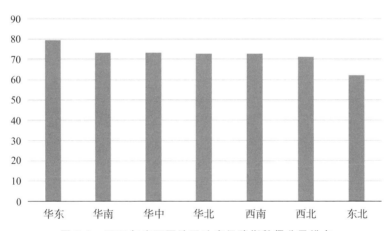

图3.3　2017年度不同地区政府保障指数得分及排名

华东地区政府保障指数排名第1，其中政府财政保障、政府法律政策保障与政府公信力指数均为第1名，政府服务保障为第2名；政府金融保障为第5名。

华南地区政府保障指数排名第 2，其中政府财政保障、政府服务保障与政府法律政策保障排名靠前，分别为第 3 名、第 3 名与第 2 名；政府金融保障与政府公信力指数分别为第 6 名与第 4 名。

华中地区政府保障指数排名第 3，其中政府财政保障、政府法律政策保障、政府公信力指数排名较高，分别为第 2 名、第 3 名、第 2 名；政府金融保障排名居中，为第 4 名；政府服务保障为第 7 名，拖累了华中地区的整体排名。

华北地区政府保障指数排名第 4，其中政府金融保障排名靠前，为第 2 名；政府财政保障与政府法律政策保障排名居中，均为第 4 名；政府服务保障与政府公信力指数均为第 5 名。

西南地区政府保障指数排名第 5，其中政府金融保障排名靠前，为第 3 名；政府服务保障排名居中，为第 4 名；政府财政保障、政府法律政策保障和政府公信力指数排名均靠后，分别为第 5 名、第 5 名和第 6 名。

西北地区政府保障指数排名第 6，其中政府服务保障与政府金融保障排名靠前，均为第 1 名；政府公信力指数为第 3 名；政府财政保障、政府法律政策保障排名靠后，均为第 6 名。

东北地区政府保障指数排名第 7，政府财政保障、政府服务保障、政府法律政策保障、政府金融保障和政府公信力指数均排名靠后。

（二）政府保障指数分项评价

1. 政府财政保障

政府财政保障主要衡量当地政府为 PPP 项目提供充裕资金保障的能力，主要考查指标为财政汲取能力、政府债务水平及经济增长等。当地经济发展水平、收入情况与债务水平都是影响政府对 PPP 项目拨款支出的重要因素，而财政资金支持的充裕与否则直接影响到 PPP 项目开展的顺利程度。政府方出资越多，社会资本方的筹资压力越小，项目开展过程中因资金链断裂而造成项目停工的风险也就越小。因此，政府财政保障是政府总体保障的重要组成部分，也是社会资本方较为关注的方面。

政府财政保障共包括四个三级指标：财政汲取能力、政府债务水平、经济增长及财政自给率。三级指标下又包含四级指标。财政汲取能力反映了当地政府的财政收入总量、财政承受能力、财政收入增长空间及稳定性，全方位衡量了地方政府的财政汲取实力。政府债务水平则主要衡量地方政府债务总量及偿债压力，与财政汲取能力相结合，分析当地政府可用的资金情况。经济增长以 GDP 增长率来衡量。财政自给率衡量的则是地方政府对中央转移支付的依赖程度。政府财政保障对政府为 PPP 项目提供资金的能力做出了较好的描述，具体指标体系如图 3.4 和表 3.3 所示。

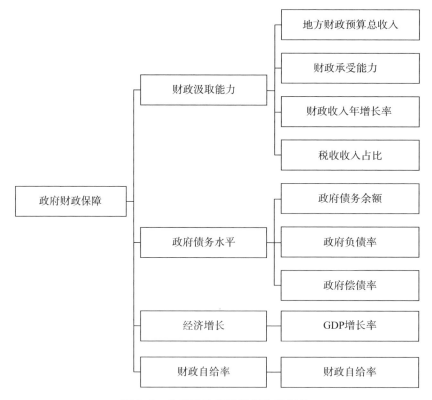

图 3.4　政府财政保障指标体系框架

表 3.3 政府财政保障指标体系构成

二级指标	三级指标	四级指标	指标的计算公式	选择该指标的原因
政府财政保障	财政汲取能力	地方财政预算总收入	地方一般公共预算收入+中央转移支付+政府性基金收入	地方财政预算收入是政府方能为 PPP 项目的开展提供的总体资金保障
		财政承受能力	一般公共预算支出×10%	中央财政和省级财政会对接近或超出 10% 红线的地区进行风险预警
		财政收入年增长率	（当年地方政府财政收入－上年地方政府财政收入）/上年地方政府财政收入	财政收入增长越快，说明当地经济发展速度越快，越有可能提供充足的财政保障
		税收收入占比	各项税收收入/地方一般公共预算收入	税收收入占一般公共预算收入的比例越高，地方政府财政收入情况越稳定，PPP 项目的资金保障越可靠
	政府债务水平	政府债务余额	直接获取数据	地方政府债务余额越大，偿债压力越大，越有可能拖欠 PPP 项目款项，造成违约；或者没有充足的资金投资于 PPP 项目
		政府负债率	地方政府债务余额/地方 GDP	地方政府还债压力越大，供给 PPP 项目的资金就越得不到保障
		政府偿债率	地方政府债务余额/地方一般公共预算收入	地方政府偿债能力越弱，偿债压力越大，供给 PPP 项目的资金就越得不到保障
	经济增长	GDP 增长率	直接获取数据	GDP 增长率反映了当地经济发展增速，经济增速越快，越有利于 PPP 项目发展
	财政自给率	财政自给率	地方一般公共预算收入/地方一般公共预算支出	财政自给率越低，说明地方财政对中央转移支付的依赖程度越严重，越有可能发生提供给 PPP 项目的资金不足的情况

根据搜集的数据,我们计算得到全国31个省份的政府财政保障得分,并根据得分进行排名,具体如表3.4和图3.5所示。

表3.4 2017年度各个省份政府财政保障得分及排名

省份	得分	排名	所属地区	省份	得分	排名	所属地区
广东	74.13	1	华南	西藏	51.14	17	西南
北京	68.83	2	华北	陕西	48.51	18	西北
浙江	67.25	3	华东	云南	44.29	19	西南
上海	66.59	4	华东	天津	43.77	20	华北
江苏	65.47	5	华东	广西	43.36	21	华南
山东	62.89	6	华东	新疆	43.08	22	西北
重庆	58.53	7	西南	海南	40.96	23	华南
福建	57.43	8	华东	黑龙江	39.33	24	东北
湖北	57.15	9	华中	宁夏	38.16	25	西北
河南	57.14	10	华中	吉林	37.73	26	东北
江西	55.36	11	华东	贵州	37.00	27	西南
四川	53.06	12	西南	辽宁	32.28	28	东北
河北	52.58	13	华北	甘肃	28.91	29	西北
山西	52.48	14	华北	内蒙古	27.22	30	华北
安徽	52.43	15	华东	青海	24.18	31	西北
湖南	52.12	16	华中				

政府保障指数得分的前五名分别为广东、北京、浙江、上海和江苏,得分分别为74.13分、68.83分、67.25分、66.59分和65.47分。得分的后五名分别为贵州、辽宁、甘肃、内蒙古和青海,分数分别为37.00分、

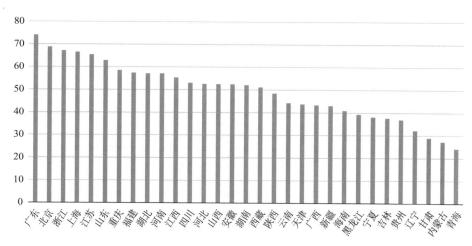

图 3.5　2017年度各个省份政府财政保障得分及排名

32.28 分、28.91 分、27.22 分及 24.18 分。整体来看，政府财政保障得分与当地经济发展状况呈明显的正相关关系。经济发达省份，政府财政收入较高、偿债压力较小，政府财政保障水平较高、得分更高；经济欠发达省份，政府收入较低、财政压力较大，政府财政保障水平较低、得分更低。不同地区的政府财政保障得分及排名如表 3.5 和图 3.6 所示。

表 3.5　2017年度不同地区政府财政保障得分及排名

排名	地区	本书涉及省份	平均得分
1	华东地区	上海、江苏、浙江、安徽、福建、江西、山东	61.06
2	华中地区	河南、湖北、湖南	55.47
3	华南地区	广东、广西、海南	52.81
4	华北地区	北京、天津、山西、河北、内蒙古	48.98
5	西南地区	四川、贵州、云南、重庆、西藏	48.81
6	西北地区	陕西、甘肃、青海、宁夏、新疆	36.57
7	东北地区	黑龙江、吉林、辽宁	36.45

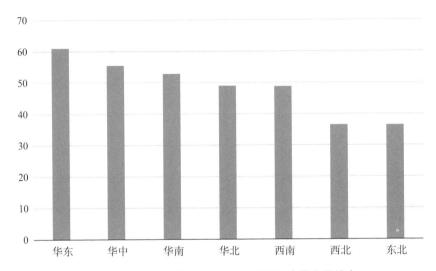

图 3.6 2017 年度不同地区政府财政保障得分及排名

如表 3.5 和图 3.6 所示，华东地区的政府财政保障得分最高，为 61.06 分；其次是华中地区和华南地区，分别为 55.47 分与 52.81 分；政府财政保障得分最低的地区为东北地区，为 36.45 分。全国各省份政府财政保障平均分为 49.46 分，华东、华中、华南三个地区位于平均水平以上，华北、西南、西北、东北四个地区位于平均水平以下。从得分结果来看，地区经济发展状况对政府财政保障得分有明显的正向影响。华东、华中等地区经济发展增速较快，水平也较高，带来了更高的财政收入水平与更小的财政压力。而东北、西北地区近年来经济增长放缓，负债率较高，对政府财政保障水平起到了一定的负面影响。

2. 政府服务保障

政府服务保障是指政府在运行过程中能够为各项政府服务提供保障的力度，限定于 PPP 项目领域。拥有较为丰富的项目运行经验的省份，能够在项目流程、项目监督及项目验收等方面对 PPP 项目的运行提供指导与保障。政府服务保障指标体系如表 3.6 所示。

表 3.6　政府服务保障指标体系构成

二级指标	三级指标	四级指标	指标的计算公式	选择该指标的原因
政府服务保障	政府办事时效	项目准备速度	该省份 PPP 项目从项目发起到采购合同签署的平均时间长度	衡量该省份 PPP 项目前期工作速度，督促省份加快审批、简化手续，缩短 PPP 项目前期审核时间，将更多精力投入到项目实际建设中
	政府绩效	政府绩效评估	暂无	政府绩效越高，在参与 PPP 项目时效率就越高
	政府经验	政府运行经验	该省份 PPP 入库项目数/全国 PPP 入库项目总数	政府有关 PPP 项目的运行经验越丰富，就越有可能为 PPP 项目的运行提供指导与保障

根据搜集的数据，我们计算得到 31 个省份的政府服务保障得分，并根据政府服务保障得分进行排名，具体如表 3.7 和图 3.7 所示。

表 3.7　2017 年度各个省份政府服务保障得分及排名

省份	得分	排名	所属地区	省份	得分	排名	所属地区
重庆	76.12	1	西南	上海	48.46	17	华东
海南	75.37	2	华南	江苏	48.19	18	华东
新疆	72.99	3	西北	贵州	48.04	19	西南
宁夏	70.97	4	西北	河北	47.93	20	华北
江西	64.26	5	华东	陕西	47.76	21	西北
山东	62.93	6	华东	内蒙古	47.33	22	华北
福建	61.82	7	华东	西藏	47.22	23	西南
北京	59.07	8	华北	天津	45.32	24	华北
浙江	57.55	9	华东	云南	43.82	25	西南

(续表)

省份	得分	排名	所属地区	省份	得分	排名	所属地区
广东	54.05	10	华南	河南	42.49	26	华中
山西	53.78	11	华北	湖南	42.46	27	华中
安徽	52.08	12	华东	青海	42.08	28	西北
吉林	51.77	13	东北	四川	39.44	29	西南
湖北	50.72	14	华中	辽宁	37.45	30	东北
黑龙江	50.16	15	东北	广西	29.10	31	华南
甘肃	49.41	16	西北				

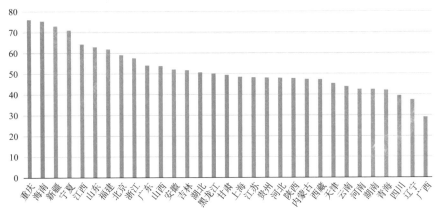

图 3.7　2017 年度各个省份政府服务保障得分及排名

政府服务保障得分的前五名分别为重庆、海南、新疆、宁夏和江西，分别为 76.12 分、75.37 分、72.99 分、70.97 分和 64.26 分；后五名为湖南、青海、四川、辽宁和广西，分别为 42.46 分、42.08 分、39.44 分、37.45 分和 29.10 分。总体来看，新疆、贵州等地 PPP 入库项目较多，PPP 运行经验较为丰富；重庆、海南、新疆等地项目准备速度较快，综合排名也较高。而北京、上海等经济发达省市由于在这两项上均不够突出，所以排名中等，可以通过增加 PPP 项目承办的方式积累经验，完善 PPP 服务保障。

通过对指标的计算，我们得到各地区在政府服务保障方面的得分及排名情况，具体如表3.8和图3.8所示。

表3.8　2017年度不同地区政府服务保障得分及排名

排名	地区	本书涉及省份	平均得分
1	西北地区	陕西、甘肃、青海、宁夏、新疆	56.64
2	华东地区	上海、江苏、浙江、安徽、福建、江西、山东	56.47
3	华南地区	广东、广西、海南	52.84
4	西南地区	四川、贵州、云南、重庆、西藏	50.93
5	华北地区	北京、天津、山西、河北、内蒙古	50.69
6	东北地区	黑龙江、吉林、辽宁	46.46
7	华中地区	河南、湖北、湖南	45.23

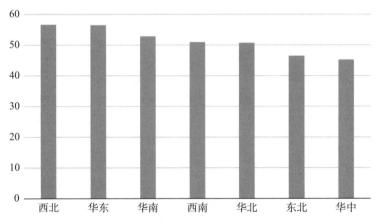

图3.8　2017年度不同地区政府服务保障得分及排名

如表3.8和图3.8所示，西北地区以56.64分排名第1，华东地区与华南地区分别以56.47分、52.84分位列第2、3名，平均得分最低的地区为华中地区，为45.23分。从各省份的情况来看，贵州入库项目比例达到12.68%，广东、广西、海南的入库项目比例仅略微超过1%，而西藏仅有0.03%。由此可见，入库项目的分布在省份及地区间都存在较大差异。

政府服务保障指标一方面可以反映一直以来政府发展PPP项目的积极性，另一方面也能体现政府为PPP项目的运行提供保障的力度。中西部地区经济发展较为落后，政府发展PPP项目的意愿也更为强烈，东南部沿海城市经济较为发达，故而对PPP的发展显得兴趣不足。

3. 政府法律政策保障

政府法律政策保障是指政府通过制定法律法规、出台相关政策等方式对PPP项目的运行提供保障。本部分通过地方政府有关PPP的法律法规数量及法治政府指数这两个指标来对政府的该项保障力度进行刻画。有关PPP的法律法规数量直接反映了政府规范PPP项目运行的举措，法治政府指数则更综合地体现了地方政府的法制建设水平。

政府法律政策保障指标体系具体如表3.9所示。

表3.9 政府法律政策保障指标体系构成

二级指标	三级指标	四级指标	指标的计算公式	选择该指标的原因
政府法律政策保障	法律法规保障	地方政府有关PPP的法律法规数量	各省份政府出台有关PPP法规的数量	直接相关。地方性的PPP法规能够进一步细化各省份的PPP相关工作要求，法律法规越完善，越能保障当地PPP的发展
	政府法治保障	法治政府指数	数据直接引用自《中国法治政府评估报告（2017）》，指标体系包括8个客观指标和1个主观指标	法治发展与经济社会的发展存在正相关关系，地方法治政府建设的水平越高，越能推进和完善PPP的发展

在政府法律政策保障方面，各地区的得分和排名情况如表3.10和图3.9所示。

表 3.10　2017 年度不同地区政府法律政策保障得分及排名

排名	地区	本书涉及省份	平均得分
1	华东地区	上海、江苏、浙江、安徽、福建、江西、山东	68.20
2	华南地区	广东、广西、海南	53.12
3	华中地区	河南、湖北、湖南	52.10
4	华北地区	北京、天津、山西、河北、内蒙古	44.13
5	西南地区	四川、贵州、云南、重庆、西藏	43.79
6	西北地区	陕西、甘肃、青海、宁夏、新疆	33.32
7	东北地区	黑龙江、吉林、辽宁	33.02

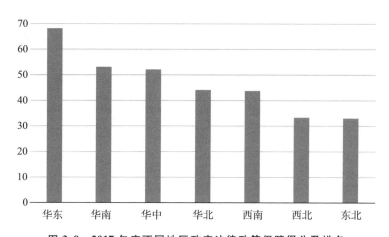

图 3.9　2017 年度不同地区政府法律政策保障得分及排名

华东地区政府法律政策保障得分排名第 1。该地区在地方政府有关 PPP 的法律法规数量方面为第 1 名；法治政府指数方面为第 2 名，且仅与第 1 名相差 1 分。

华南地区政府法律政策保障得分排名第 2。该地区在地方政府有关 PPP 的法律法规数量方面表现较差，为第 5 名；法治政府指数方面为第 1 名。

华中地区政府法律政策保障得分排名第 3。该地区在地方政府有关

PPP 的法律法规数量方面为第 2 名；法治政府指数方面为第 3 名。

华北地区政府法律政策保障得分排名第 4。该地区在地方政府有关 PPP 的法律法规数量方面及法治政府指数方面均为第 4 名，表现较为平衡。

西南地区政府法律政策保障得分排名第 5。该地区在地方政府有关 PPP 的法律法规数量方面为第 3 名；法治政府指数方面为第 6 名，政府法治程度有待提高。

西北地区政府法律政策保障得分排名第 6。该地区在地方政府有关 PPP 的法律法规数量方面为第 6 名；法治政府指数方面为第 7 名，表现较差。

东北地区政府法律政策保障得分排名第 7。该地区在地方政府有关 PPP 的法律法规数量方面为第 7 名，亟须有针对性地改进；法治政府指数方面为第 5 名。

从具体得分来看，华东地区在法律政策保障方面表现较好，以 68.20 的得分排名第 1，且与其他地区的分差较大。西北地区及东北地区得分偏低，分别为 33.32 分及 33.02 分，位列最后。就各省份的表现来看，江苏出台了最多的法规来保障 PPP 项目的运行，同时也具有较高的法治程度，其综合得分高达 93.87 分。新疆在这两个方面的表现都不尽如人意，加权平均分仅为 25.63 分。

法治意识与经济发展水平息息相关，东南部沿海地区在法治政府建设方面卓有成效，西部地区及东北地区仍有待提高。

4. 政府金融保障

政府金融保障指政府在金融方面对 PPP 项目所给予的帮助，直接体现在政府对项目的资金支持力度上。中国 PPP 基金（经国务院批准设立，注册资本为 1 800 亿元人民币）和地方政府 PPP 引导基金能够为项目的开展提供有力支持；政府资本的参与程度则从项目资金构成的角度体现政府保障。政府金融保障指标体系如表 3.11 所示。

表 3.11 政府金融保障指标体系构成

二级指标	三级指标	四级指标	指标的计算公式	选择该指标的原因
政府金融保障	政府基金保障	中国 PPP 基金分省投资项目数量	截至 2017 年年末，中国 PPP 基金在当地已决策的项目数量	作为财政部牵头成立的基金，中国 PPP 基金能为相关项目提供有力的资金支持与保障
		地方政府 PPP 引导基金规模	地方政府已成立的 PPP 引导基金规模	地方政府设立的 PPP 基金能够更有针对性地支持本省 PPP 项目的发展
	政府资本保障	政府资本参与程度	PPP 中心提供数据：政府拟出资额/（拟引入社会资本额度+政府拟出资额）	与社会资本相比，政府资本对 PPP 项目的发展有着更强的保障力度

通过对所获得的数据进行打分，我们得到各地区在政府金融保障方面的得分及排名情况，具体如表 3.12 和图 3.10 所示。

表 3.12 2017 年度不同地区政府金融保障得分及排名

排名	地区	本书涉及省份	平均得分
1	西北地区	陕西、甘肃、青海、宁夏、新疆	29.37
2	华北地区	北京、天津、山西、河北、内蒙古	29.33
3	西南地区	四川、贵州、云南、重庆、西藏	22.52
4	华中地区	河南、湖北、湖南	15.76
5	华东地区	上海、江苏、浙江、安徽、福建、江西、山东	15.42
6	华南地区	广东、广西、海南	14.30
7	东北地区	黑龙江、吉林、辽宁	12.81

西北地区政府金融保障得分排名第 1。该地区在中国 PPP 基金分省投资项目数量方面为第 6 名，获投资项目数量较少；地方政府 PPP 引导基金

规模方面为第 1 名；政府资本参与程度方面为第 2 名。

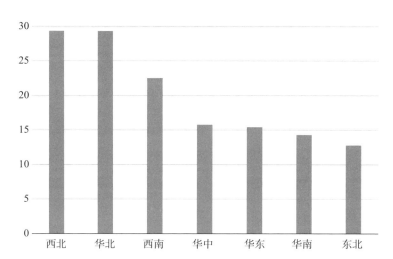

图 3.10　2017 年度不同地区政府金融保障得分及排名

华北地区政府金融保障得分排名第 2。该地区在中国 PPP 基金分省投资项目数量方面为第 3 名；地方政府 PPP 引导基金规模方面为第 4 名；政府资本参与程度方面为第 1 名，政府资本参与程度较高。

西南地区政府金融保障得分排名第 3。该地区在中国 PPP 基金分省投资项目数量方面为第 2 名；地方政府 PPP 引导基金规模方面为第 6 名，基金规模有待提高；政府资本参与程度方面为第 3 名。

华中地区政府金融保障得分排名第 4。该地区在中国 PPP 基金分省投资项目数量方面为第 1 名，获投资项目数量较多；地方政府 PPP 引导基金规模方面为第 5 名；政府资本参与程度方面为第 6 名。

华东地区政府金融保障得分排名第 5。该地区在中国 PPP 基金分省投资项目数量方面为第 5 名；地方政府 PPP 引导基金规模方面为第 3 名；政府资本参与程度方面为第 4 名。

华南地区政府金融保障得分排名第 6。该地区在中国 PPP 基金分省投资项目数量方面为第 7 名；地方政府 PPP 引导基金规模方面为第 7 名，基金对项目的保障能力有待提高；政府资本参与程度方面为第 5 名。

东北地区政府金融保障得分排名第 7。该地区在中国 PPP 基金分省投资项目数量方面为第 4 名;地方政府 PPP 引导基金规模方面为第 4 名;政府资本参与程度方面为第 7 名。

综合来看,各地区在政府金融保障方面的表现均较差,西北地区也较为反常地在此项取得了第 1 名。究其原因,主要是新疆建立了规模极大的 PPP 引导基金,这也从一方面反映出 PPP 发展较为落后的地区正积极采取措施推进相关项目的发展。

5. 政府公信力指数

政府公信力即政府受公众信任的程度。本文选取了债务违约数量、债务违约公司数量、行政诉讼案件数、腐败发生率、职务犯罪率及政府透明度指数等多个指标来综合体现一省政府的公信度(见表 3.13)。前四项(不含"腐败发生率")指标过高,意味着政府运行的效率及规范性需要被质疑;政府透明度指数则更直观地体现了其信息、程序等方面的公开性,与公信力直接相关。

表 3.13 政府公信力指数指标体系构成

二级指标	三级指标	四级指标	指标的计算公式	选择该指标的原因
政府公信力指数	政府公信程度	债务违约数量	Wind 资讯金融终端中检索得到某省份债券违约的数量	一个省份债券发生违约,且当地政府未及时采取措施帮助企业维护投资者利益,则侧面反映了政府的公信力不足
		债务违约公司数量	Wind 资讯金融终端中检索得到某省份债券违约公司的数量	
		行政诉讼案件数	通过在中国裁判文书网进行检索,设定行政案件裁判年份为 2017 年,可得到各省份的案件数量	行政诉讼案件数越多,则说明当地政府行政制度不合理或执行力不佳

（续表）

二级指标	三级指标	四级指标	指标的计算公式	选择该指标的原因
		腐败发生率	暂无	腐败数量越多说明政府公信力越低
		职务犯罪率	在纪检委网站统计某省份干部受党纪政务处分人次	较高的职务犯罪率从侧面反映了当地政府在机制体制方面存在的问题，及其干部班子中存在的不正之风
	信息公开程度	政府透明度指数	数据直接选自《中国法治发展报告 No.16（2018）》，其中的政府透明度指数由八个量化指标构成	较高的政府透明度更能满足公众对相关信息的需求，从而提升政府的公信力

在政府公信力方面，各地区的综合评分结果如表3.14和图3.11所示。

表3.14 2017年度不同地区政府公信力指数得分及排名

排名	地区	本书涉及省份	平均得分
1	华东地区	上海、江苏、浙江、安徽、福建、江西、山东	82.13
2	华中地区	河南、湖北、湖南	82.02
3	西北地区	陕西、甘肃、青海、宁夏、新疆	81.44
4	西南地区	四川、贵州、云南、重庆、西藏	81.08
5	华南地区	广东、广西、海南	77.16
6	华北地区	北京、天津、山西、河北、内蒙古	77.11
7	东北地区	黑龙江、吉林、辽宁	65.89

华东地区政府公信力指数得分排名第1。该地区具体得分情况：债务违约数量方面并列为第1名；债务违约公司数量方面并列为第1名；行政诉讼案件数方面为第6名，相关案件发生率较高；职务犯罪率方面为第3名；政府透明度指数方面为第2名。

华中地区政府公信力指数得分排名第 2。该地区具体得分情况：债务违约数量方面并列为第 1 名；债务违约公司数量方面并列为第 1 名；行政诉讼案件数方面排为第 7 名，相关案件发生率较高；职务犯罪率方面为第 5 名，受党纪处分人次较高；政府透明度指数方面为第 1 名。

西北地区政府公信力指数得分排名第 3。该地区具体得分情况：债务违约数量方面并列为第 1 名；债务违约公司数量方面并列为第 1 名；行政诉讼案件数方面为第 1 名；职务犯罪率方面为第 1 名；政府透明度指数方面为第 6 名，政府公开程度有待提高。

西南地区政府公信力指数得分排名第 4。该地区具体得分情况：债务违约数量方面为第 6 名；债务违约公司数量方面为第 5 名，债务违约率较高；行政诉讼案件数方面为第 2 名；职务犯罪率方面为第 2 名；政府透明度指数方面为第 4 名。

华南地区政府公信力指数得分排名第 5。该地区具体得分情况：债务违约数量方面为第 5 名；债务违约公司数量方面为第 7 名；行政诉讼案件数方面为第 3 名；职务犯罪率方面为第 6 名；政府透明度指数方面为第 3 名，政府透明度表现较好。

华北地区政府公信力指数得分排名第 6。该地区具体得分情况：债务违约数量方面为第 4 名；债务违约公司数量方面为第 3 名；行政诉讼案件数方面为第 5 名；职务犯罪率方面为第 7 名，职务犯罪人次较多；政府透明度指数方面为第 5 名。

东北地区政府公信力指数得分排名第 7。该地区具体得分情况：债务违约数量方面为第 7 名；债务违约公司数量方面为第 6 名；行政诉讼案件数方面为第 4 名；职务犯罪率方面为第 4 名；政府透明度指数方面为第 7 名，综合表现较差。

从具体分数来看，如图 3.11 所示，华东地区及华中地区得分分别为 82.13 分和 82.02 分，位列前两名。第 3、4、5、6 名得分较为接近，为 77—82 分。相比之下，东北地区的表现较差，仅获得了 65.89 分的综合均分。就各省份的情况来看,云南及贵州公信程度较高,综合得分均大于90分;辽宁得分垫底,仅为34.24分,与其他各省份差距较大。

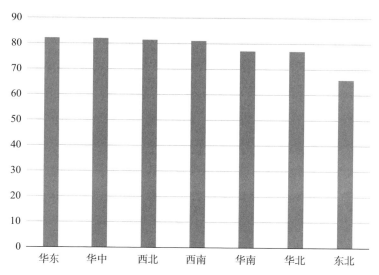

图 3.11 2017 年度不同地区政府公信力指数得分及排名

从图 3.11 中可以看出,除东北地区之外,其他各地区在政府公信力方面差距不大,随着社会大众全面参与到政府治理的各个环节,公众对政府的信任有了大幅提升。东北地区则应更加重视为人民服务的理念,进一步扩大政务公开内容与决策程序,降低行政诉讼发生率及职务犯罪率,为PPP项目的发展营造更加便利的环境。

二、社会参与指数排名

(一)社会参与总体评价

所谓"社会资本",即以企业为代表的社会力量参与PPP项目的能力,它一方面代表企业参与PPP项目的意愿,另一方面衡量企业自身的资金实力、信誉与专业化程度。社会资本依靠市场主体的力量,有效防控过高的财政赤字,推动PPP项目健康发展。从政府财力的角度思考,财政资金状况制约着政府职能的实现，而社会的发展意味着公民需要更优质的公共服务。

国家财政的现实压力意味着基础设施项目的融资需要社会力量的参与。历史上，以英美实践经验看，财政资金短缺阻碍公共项目实施的情况十分常见。进入新时代以来，我国政府的财政收入逐年稳步升高，但是政府特别是地方政府相对较高的杠杆率仍不容忽视，引入社会资本参与公共项目、防范过高财政赤字是必然的。

我国政府对社会资本高度重视，颁布了多部关于引入社会资本进入基础设施、公用事业和公益事业等领域的文件：2001年12月11日，国家计委印发了《关于促进和引导民间投资的若干意见的通知》（计投资〔2001〕2653号），鼓励和引导民间投资参与经营性的基础设施和公益事业项目建设；2003年10月14日，中国共产党第十六届三中全会通过《中共中央关于完善社会主义市场经济体制若干问题的决定》，允许非公有资本进入法律法规未禁入的基础设施、公用事业及其他行业和领域；2010年5月7日，国务院发布了《国务院关于鼓励和引导民间投资健康发展的若干意见》（国发〔2010〕13号）；2013年9月发布了《国务院办公厅关于政府向社会力量购买服务的指导意见》（国办发〔2013〕96号）。这些文件都表明了政府对社会资本的重视。

除了社会资本，社会上还有提供相应服务的第三方，其中主要包括金融服务、法律服务和咨询服务，因为融资对于PPP来说非常重要，因此我们将其从金融中提出来单独分析，在金融这一项中主要分析金融机构和金融市场。这些第三方加上社会资本都属于社会，因而第二个一级指数叫社会参与指数。

社会参与指数由PPP企业参与程度、企业信誉水平、社会资本融资、金融服务、法律服务、咨询服务六个分项指标构成，具体如图3.12所示。

经过计算，我们得出了2017年全国31个省份的社会参与指数。如表3.15和图3.13所示，31个省份的得分平均为57.80，高于平均值的省份共计13个，低于平均值的省份共计18个。大部分省份的社会参与指数

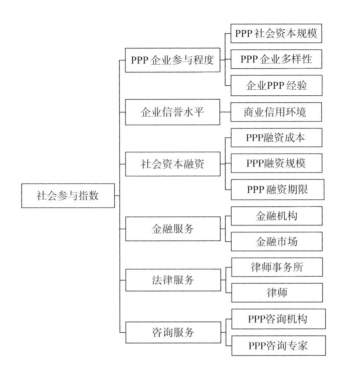

图 3.12　社会参与指数指标体系框架

得分集中于 50 和 60 之间。根据数据分布，我们将社会参与指数得分在 55 分以上的省份界定为社会力量参与 PPP 项目活跃度高，将社会参与指数得分在 55 分以下的省份界定为社会力量参与 PPP 项目活跃度低，活跃度高的省份共计 18 个，活跃度低的省份共计 13 个。

其中北京以 90.42 分排名第 1，广东、浙江、江苏等紧随其后。根据得分，社会参与指数得分较为靠前的省份多集中于经济发达地区，反映出这些省份社会资本实力雄厚，营商环境良好，企业注重信誉，同时金融、法律等均有较好的保障；而社会参与指数得分较为落后的省份多集中于经济欠发达地区，在社会资本实力、营商环境、金融法律配套服务建设等方面均有较大的提升空间。值得注意的是，新疆（不含新疆生产建设兵团）社会参与指数得分位列第 10 名，为西北地区第 1 名，这与当地积极鼓励 PPP 项目、为 PPP 项目提供各项保障措施有着密不可分的关系。

表 3.15　2017 年度各个省份社会参与指数得分及排名

省份	得分	排名	所属地区	省份	得分	排名	所属地区
北京	90.42	1	华北	云南	55.63	17	西南
广东	73.35	2	华南	辽宁	55.33	18	东北
浙江	67.75	3	华东	海南	54.72	19	华南
江苏	67.60	4	华东	安徽	54.36	20	华东
山东	65.70	5	华东	广西	54.15	21	华南
河南	64.23	6	华中	黑龙江	53.88	22	东北
上海	62.43	7	华东	山西	52.68	23	华北
四川	61.72	8	西南	内蒙古	52.27	24	华北
湖北	60.03	9	华中	陕西	51.51	25	西北
新疆	59.40	10	西北	江西	51.45	26	华东
福建	59.25	11	华东	甘肃	50.52	27	西北
吉林	58.34	12	东北	青海	47.65	28	西北
湖南	58.27	13	华中	天津	47.26	29	华北
河北	56.98	14	华北	宁夏	46.23	30	西北
贵州	56.38	15	西南	西藏	46.14	31	西南
重庆	56.27	16	西南				

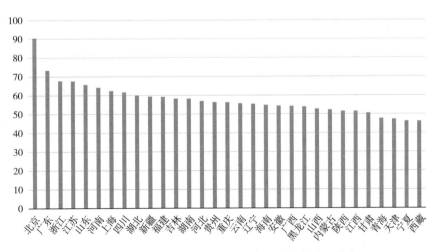

图 3.13　2017 年度各个省份社会参与指数得分及排名

社会力量参与PPP项目活跃的省份集中于华东、华中、华南等地区，社会力量参与PPP项目活跃度相对较低的省份集中于东北、西南、西北地区。各地区间所包含省份社会参与指数得分排名基本位于同一梯队。华东地区所包含的江苏、浙江、山东等省份社会参与指数得分在全国位居前列；而排名较为靠后的西北地区、西南地区所包含的大部分省份得分也较为接近，全国排名中等偏后。值得注意的是，北京、四川、新疆全国排名均位列前10，PPP社会参与程度显著高于同地区其他省份。不同地区的社会参与指数得分及排名如表3.16和图3.14所示。

表3.16 2017年度不同地区社会参与指数得分及排名

排名	地区	本书涉及省份	平均得分
1	华东地区	上海、江苏、浙江、安徽、福建、江西、山东	61.22
2	华中地区	河南、湖北、湖南	60.84
3	华南地区	广东、广西、海南	60.74
4	华北地区	北京、天津、山西、河北、内蒙古	59.92
5	东北地区	黑龙江、吉林、辽宁	55.85
6	西南地区	四川、贵州、云南、重庆、西藏	55.23
7	西北地区	陕西、甘肃、青海、宁夏、新疆	51.06

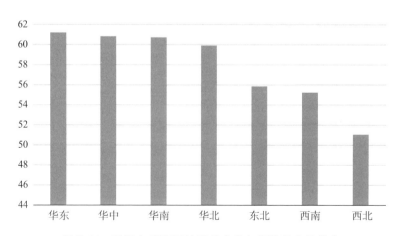

图3.14 2017年度不同地区社会参与指数得分及排名

华东地区社会参与指数排名第 1。金融服务、法律服务两项均为第 1 名;咨询服务、PPP 企业参与程度均为第 2 名;社会资本融资为第 7 名,存在进一步提升空间。

华中地区社会参与指数排名第 2。PPP 企业参与程度为第 1 名;金融服务、法律服务和咨询服务均为第 3 名;在社会资本融资和企业信誉水平方面排名落后,导致其整体排名受拖累。

华南地区社会参与指数排名第 3。企业信誉水平为第 1 名;金融服务、法律服务均为第 2 名;PPP 企业参与程度、社会资本融资和咨询服务表现中等,存在进一步提升的空间。

华北地区社会参与指数排名第 4。咨询服务、企业信誉水平表现突出,分别为第 1 名、第 3 名;金融服务、法律服务均为第 4 名,表现中等;PPP 企业参与程度、社会资本融资排名落后,导致整体排名受拖累。

东北地区社会参与指数排名第 5。社会资本融资、PPP 企业参与程度表现突出,分别为第 1 名、第 3 名;但是金融服务、法律服务、咨询服务、企业信誉水平等排名较为靠后,拖累了整体排名。

西南地区社会参与指数排名第 6。企业信誉水平、社会资本融资表现突出,均为第 2 名;咨询服务表现中等,为第 4 名;但是 PPP 企业参与程度、金融服务、法律服务排名靠后,均为第 6 名或第 7 名,导致整体排名受拖累。

西北地区社会参与指数排名第 7。除社会资本融资排第 3 名外,其余排名均为第 5 名至第 7 名,存在较大的提升空间。

(二)社会参与指数分项评价

1. PPP 企业参与程度

PPP 企业参与程度从 PPP 社会资本规模、PPP 企业多样性和企业 PPP 经验三个维度进行构造。PPP 社会资本规模从社会资本平均投资额、拟引入社会资本投资额、社会资本平均投资比例、项目公司社会资本占比、

PPP 项目企业注册资本规模均值、PPP 参与企业上市率等方面构建指标；PPP 企业多样性从签约民营企业资本率和签约外商及港澳台企业率两方面构建指标；企业 PPP 经验从中标项目数/企业数角度构建指标。

社会资本平均投资额、PPP 参与企业上市率、PPP 项目企业注册资本规模均值有效反映了社会参与方的投资能力与参与意愿，社会资本平均投资比例反映了社会资本对项目资金的负担程度。PPP 企业多样性通过民营、外商及港澳台企业参与比例，反映了各省份 PPP 项目中实际利用非公有资产的程度，更能刻画社会资本活跃与否，衡量 PPP 项目是否真正做到了"政府与社会资本合作"。企业 PPP 经验这一"隐形资本"会助推 PPP 项目稳健、顺利地进行，拥有丰富 PPP 项目经验的企业往往在资金筹措与运营、项目建设运营等方面拥有更多经验，能更好地处理与政府的关系，使得 PPP 项目的落地率、完工率、收益率均有优异的表现。具体如表 3.17 和图 3.15 所示。

表 3.17　PPP 企业参与程度指标体系构成

二级指标	三级指标	四级指标	指标的计算公式	选择该指标的原因
PPP 企业参与程度	PPP 社会资本规模	社会资本平均投资额	$\dfrac{\sum \text{PPP 项目社会资本出资额}}{\text{总项目数}}$	社会资本平均投资额反映社会资本参与活跃度，衡量项目的平均社会资本出资规模
		拟引入社会资本投资额	$\sum \text{PPP 项目社会资本出资额}$	拟引入社会资本投资额衡量各省份的社会资本总出资额
		社会资本平均投资比例	$\sum \dfrac{\text{社会资本出资额}}{\text{项目总投资额}} \Big/ \text{项目数}$	社会资本平均投资比例考察项目的社会资本出资占比
		项目公司社会资本占比	$\sum \dfrac{\text{社会资本出资额}}{\text{项目公司注册资本}} \Big/ \text{项目数}$	与社会资本平均投资比例一样，均是对社会资本出资情况的衡量
		PPP 项目企业注册资本规模均值	$\dfrac{\sum \text{PPP 项目公司注册资本}}{\text{总项目数}}$	注册资本作为对企业资产、资金能力的间接衡量指标，可以衡量该企业是否有充足的资金

（续表）

二级指标	三级指标	四级指标	指标的计算公式	选择该指标的原因
PPP企业参与程度	PPP企业多样性	PPP参与企业上市率	$\sum \dfrac{\text{社会资本方中上市公司（含新三板）数量}}{\text{社会资本方总数}}$	上市公司一般有较为雄厚的经济实力与管理能力，能更好地运行PPP项目
		签约民营企业资本率	$\sum \dfrac{\text{社会资本方中民营企业数量}}{\text{社会资本方总数}}$	衡量民营资本参与PPP项目的积极性与中标率，反映PPP项目的民营资本参与程度
		签约外商及港澳台企业率	$\sum \dfrac{\text{社会资本方中外资及港澳台企业数量}}{\text{社会资本方总数}}$	衡量外商及港澳台企业参与程度，反映PPP项目吸引外资以及港澳台资金的能力
	企业PPP经验	中标项目数/企业数	$\sum \dfrac{\text{社会资本方累计中标项目}}{\text{社会资本方总数}}$	衡量企业PPP项目经验，预估项目落地率及收益

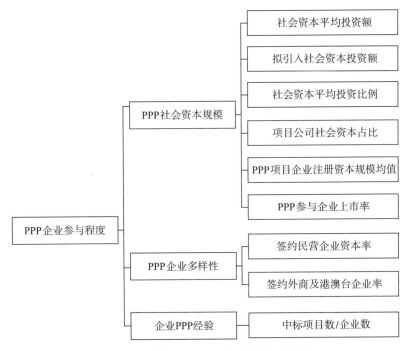

图 3.15　PPP企业参与程度指标体系框架

经过计算，我们得出了 2017 年全国 31 个省份的 PPP 企业参与程度得分。如表 3.18 和图 3.16 所示，31 个省份的得分平均为 38.50 分，高于平均值的省份共计 19 个，低于平均值的省份共计 12 个。大部分省份的社会参与指数得分集中于 30 分至 45 分。根据数据分布，将 PPP 企业参与程度得分在 37.5 分以上的省份界定为社会力量参与 PPP 项目活跃度高，将 PPP 企业参与程度得分在 37.5 分以下的省份界定为社会力量参与 PPP 项目活跃度低，活跃度高的省份共计 19 个，活跃度低的省份共计 12 个。

表 3.18　2017 年度各个省份 PPP 企业参与程度得分及排名

省份	得分	排名	所属地区	省份	得分	排名	所属地区
新疆	62.34	1	西北	安徽	41.10	17	华东
河南	55.95	2	华中	江西	40.49	18	华东
山东	51.77	3	华东	四川	38.60	19	西南
吉林	48.70	4	东北	贵州	33.96	20	西南
云南	47.91	5	西南	青海	33.42	21	西北
湖南	46.82	6	华中	陕西	30.89	22	西北
湖北	45.66	7	华中	西藏	30.83	23	西南
江苏	45.54	8	华东	甘肃	29.30	24	西北
山西	45.50	9	华北	海南	27.72	25	华南
内蒙古	45.02	10	华北	北京	27.07	26	华北
广西	43.26	11	华南	天津	26.38	27	华北
黑龙江	42.40	12	东北	辽宁	22.38	28	东北
广东	42.03	13	华南	上海	22.15	29	华东
浙江	41.78	14	华东	重庆	21.56	30	西南
福建	41.60	15	华东	宁夏	19.97	31	西北
河北	41.26	16	华北				

值得注意的是，新疆的 PPP 企业参与程度得分最高，这与当地鼓励 PPP 项目发展、积极吸纳社会资本存在一定联系；另外，四个直辖市均属

于企业参与不活跃的省级行政区，这与当地财政实力雄厚或城投公司业务发展较好存在关系。

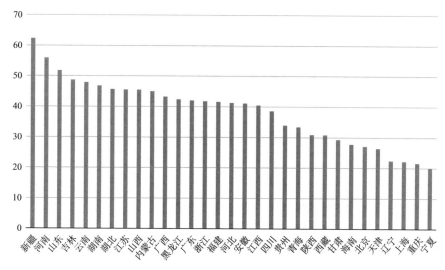

图 3.16　2017 年度各个省份 PPP 企业参与程度得分及排名

社会参与活跃的省份集中于华东、华中、东北等地区，社会参与度相对较低的省份集中于华北、西南、西北地区。各地区间所包含省份 PPP 企业参与程度得分排名基本位于同一梯队。值得注意的是，东北地区的 PPP 企业参与程度得分居前，特别是吉林 PPP 企业参与程度得分位居全国第 4 名。不同地区具体排名如表 3.19 和图 3.17 所示。

表 3.19　2017 年度不同地区 PPP 企业参与程度得分及排名

排名	地区	本书涉及省份	平均得分
1	华中地区	河南、湖北、湖南	49.47
2	华东地区	上海、江苏、浙江、安徽、福建、江西、山东	40.63
3	东北地区	黑龙江、吉林、辽宁	37.83
4	华南地区	广东、广西、海南	37.67
5	华北地区	北京、天津、山西、河北、内蒙古	37.05
6	西北地区	陕西、甘肃、青海、宁夏、新疆	35.19
7	西南地区	四川、贵州、云南、重庆、西藏	34.57

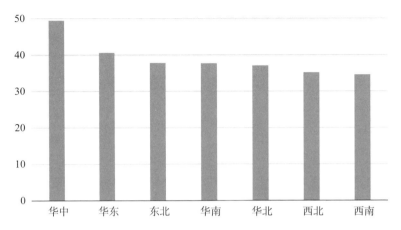

图 3.17　2017 年度不同地区 PPP 企业参与程度得分及排名

华中地区 PPP 企业参与程度得分排名第 1。PPP 社会资本规模、企业 PPP 经验均为第 1 名；PPP 企业多样性得分为第 5 名。

华东地区 PPP 企业参与程度得分排名第 2。企业 PPP 经验表现突出，为第 2 名；PPP 社会资本规模和 PPP 企业多样性均为第 4 名，表现中等。

东北地区 PPP 企业参与程度得分排名第 3。PPP 企业多样性表现突出，为第 2 名；PPP 社会资本规模和企业 PPP 经验排名较为靠后，分别为第 5 名、第 7 名。

华南地区 PPP 企业参与程度得分排名第 4。PPP 企业多样性表现突出，为第 1 名；PPP 社会资本规模和企业 PPP 经验排名较为靠后，均为第 6 名。

华北地区 PPP 企业参与程度得分排名第 5。PPP 社会资本规模表现突出，为第 3 名；企业 PPP 经验为第 4 名，表现适中；PPP 企业多样性较为靠后，为第 6 名。

西北地区 PPP 企业参与程度得分排名第 6。PPP 企业多样性表现突出，为第 3 名；企业 PPP 经验、PPP 社会资本规模较为靠后，分别为第 5、7 名。

西南地区 PPP 企业参与程度得分排名第 7。企业 PPP 经验、PPP 社会资本规模表现突出，分别为第 2 名、第 3 名，但是 PPP 企业多样性得分严重偏低，拖累了综合排名。

2. 企业信誉水平

企业信誉水平从商业信用环境这一维度衡量，不仅指诚信程度，而且注重衡量营商环境、企业稳健经营可能性，分为不良企业率和城市商业信用环境指数两个四级指标，衡量各省企业的综合信誉水平。若该省企业的信誉状况越良好，遵纪守法意识越强烈，进而出现违约、违规、违法事件的可能性越小，PPP项目质量、完工率越有保证，因此PPP项目发展得越好，成功率越高。从商业信用环境这一维度衡量，主要包括各省不良企业率和城市商业信用环境指数。

表 3.20 企业信誉水平指标体系构成

二级指标	三级指标	四级指标	指标的计算公式	选择该指标的原因
企业信誉水平	商业信用环境	不良企业率	$\sum \dfrac{\text{不良企业数}}{\text{企业总数}}$	不良企业率衡量各省的企业经营状况，借以衡量企业潜在的违约、违法、违规可能性
		城市商业信用环境指数	引用中国城市商业信用环境指数	衡量各省的整体营商环境，从而预估PPP项目的落地率及后期运营效益

七大地理地区的企业信誉水平指标之间存在一定的相似性，不同地区的平均得分及排名如表3.21和图3.18所示。

表 3.21 2017年度不同地区企业信誉水平得分及排名

排名	地区	本书涉及省份	平均得分
1	华南地区	广东、广西、海南	52.29
2	西南地区	四川、贵州、云南、重庆、西藏	49.26
3	华北地区	北京、天津、山西、河北、内蒙古	48.76
4	华东地区	上海、江苏、浙江、安徽、福建、江西、山东	46.18

（续表）

排名	地区	本书涉及省份	平均得分
5	西北地区	陕西、甘肃、青海、宁夏、新疆	44.27
6	华中地区	河南、湖北、湖南	41.65
7	东北地区	黑龙江、吉林、辽宁	41.05

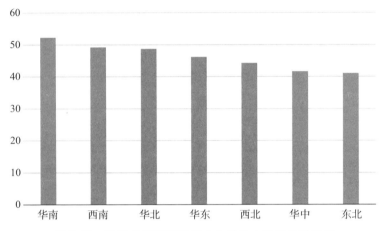

图 3.18　2017 年度不同地区企业信誉水平得分及排名

华南地区企业信誉水平排名第 1。其中不良企业率得分为第 1 名；城市商业信用环境指数得分为第 3 名；

西南地区企业信誉水平排名第 2。其中不良企业率得分为第 2 名；城市商业信用环境指数得分为第 4 名。

华北地区企业信誉水平排名第 3。其中不良企业率得分为第 7 名；城市商业信用环境指数得分为第 1 名。

华东地区企业信誉水平排名第 4。其中不良企业率得分为第 6 名；城市商业信用环境指数得分为第 2 名。

西北地区企业信誉水平排名第 5。其中不良企业率得分为第 3 名；城市商业信用环境指数得分为第 5 名。

华中地区企业信誉水平排名第 6。其中不良企业率得分为第 5 名；城市商业信用环境指数得分为第 6 名。

东北地区企业信誉水平排名第 7。其中不良企业率得分为第 4 名;城市商业信用环境指数得分为第 7 名。

3. 社会资本融资

社会资本融资这一指标是指社会资本在参与 PPP 项目融资时的难度。社会资本融资难会降低企业参与 PPP 项目的积极性,不利于在地方形成 PPP 运营的良好氛围。社会资本融资分为 PPP 融资成本、PPP 融资规模和 PPP 融资期限三个三级指标,分别从利率、资金数量和时间三个角度衡量。进一步,三级指标各由一个或两个三级指标来表征,如图 3.19 和表 3.22 所示。

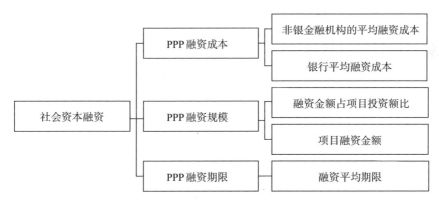

图 3.19　社会资本融资指标体系框架

表 3.22　社会资本融资指标体系构成

二级指标	三级指标	四级指标	指标的计算公式	选择该指标的原因
社会资本融资	PPP融资成本	非银金融机构的平均融资成本	直接引用	非银金融机构的平均融资成本可以衡量 PPP 项目融资难易程度
		银行平均融资成本	$[\sum(融资金额 \times 融资成本)]/(\sum 融资金额)$	可补充非银机构数据。注:该部分仅选用前三批示范项目融资相关数据中的银行和政策性银行的利率

（续表）

二级指标	三级指标	四级指标	指标的计算公式	选择该指标的原因
社会资本融资	PPP融资规模	融资金额占项目投资额比	融资金额/项目投资额	融资金额占项目投资额比可以衡量项目的开展是否有保障
		项目融资金额	直接引用	项目融资金额直接衡量融资的规模
	PPP融资期限	融资平均期限	[∑（融资金额×融资期限）]/(∑融资金额)	融资期限可以衡量项目资金的持续性。融资期限越长，长期项目的开展更有保障

我们根据搜集的数据，计算得到31个省份的社会资本融资得分，并根据社会资本融资得分进行排名，具体如表3.23和图3.20所示。

表3.23 2017年度各个省份社会资本融资得分及排名

省份	得分	排名	所属地区	省份	得分	排名	所属地区
北京	76.01	1	华北	河南	48.95	17	华中
吉林	70.04	2	东北	青海	48.49	18	西北
宁夏	69.15	3	西北	海南	47.54	19	华南
辽宁	64.98	4	东北	西藏	46.98	20	西南
重庆	63.27	5	西南	安徽	45.89	21	华东
江苏	60.86	6	华东	新疆	44.18	22	西北
黑龙江	58.86	7	东北	湖南	43.91	23	华中
贵州	58.43	8	西南	四川	43.55	24	西南
甘肃	58.06	9	西北	河北	42.44	25	华北
天津	57.20	10	华北	陕西	39.87	26	西北
湖北	56.58	11	华中	上海	38.85	27	华东
浙江	55.77	12	华东	山西	38.08	28	华北
广东	55.16	13	华南	江西	34.06	29	华东
福建	54.66	14	华东	内蒙古	32.57	30	华北

（续表）

省份	得分	排名	所属地区	省份	得分	排名	所属地区
广西	51.29	15	华南	山东	28.84	31	华东
云南	50.37	16	西南				

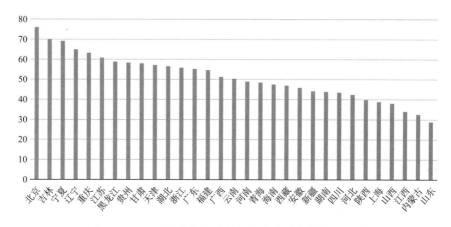

图 3.20　2017 年度各个省份社会资本融资得分及排名

吉林排名第 2，主要源于 PPP 融资成本、PPP 融资规模和 PPP 融资期限排名均靠前，分别为第 7 名、第 3 名和第 3 名。

宁夏排名第 3，主要源于 PPP 融资成本、PPP 融资规模和 PPP 融资期限排名均靠前，分别为第 9 名、第 8 名和第 2 名，均对社会资本融资得分呈现积极的影响。

辽宁排名第 4，主要源于 PPP 融资成本和 PPP 融资规模排名均靠前，分别为第 1 名和第 6 名。其中 PPP 融资成本排名最高，主要源于银行平均融资成本排名靠前，为第 3 名；PPP 融资期限排名居中，为第 20 名。

黑龙江排名第 7，主要源于 PPP 融资期限排名靠前，为第 1 名。PPP 融资成本排名居中，为第 11 名，对黑龙江社会融资得分呈现相对中性的影响；PPP 融资规模排名相对靠后，为第 28 名，对黑龙江的社会资本融资得分有所拖累。

贵州排名第8，主要源于PPP融资规模和PPP融资期限均为第5名，相对靠前，对贵州社会融资得分呈现相对中性的影响；PPP融资成本为22名，相对靠后，对贵州的社会资本融资得分有所拖累。

甘肃排名第9，主要源于PPP融资成本为第5名，相对靠前，对甘肃社会融资得分呈现相对积极的影响；PPP融资规模和PPP融资期限分别为第20名和第12名，对甘肃社会资本融资得分呈现相对中性的影响。

上海排名第27，主要源于PPP融资成本为第30名，对上海社会资本融资得分有严重的拖累；PPP融资规模和PPP融资期限分别为第15名和第17名，对上海社会资本融资得分呈现相对中性的影响。

七大地理地区的社会资本融资之间存在一定的相似性，不同地区的平均得分及排名如表3.24和图3.21所示。

表3.24　2017年度不同地区社会资本融资得分及排名

排名	地理区域	本书涉及省份	平均得分
1	东北地区	黑龙江、吉林、辽宁	64.63
2	西南地区	四川、贵州、云南、重庆、西藏	52.52
3	西北地区	陕西、甘肃、青海、宁夏、新疆	51.95
4	华南地区	广东、广西、海南	51.33
5	华中地区	河南、湖北、湖南	49.82
6	华北地区	北京、天津、山西、河北、内蒙古	49.26
7	华东地区	上海、江苏、浙江、安徽、福建、江西、山东	45.56

东北地区排名第1，其社会资本融资得分的绝对值也显著高于其他各地区，主要源于PPP融资成本、PPP融资规模和PPP融资期限排名均靠前，分别为第1名、第2名和第1名。

西南地区排名第2，主要源于PPP融资规模和PPP融资期限分别为第1名和第2名，相对靠前，对西南地区的社会资本融资得分呈现积极的影响；PPP融资成本为第5名，对西南地区的社会资本融资得分有所拖累。

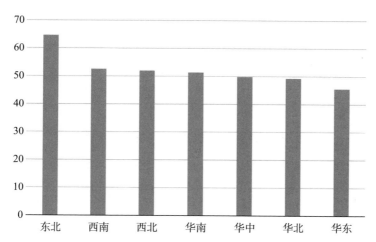

图 3.21 2017 年度不同地区社会资本融资得分及排名

西北地区排名第 3，主要源于 PPP 融资成本和 PPP 融资期限均为第 3 名，对西北地区社会资本融资得分呈现相对中性的影响；PPP 融资规模为第 5 名，对西北地区的社会资本融资得分有所拖累。

华南地区排名第 4，主要源于 PPP 融资成本为第 2 名，相对靠前；PPP 融资规模和 PPP 融资期限分别为第 7 名和第 5 名，对华南地区的社会资本融资得分有所拖累。

华中地区排名第 5 名，主要源于 PPP 融资成本为第 7 名，对华中地区的社会资本融资得分有所拖累；PPP 融资规模和 PPP 融资期限排名相对居中，均为第 4 名。

华北地区排名第 6，主要源于 PPP 融资期限排名第 6 名，对华北地区的社会资本融资得分有所拖累；PPP 融资成本和 PPP 融资规模分别为第 4 名和第 3 名，对华北地区的社会资本融资得分呈现相对中性的影响。

华东地区排名第 7，华东地区社会资本融资得分的绝对值显著低于其他地区，主要源于 PPP 融资成本、PPP 融资规模和 PPP 融资期限均相对靠后，分别为第 6 名、第 6 名和第 7 名，对华东地区的社会资本融资得分呈现负面的影响。

4. 金融服务

金融服务是指该地区金融行业的完善程度。引入这一指标的目的是衡量当地金融行业是否足以为PPP项目的健康运转提供优质的金融服务。金融服务下设金融机构和金融市场两个子指标。其中，金融机构通过金融机构资产总额、金融机构数量和金融机构从业人员数量来表征，金融市场通过金融市场发展程度来表征，具体如图3.22和表3.25所示。

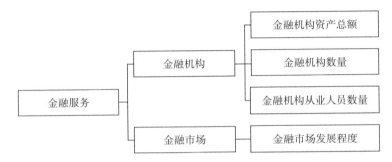

图 3.22　金融服务指标体系框架

表 3.25　金融服务指标体系构成

二级指标	三级指标	四级指标	指标的计算公式	选择该指标的原因
金融服务	金融机构	金融机构资产总额	$\sum$ 金融机构资产	金融机构资产总额越充足，为PPP项目融资越容易，且提供越充分的保障
		金融机构数量	直接计算	金融机构数量越多，PPP项目融资的选择余地越大，越有利于做出最优选择
		金融机构从业人员数量	$\sum$ 金融机构从业人员数量	金融机构从业人员数量越多，为PPP项目融资的服务人员越多，融资越有效率，且越有保障
	金融市场	金融市场发展程度	直接引用	金融市场发展程度越高，金融市场越完善，越有利于PPP项目融资

根据搜集的数据，我们计算得到 31 个省份的金融服务得分，并根据金融服务得分进行排名，具体排名如表 3.26 和图 3.23 所示。

表 3.26　2017 年度各个省份金融服务得分及排名

省份	得分	排名	所属地区	省份	得分	排名	所属地区
广东	86.30	1	华南	山西	33.45	17	华北
江苏	71.36	2	华东	贵州	31.98	18	西南
北京	69.01	3	华北	江西	31.30	19	华东
浙江	66.40	4	华东	天津	29.28	20	华北
山东	63.29	5	华东	甘肃	28.39	21	西北
四川	56.76	6	西南	重庆	26.39	22	西南
上海	53.38	7	华东	广西	26.33	23	华南
河南	50.13	8	华中	吉林	26.22	24	东北
辽宁	47.32	9	东北	云南	25.77	25	西南
河北	46.72	10	华北	新疆	24.32	26	西北
福建	44.38	11	华东	黑龙江	23.47	27	东北
陕西	42.90	12	西北	青海	23.11	28	西北
湖南	40.91	13	华中	内蒙古	15.52	29	华北
海南	39.39	14	华南	宁夏	9.02	30	西北
湖北	39.36	15	华中	西藏	4.35	31	西南
安徽	38.55	16	华东				

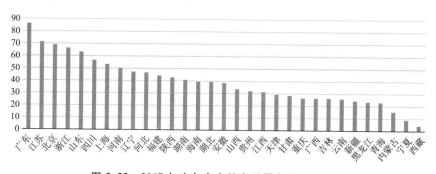

图 3.23　2017 年度各个省份金融服务得分及排名

辽宁排名第 9，主要源于金融机构和金融市场排名均相对靠前，分别为第 9 名和第 10 名，对辽宁的金融服务得分呈现相对积极的影响。

陕西排名第 12，主要源于金融市场为第 3 名，相对靠前，对陕西的金融服务得分呈现相对积极的影响；金融机构这一指标为第 17 名，相对居中，对陕西的金融服务得分呈现相对中性的影响。

贵州排名第 18，主要源于金融市场排名相对靠前，为第 8 名，对贵州的金融服务得分呈现相对积极的影响；但金融机构排名相对靠后，为第 24 名，对贵州的金融服务得分呈现相对负面的影响。

天津排名第 20，主要源于金融机构排名相对靠后，为第 27 名，对天津的金融服务得分呈现相对负面的影响；但金融市场排名相对靠前，是第 9 名，对天津的金融服务得分呈现相对积极的影响。

重庆排名第 22，主要源于金融机构和金融市场的排名均相对靠后，分别为第 25 名和第 22 名，对金融服务的得分呈现相对负面的影响。

七大地理地区的金融服务之间存在一定的相似性，不同地区的平均得分及排名如表 3.27 和图 3.24 所示。

表 3.27　2017 年度不同地区金融服务得分及排名

排名	地理区域	本书涉及省份	平均得分
1	华东地区	上海、江苏、浙江、安徽、福建、江西、山东	52.67
2	华南地区	广东、广西、海南	50.67
3	华中地区	河南、湖北、湖南	43.47
4	华北地区	北京、天津、山西、河北、内蒙古	38.79
5	东北地区	黑龙江、吉林、辽宁	32.34
6	西南地区	四川、贵州、云南、重庆、西藏	29.05
7	西北地区	陕西、甘肃、青海、宁夏、新疆	25.55

华东地区排名第 1。主要源于金融机构为第 1 名，金融市场为第 2 名，均相对靠前，对华东地区的金融服务得分呈现相对积极的影响。

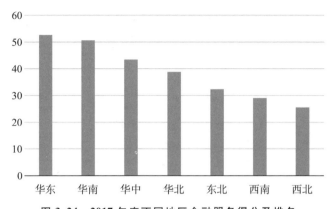

图 3.24　2017 年度不同地区金融服务得分及排名

华南地区排名第 2。主要源于金融机构为第 1 名，相对靠前；但金融市场得分为第 4 名，对华南地区的金融服务得分呈现相对中性的影响。

华中地区排名第 3。主要源于金融机构为第 3 名，相对居中；但金融市场为第 5 名，相对靠后，对华中地区金融服务得分呈现相对负面的影响。

华北地区排名第 4。主要源于金融机构和金融市场得分均相对居中，分别为第 4 名和第 3 名，对华北地区金融服务得分呈现相对中性的影响。

东北地区排名第 5。主要源于金融机构和金融市场得分均相对靠后，分别为第 5 名和第 7 名，均不利于东北地区金融服务的得分排名。

西南地区排名第 6。主要源于金融机构和金融市场为均为第 6 名，对西南地区的金融服务的得分呈现相对负面的影响。

西北地区排名第 7。主要源于金融机构为第 7 名，相对靠后，对西北地区的金融服务得分呈现相对负面的影响；但金融市场为第 2 名，相对较好。

5. 法律服务

法律服务是指与法律事务相关的服务。法律服务旨在通过规范 PPP 市场参与者的行为、PPP 项目开展的流程与相关文件，有效规范 PPP 市场，有利于 PPP 市场的有效运行。法律服务由律师事务所和律师两个方面表征，具体如图 3.25 和表 3.28 所示。

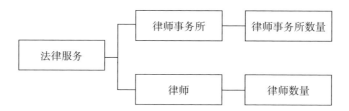

图 3.25 法律服务指标体系框架

表 3.28 法律服务指标体系构成

二级指标	三级指标	四级指标	指标的计算公式	选择该指标的原因
法律服务	律师事务所	律师事务所数量	直接计算	律师事务所数量越多，PPP项目关于法律保障的选择余地越大，有利于做出最优选择
	律师	律师数量	直接计算	律师数量越多，为PPP项目提供法律保障的服务人员越多，更有保障

根据搜集的数据，我们计算得到 31 个省份的法律服务得分，并根据法律服务得分进行排名，具体如表 3.29 和图 3.26 所示。

表 3.29 2017 年度各个省份法律服务得分及排名

省份	得分	排名	所属地区	省份	得分	排名	所属地区
广东	100.00	1	华南	天津	20.26	17	华东
北京	88.89	2	华北	安徽	18.52	18	西北
山东	65.36	3	华东	陕西	18.15	19	华北
江苏	60.58	4	华东	内蒙古	15.55	20	华东
上海	58.32	5	华东	江西	14.60	21	东北
河南	49.44	6	华中	吉林	14.46	22	西南
浙江	47.25	7	华东	贵州	14.27	23	西北
四川	44.49	8	西南	新疆	13.34	24	华南

（续表）

省份	得分	排名	所属地区	省份	得分	排名	所属地区
辽宁	31.89	9	东北	广西	12.52	25	西北
湖南	31.64	10	华中	甘肃	10.01	26	华北
河北	29.90	11	华北	山西	8.96	27	西北
湖北	27.91	12	华中	宁夏	4.26	28	西北
重庆	25.66	13	西南	青海	2.38	29	华南
云南	23.84	14	西南	海南	1.26	30	西南
福建	23.48	15	华东	西藏	0.00	31	华东
黑龙江	21.95	16	东北				

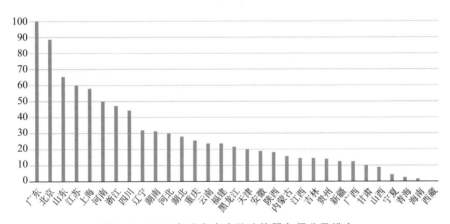

图 3.26　2017 年度各个省份法律服务得分及排名

辽宁排名第 9，主要源于律师事务所得分为第 9 名，律师得分为第 10 名，均相对靠前，对辽宁的法律服务得分呈现相对中性的影响。

重庆排名第 13，主要源于律师事务所得分为第 12 名，律师得分为第 13 名，均相对居中，对重庆的法律服务得分呈现中性的影响。

云南排名第 14，主要源于律师事务所得分为第 13 名，律师得分为第 15 名，均相对居中，对云南的法律服务得分呈现相对中性的影响。

天津排名第 17，主要源于律师事务所得分为第 17 名，律师得分为第

18名,均相对居中,对天津的法律服务得分呈现相对中性的影响。

山西排名第27,主要源于律师事务所和律师得分分别为第27名和第23名,均相对靠后,对山西的法律服务得分呈现相对负面的影响。

七大地理地区的法律服务之间存在一定的相似性,不同地区的平均得分和具体排名如表3.30和图3.27所示。

表3.30 2017年度不同地区法律服务得分及排名

排名	地理区域	本书涉及省份	平均得分
1	华东	上海、江苏、浙江、安徽、福建、江西、山东	41.16
2	华南	广东、广西、海南	37.93
3	华中	河南、湖北、湖南	36.33
4	华北	北京、天津、山西、河北、内蒙古	32.71
5	东北	黑龙江、吉林、辽宁	22.77
6	西南	四川、贵州、云南、重庆、西藏	21.65
7	西北	陕西、甘肃、青海、宁夏、新疆	9.63

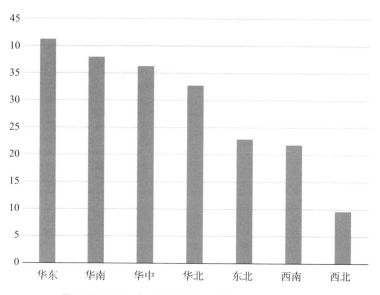

图3.27 2017年度不同地区法律服务得分及排名

华东地区排名第 1，主要源于律师事务所得分为第 1 名，律师得分为第 2 名，均相对靠前，对华东地区的法律服务得分呈现相对积极的影响。

华南地区排名第 2，主要源于律师事务所得分为第 2 名，相对靠前；律师得分为第 3 名，对华南地区的法律服务得分呈现相对中性的影响。

华中地区排名第 3，主要源于律师得分为第 1 名，相对靠前；律师事务所得分为第 4 名，对华中地区的法律服务得分呈现相对中性的影响。

华北地区排名第 4，主要源于律师事务所得分为第 3 名，律师得分排名第 4 名，均相对居中，对华北地区的法律服务得分呈现相对中性的影响。

东北地区排名第 5，主要源于律师事务所为第 5 名，律师得分为第 6 名，均相对靠后，对东北地区的法律服务得分呈现相对负面的影响。

西南地区排名第 6，主要源于律师事务所为第 6 名，律师得分为第 5 名，均相对靠后，对西南地区的法律服务得分呈现相对负面的影响。

西北地区排名第 7，主要源于律师事务所和律师得分均为第 7 名，相对靠后，对西北地区的法律服务得分呈现相对负面的影响。

6. 咨询服务

咨询服务是指为 PPP 项目的开展提供信息资料的整合、项目流程的指导等相关业务的一类服务。咨询服务有利于引导社会资本积极有序参与 PPP 项目，有利于加快我国 PPP 项目规范化的进程。咨询服务由 PPP 咨询机构和 PPP 咨询专家两类指标表征。其中，PPP 咨询机构从数目、项目总投资、项目总数、服务类别平均数和 PPP 咨询费率几个方面表征，PPP 咨询专家由数目、科研能力、咨询经验和参与经验等几个方面表征（见图 3.28 和表 3.31）。

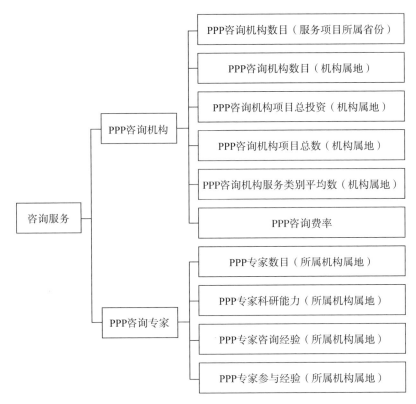

图 3.28 咨询服务指标体系框架

表 3.31 咨询服务指标体系构成

二级指标	三级指标	四级指标	指标的计算公式	选择该指标的原因
咨询服务	PPP咨询机构	PPP咨询机构数目（服务项目所属省份）	$\sum$ 咨询机构数目	咨询机构数目越多，在一定程度上说明该地区咨询服务越充分
		PPP咨询机构数目（机构属地）	$\sum$ 咨询机构数目	
		PPP咨询机构项目总投资（机构属地）	$\sum$ 咨询机构项目投资	咨询机构项目投资越多，在一定程度上说明该地区咨询服务越充分
		PPP咨询机构项目总数（机构属地）	$\sum$ 咨询机构项目数	咨询机构项目数越多，在一定程度上说明该地区咨询服务越充分

(续表)

二级指标	三级指标	四级指标	指标的计算公式	选择该指标的原因
咨询服务		PPP 咨询机构服务类别平均数（机构属地）	$\sum$ 咨询机构服务类别数目/$\sum$ 咨询机构数目	咨询机构服务类别平均数越多，在一定程度上说明该地区咨询服务越充分
		PPP 咨询费率	直接引用	咨询费率越低，在一定程度上说明该地区咨询服务越容易获得，越有利于开展 PPP 项目
	PPP 咨询专家	PPP 专家数目（所属机构属地）	$\sum$ 专家数	专家数目越多，在一定程度上说明该地区咨询服务越充分
		PPP 专家科研能力（所属机构属地）	$\sum$ 科研课题数	科研课题数越多，在一定程度上说明专家科研能力越强，该地区咨询服务越充分
		PPP 专家咨询经验（所属机构属地）	$\sum$ 专家咨询项目数	专家咨询项目越多，在一定程度上说明专家咨询经验越丰富，该地区咨询服务越充分
		PPP 专家参与经验（所属机构属地）	$\sum$ 专家参与项目数	专家参与项目越多，在一定程度上说明专家咨询经验越丰富，该地区咨询服务越充分

根据搜集的数据，我们计算得到 31 个省份的咨询服务得分，并根据咨询服务得分进行排名，具体如图 3.29 和表 3.32 所示。

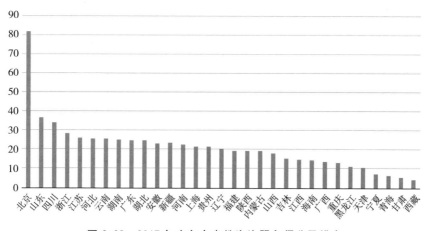

图 3.29　2017 年度各个省份咨询服务得分及排名

表 3.32　2017 年度各个省份咨询服务得分及排名

省份	得分	排名	所属地区	省份	得分	排名	所属地区
北京	81.41	1	华北	福建	19.93	17	华东
山东	37.28	2	华东	陕西	19.72	18	西北
四川	34.80	3	西南	内蒙古	19.59	19	华北
浙江	29.17	4	华东	山西	18.61	20	华北
江苏	26.85	5	华东	吉林	16.17	21	东北
河北	26.40	6	华北	江西	15.66	22	华东
云南	26.18	7	西南	海南	15.16	23	华南
湖南	26.02	8	华中	广西	14.11	24	华南
广东	25.57	9	华南	重庆	13.89	25	西南
湖北	25.54	10	华中	黑龙江	11.75	26	东北
安徽	24.18	11	华东	天津	11.02	27	华北
新疆	23.87	12	西北	宁夏	7.91	28	西北
河南	23.33	13	华中	甘肃	7.24	29	西北
上海	22.16	14	华东	青海	5.86	30	西北
贵州	21.82	15	西南	西藏	4.86	31	西南
辽宁	20.90	16	东北				

云南排名第 7，主要源于 PPP 咨询机构得分为第 7 名，相对靠前，对云南咨询服务得分呈现相对积极的影响；PPP 咨询专家得分为第 11 名，对云南咨询服务得分呈现相对中性的影响。

新疆排名第 12，主要源于 PPP 咨询机构得分为第 6 名，相对靠前；PPP 咨询专家得分为第 16 名，对新疆咨询服务得分呈现相对中性的影响。

上海排名第 14，主要源于 PPP 咨询专家得分为第 2 名，相对靠前，说明有许多咨询机构属地位于上海；PPP 咨询机构得分为第 26 名，对上海咨询服务得分有所拖累。

贵州排名第 15，主要源于 PPP 咨询机构得分和 PPP 咨询专家得分排名均相对居中，分别为第 13 名和第 19 名，对贵州咨询服务得分呈现相对中性的影响。

重庆排名第 25，主要源于 PPP 咨询机构得分排名相对靠后，为第 25 名，对重庆咨询服务得分有所拖累，其主要原因是 PPP 咨询机构数目（服务项目所属省份）、PPP 咨询机构服务类别平均数（机构属地）和 PPP 咨询机构项目总数（机构属地）排名均相对靠后；PPP 咨询专家得分排名相对靠前，为第 6 名。

天津排名第 27，主要源于 PPP 咨询机构得分排名相对靠后，为第 27 名，对天津咨询服务得分有所拖累，其主要原因是 PPP 咨询机构数目、投资额、项目数和服务类别平均数都相对较少，排名靠后；PPP 咨询专家得分排名相对居中，为第 13 名。

七大地理地区的咨询服务之间存在一定的相似性，将不同地区的具体排名如表 3.33 和图 3.30 所示。

表 3.33 2017 年度不同地区咨询服务得分及排名

排名	地理区域	本书涉及省份	平均得分
1	华北地区	北京、天津、山西、河北、内蒙古	31.41
2	华东地区	上海、江苏、浙江、安徽、福建、江西、山东	25.03
3	华中地区	河南、湖北、湖南	24.96
4	西南地区	四川、贵州、云南、重庆、西藏	20.31
5	华南地区	广东、广西、海南	18.28
6	东北地区	黑龙江、吉林、辽宁	16.27
7	西北地区	陕西、甘肃、青海、宁夏、新疆	12.92

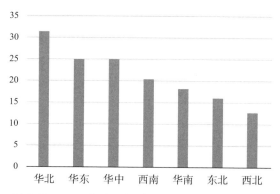

图 3.30　2017 年度不同地区咨询服务得分及排名

华北地区排名第 1，主要源于 PPP 咨询机构得分和 PPP 咨询专家得分排名均相对靠前，分别为第 2 名和第 1 名，对华北地区咨询服务得分呈现相对积极的影响。

华东地区排名第 2，主要源于 PPP 咨询机构得分和 PPP 咨询专家得分排名均相对靠前，分别为第 3 名和第 2 名，对华东地区咨询服务得分呈现相对积极的影响。

华中地区排名第 3，主要源于 PPP 咨询机构得分为第 1 名，相对靠前；PPP 咨询专家得分排名相对居中，为第 4 名，对华中地区咨询服务得分呈现相对中性的影响。

西南地区排名第 4，主要源于 PPP 咨询机构得分和 PPP 咨询专家得分排名均相对居中，分别为第 4 名和第 3 名，对西南地区咨询服务得分呈现相对中性的影响。

华南地区排名第 5，主要源于 PPP 咨询机构得分和 PPP 咨询专家得分排名均相对靠后，均为第 5 名，对华南地区咨询服务得分呈现相对负面的影响。

东北地区排名第 6，主要源于 PPP 咨询机构得分和 PPP 咨询专家得分排名均为第 6 名，相对靠后，对华南地区咨询服务得分呈现相对负面的影响。

西北地区排名第 7，主要源于 PPP 咨询机构得分和 PPP 咨询专家得分排名均相对靠后，均为第 7 名，对华南地区咨询服务得分呈现相对负面的影响。

三、项目运行指数排名

（一）项目运行总体评价

项目运行指数是衡量地区 PPP 项目过去的发展成果、当前的发展局势、未来的发展潜力的全面性和综合性指标。相比于政府保障和社会参与，项目运行着重从 PPP 项目本身出发，根据发展的规模、质量、分布结构、执行过程与结果、未来发展空间等多个维度构建指标体系，旨在对地区 PPP 市场的现状和态势作出整体性的评估。

该指数由 PPP 发展程度、PPP 风险收益、PPP 发展空间三个二级指标构成。其中 PPP 发展程度包括项目发展规模、PPP 项目分布、PPP 工作进展、PPP 规范化程度、PPP 透明化程度、PPP 执行情况、PPP 移交情况等七个三级指标，描述了一个地区现有 PPP 项目的宏观面貌；PPP 风险收益包括项目收益、项目风险、外部效益等三个三级指标，目的是着重考察收益和风险这两个最重要的项目属性；PPP 发展空间包括基础设施现状、城镇化率、基建投资潜力、储备项目规模等四个三级指标，度量了未来 PPP 市场可待开拓的空间。指标框架如图 3.31 所示。

图 3.31　PPP 项目运行指数指标体系框架

三部分内容分别刻画了地区 PPP 市场的三个方面：已有 PPP 市场总体表现如何，蕴含的价值大小如何，将来增长的潜力如何。健康繁荣的

PPP 市场有着规模大、增长快、行业和地区分布均衡、落地率高、规范透明等特点，本身是 PPP 发展所追求的方向；有合理内外部收益、较低风险的项目有着更大的投资价值，是采取 PPP 模式创造效益的保证，也是吸引各方参与的关键；更高的增长潜力则意味着未来更多的发展机会，是推动 PPP 市场持续增长的内在动力，预示着未来的可发展程度。选取这三个指标以作为对 PPP 项目运行成绩和前景的综合打分，是较为全面和准确的。

根据搜集的数据，我们计算得到 31 个省份的项目运行指数得分，并根据项目运行指数得分进行排名，具体如表 3.34 和图 3.32 所示。

表 3.34　2017 年度各个省份项目运行指数得分及排名

序号	省份	项目运行指数		PPP 发展程度		PPP 风险收益		PPP 发展空间	
		得分	排名	得分	排名	得分	排名	得分	排名
1	河南	86.89	1	89.10	4	93.80	3	78.61	3
2	山东	86.55	2	95.21	1	94.68	2	66.70	19
3	新疆	84.84	3	88.23	6	84.89	6	79.15	2
4	贵州	83.94	4	78.18	23	98.49	1	83.85	1
5	四川	82.86	5	89.70	3	75.27	10	76.51	7
6	安徽	82.71	6	95.20	2	74.58	12	67.32	17
7	云南	82.27	7	84.89	14	82.14	7	77.98	5
8	湖北	80.89	8	84.58	15	75.64	8	78.26	4
9	湖南	80.83	9	86.18	11	85.39	5	68.88	12
10	河北	79.84	10	87.77	8	75.46	9	69.53	11
11	内蒙古	79.03	11	87.13	10	89.91	4	58.30	25
12	福建	77.32	12	85.92	12	71.21	14	67.07	18
13	陕西	77.00	13	84.21	17	69.98	16	69.67	10
14	浙江	76.21	14	88.32	5	75.05	11	56.78	29
15	江苏	75.60	15	87.30	9	74.18	13	57.06	28

(续表)

序号	省份	项目运行指数		PPP 发展程度		PPP 风险收益		PPP 发展空间	
		得分	排名	得分	排名	得分	排名	得分	排名
16	吉林	75.37	16	88.01	7	64.35	18	61.67	22
17	山西	74.83	17	84.45	16	68.13	17	63.27	20
18	广东	73.75	18	85.19	13	61.95	23	62.54	21
19	江西	73.17	19	80.00	19	60.34	25	70.32	9
20	广西	72.12	20	72.62	27	70.33	15	72.47	8
21	黑龙江	71.30	21	77.14	24	60.96	24	68.47	14
22	海南	71.01	22	76.29	25	62.84	21	67.68	15
23	西藏	70.73	23	71.61	28	58.59	27	77.34	6
24	宁夏	70.39	24	79.80	20	64.20	19	58.82	24
25	青海	69.68	25	78.38	22	51.08	30	67.59	16
26	甘肃	68.03	26	73.74	26	52.82	28	68.64	13
27	上海	66.57	27	80.22	18	63.67	20	45.76	30
28	天津	63.94	28	68.61	31	62.10	22	57.38	27
29	辽宁	63.77	29	69.13	29	59.61	26	57.61	26
30	重庆	63.42	30	68.88	30	52.44	29	61.63	23
31	北京	62.65	31	78.82	21	50.46	31	43.83	31

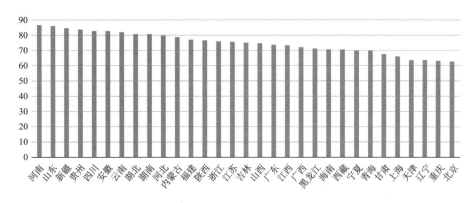

图 3.32　2017 年度各个省份项目运行指数得分及排名

河南排名第 1，主要源于 PPP 发展程度、PPP 风险收益、PPP 发展空间等状况较好，分别为第 4 名、第 3 名、第 3 名。可见该省名列第 1 源于其各项指标都有好的表现，PPP 发展程度中 PPP 发展规模、PPP 项目分布等情况优良，PPP 外部效益突出，且在基础设施现状和储备项目规模上创造了较大的发展空间。

山东排名第 2，主要源于 PPP 发展程度、PPP 风险收益等状况较好，分别为第 1 名、第 2 名；PPP 发展空间呈现相对中性影响，为第 19 名。该省 PPP 发展空间虽如预料中不突出，但凭借 PPP 项目高质量的发展提高得分，如 PPP 项目分布均衡，透明化规范化程度高、外部效益尤其是基础公共服务、污染防治和绿色保护领域明显。

新疆排名第 3，主要源于 PPP 发展程度、PPP 风险收益、PPP 发展空间等状况较好，分别为第 6 名、第 6 名、第 2 名。新疆等西北地区往往有巨大的基建投资和 PPP 发展空间，此外，该省也比较重视已有 PPP 项目的发展，投资规模大、分布广，外部效益尤其是污染防治和绿色保护上做得好。

贵州排名第 4，主要源于 PPP 风险收益、PPP 发展空间等状况较好，均为第 1 名；但 PPP 发展程度拖累了其项目运行指数，为第 23 名。该省的特点是储备项目多、增长快，同时基础设施缺口大，有很大的 PPP 发展需求。虽在 PPP 发展程度上落后，但项目风险程度低，且在贫困治理上贡献大。

北京排名第 31，主要源于 PPP 发展程度、PPP 风险收益、PPP 发展空间等表现相对较差，分别为第 21 名、第 31 名、第 31 名。以北京为代表的经济发达地区基建投资需求相对少，PPP 发展空间小。未来需在 PPP 项目的规范化透明化运行方面改善，并降低项目风险、扩展外部效益。但北京 PPP 落地率、开工率高应加以肯定。

本书选取不同地理地区作为整体，统计不同地区的平均得分，并进行排名，具体排名如表 3.35 和图 3.33 所示。

表 3.35 2017 年度不同地区项目运行指数得分及排名

序号	地区	项目运行指数		PPP 发展程度		PPP 风险收益		PPP 发展空间	
		得分	排名	得分	排名	得分	排名	得分	排名
1	华中	82.87	1	66.62	2	64.94	1	55.25	2
2	华东	76.88	2	67.45	1	53.39	2	41.57	6
3	西南	76.64	3	58.66	5	53.39	3	55.46	1
4	西北	73.99	4	60.87	4	44.60	6	48.77	3
5	华南	72.29	5	58.03	7	45.04	5	47.56	4
6	华北	72.06	6	61.35	3	49.21	4	38.46	7
7	东北	70.15	7	58.09	6	41.64	7	42.58	5

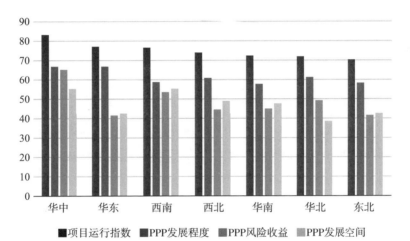

图 3.33 2017 年度不同地区项目运行指数得分及排名

华中地区排名第 1，主要源于 PPP 发展程度、PPP 风险收益、PPP 发展空间等状况较好，分别为第 2 名、第 1 名、第 2 名。

华东地区排名第 2，主要源于 PPP 发展程度、PPP 风险收益等状况较好，分别为第 1 名、第 2 名；但 PPP 发展空间拖累了其项目运行指数，为第 6 名。

西南地区排名第 3，主要源于 PPP 风险收益、PPP 发展空间等状况较好，分别为第 2 名、第 1 名；PPP 发展程度排名相对居中，为第 5 名。

西北地区排名第4，PPP发展程度、PPP发展空间等排名均相对居中，分别为第4名、第3名；但PPP风险收益相对较差，为第6名，对其项目运行指数拖累较大。

华南地区排名第5，PPP风险收益、PPP发展空间等排名均相对居中，分别为第5名、第4名；但PPP发展程度相对较差，为第7名，对其项目运行指数拖累较大。

华北地区排名第6，主要源于PPP发展空间相对较差，为第7名；PPP发展程度、PPP风险收益等排名均相对居中，分别为第3名、第4名。

东北地区排名第7，主要源于PPP发展程度、PPP风险收益等相对较差，分别为第6名、第7名；PPP发展空间排名相对居中，为第5名。

（二）PPP发展程度评价

PPP发展程度评价部分旨在衡量各省份已开展所有PPP项目的总体运营状况，从而反映各省份PPP工作的质量和进展，同时实现对高质高量的正向激励和对问题缺陷的负面警示。该指标有助于督促相关部门不仅关注PPP项目的发展增长，更要重视PPP项目的质控管理，以实现PPP市场良好运转、平稳增长，真正发挥PPP项目服务经济、高效运作的作用。

该部分主要依据PPP项目已公开信息构建，从PPP发展规模、PPP项目分布、PPP工作进展、PPP规范程度、PPP透明化程度、PPP执行情况、PPP移交情况七个维度，对评价对象所有PPP项目质量进行综合评价，如图3.34所示。数据主要采用项目数量、投资额等定量数据，以保证客观公正，辅以定性数据进一步完善。数据来源绝大部分为财政部PPP项目库2017年各省年报，还包括库内信息统计、各省级财政厅网站、财政部PPP退库信息、荣邦瑞明"PPP有例"数据库及《2017中国PPP市场透明度报告》。计算时，我们运用（GDP调整）绝对值加总、计算集合度等方法处理，选择单向或合意水平排序，对每个维度进行打分，再对分维度分数进行加权,得到 PPP 发展程度总体得分。最终通过对各省份的分维度和总体分数分别比较,得出分析和评价。

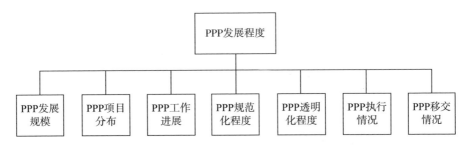

图 3.34　PPP 发展程度指标体系框架

PPP 发展程度各个省份分数排名如表 3.36 和图 3.35 所示。其中,排前三名的省级行政区为山东、安徽、四川,分数分别为 75.21 分、75.20 分、69.70 分,排后三名的省份为辽宁、重庆、天津,分数分别为 49.13 分、48.88 分、48.61 分。

表 3.36　2017 年度各个省份 PPP 发展程度得分及排名

省份	得分	排名	所属地区	省份	得分	排名	所属地区
山东	75.21	1	华东	陕西	64.21	17	西北
安徽	75.20	2	华东	上海	60.22	18	华东
四川	69.70	3	西南	江西	60.00	19	华东
河南	69.10	4	华中	宁夏	59.80	20	西北
浙江	68.32	5	华东	北京	58.82	21	华北
新疆	68.23	6	西北	青海	58.38	22	西北
吉林	68.01	7	东北	贵州	58.18	23	西南
河北	67.77	8	华北	黑龙江	57.14	24	东北
江苏	67.30	9	华东	海南	56.29	25	华南
内蒙古	67.13	10	华北	甘肃	53.74	26	西北
湖南	66.18	11	华中	广西	52.62	27	华南
福建	65.92	12	华东	西藏	51.61	28	西南

（续表）

省份	得分	排名	所属地区	省份	得分	排名	所属地区
广东	65.19	13	华南	辽宁	49.13	29	东北
云南	64.89	14	西南	重庆	48.88	30	西南
湖北	64.58	15	华中	天津	48.61	31	华北
山西	64.45	16	华北				

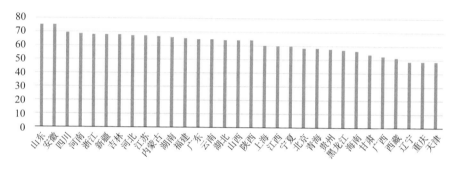

图 3.35　2017 年度各个省份 PPP 发展程度得分及排名

辽宁 PPP 发展程度得分排名第 29，主要源于 PPP 发展规模为第 30 名，出现数量和投资额双负增长，且其 PPP 规范化程度、PPP 透明化程度分别为第 30 名、第 28 名，项目运作和信息公开没有到位。尽管经济面临下行压力，辽宁仍需对 PPP 规模拓展和质量管理工作引起足够重视。

重庆 PPP 发展程度得分排名第 30，主要源于 PPP 规范化程度和 PPP 透明化程度均为第 31 名，且得分远远落后于其他省级行政区，因此尽管其他指标排名中游，仍导致发展程度总体排名很低。重庆需要通过重视前期论证、增强示范效应提高项目质量，通过建立信息公开专栏、完善项目信息公开提高运营透明度。

天津 PPP 发展程度得分排名第 31，部分由于行政区划的客观原因导致 PPP 项目存量小且分布较集中，使 PPP 发展规模和 PPP 项目分布两项指标均为第 31 名，拖累了总体排名。其余指标中，PPP 工作进展表现中游偏上，PPP 规范化程度和 PPP 透明化程度仍显出弱势，有待加强。

PPP 发展程度地区分数排名如表 3.37 和图 3.36 所示。

表 3.37　2017 年度不同地区 PPP 发展程度得分及排名

排名	地区	本书涉及省份	平均得分
1	华东地区	上海、江苏、浙江、安徽、福建、江西、山东	67.45
2	华中地区	河南、湖北、湖南	66.62
3	华北地区	北京、天津、山西、河北、内蒙古	61.35
4	西北地区	陕西、甘肃、青海、宁夏、新疆	60.87
5	西南地区	四川、贵州、云南、重庆市、西藏	58.66
6	东北地区	黑龙江、吉林、辽宁	58.09
7	华南地区	广东、广西、海南	58.03

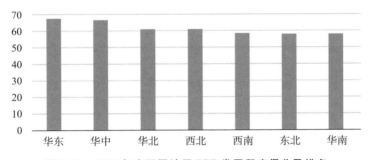

图 3.36　2017 年度不同地区 PPP 发展程度得分及排名

华东地区 PPP 发展程度得分排名第 1，主要源于 PPP 工作进展、PPP 透明化程度为第 1 名，PPP 发展规模、PPP 项目分布和 PPP 规范化程度均为第 2 名，整体发展增长较快，落实较好，综合发展程度高。

华中地区 PPP 发展程度得分排名第 2，主要源于 PPP 发展规模、PPP 项目分布、PPP 规范化程度为第 1 名，但 PPP 工作进展排名最末，PPP 透明化程度也仅为第 4 名，项目落地开工和信息公开工作不到位拖累了整体排名，需要针对这两个问题提出措施加以改进。

华北地区 PPP 发展程度得分排名第 3，主要源于 PPP 工作进展、PPP

透明化程度排名较高，分别为第3名、第2名，相较之下PPP发展规模和PPP项目分布排名居于中游偏下位置，仍有较大提升空间。

西北地区PPP发展程度得分排名第4，主要源于PPP透明化程度排名较高，为第3名；PPP规范化程度排名稍低，为第5名；其余各项指标均居于中游。项目各项指标表现比较均衡，但综合规模和水平仍有待提升。

西南地区PPP发展程度得分排名第5，虽然PPP发展规模和PPP项目分布排名分列第2、3位，但其余指标排名过低，PPP规范化程度与PPP透明化程度均居于第7名。该结果除部分由于西藏情况特殊外，反映出该地区在PPP落地工作、项目质量、信息公开等方面问题突出，需要引起重视。

东北地区PPP发展程度得分排名第6，主要源于PPP发展规模为第7名，PPP规模增长乏力；PPP项目分布、PPP规范化程度、PPP透明化程度均为第6名，整体排名较为落后。尽管该地区已入库项目工作进展较快，但需要重视提升项目质量和信息公开水平；同时，需进一步拓展PPP的应用空间，发挥PPP助力地区经济增长的作用。

华南地区PPP发展程度得分排名第7，虽然PPP工作进展、PPP规范化程度、PPP透明化程度排名大体居于中游，但PPP发展规模为第6名、PPP项目分布为第7名，特别是PPP项目分布拖累了整体排名，反映出该地区在PPP资源调动和分配上存在问题，华南地区地方政府应积极拓展社会资本合作空间，同时重视PPP资源在行业和空间上的均衡分配。

1. PPP发展规模

PPP发展规模由五项四级指标构成，具体如表3.38所示。数据来自财政部PPP管理库2017年各省年报，资产寿命由管理库项目信息统计获得，衡量了各省级行政区PPP项目在总体层面的数量、投资、持续期、发展空间水平。其中，对数量和投资水平，分别考察其存量和增量，以达到既反映过去所有工作成果，又激励当期工作推进的效果。考虑到各省份经济发展程度不同，会使其在 PPP 项目上的社会需求和供给能力不同，故我们在对上述两项指标打分时，将指标根据各省的 GDP 数据进行了调整。持续期在时间维度上反映了 PPP 项目未来可发挥效益时期的平均长度。

表 3.38 PPP 发展规模指标体系构成

三级指标	四级指标	指标的计算公式	选择该指标的原因
PPP 发展规模	项目总投资	该省份所有入库项目投资额加总	衡量省份所有 PPP 项目资金投入的存量，反映过去所有 PPP 项目的发展规模。该指标数值越大，说明该省份运用 PPP 进行融资的能力越强，PPP 项目对经济的贡献越重要
	项目投资增速	该省份当年新入库项目投资额占往年所有入库项目投资额的比率	衡量省份过去一年 PPP 项目资金投入增长快慢，反映该年度 PPP 工作积极程度。以增量形式激励 PPP 现有项目基数小的省份开展 PPP 工作
	项目总数量	该省份所有入库项目个数统计	衡量省份所有 PPP 项目数量的存量，反映过去运作的 PPP 项目的数目规模。该指标数值越大，说明该省份运用 PPP 项目的经验越丰富，能力越强
	项目数量增速	该省份当年新入库项目数量占往年所有入库项目数量的比率	衡量省份过去一年内 PPP 项目数量增长快慢，反映该年度 PPP 工作积极程度。以增量形式激励 PPP 现有项目基数小的省份开展 PPP 工作
	项目资产寿命	该省份所有入库项目预期使用寿命年限（运营期）的资产加权平均值	类似于久期的概念，衡量省份当前 PPP 项目资产的预期持续期。该指标数值越大，项目时间维度上规模越大，实际运营、发挥效益的时间越长

PPP 发展规模分数如表 3.39 和图 3.37 所示。其中，排前三名的省份为山东、西藏、河南，得分分别为 57.84 分、52.00 分、50.03 分；排后三名的省份为海南、辽宁、天津，得分分别为 15.30 分、13.34 分、5.47 分。

西藏由于现存 2 个 PPP 项目均为 2017 年新增项目,故投资增速和数量增速得分为 100 分,使其发展规模最终分数很高。

表 3.39 2017 年度各个省份 PPP 发展规模得分及排名

省份	得分	排名	所属地区	省份	得分	排名	所属地区
山东	57.84	1	华东	上海	33.57	17	华东
西藏	52.00	2	西南	宁夏	32.74	18	西北
河南	50.03	3	华中	江西	32.40	19	华东
四川	47.62	4	西南	青海	32.38	20	西北
江苏	47.03	5	华东	陕西	31.68	21	西北
湖南	44.36	6	华中	福建	29.60	22	华东
新疆	43.68	7	西北	甘肃	28.59	23	西北
广东	43.32	8	华南	重庆	25.40	24	西南
贵州	40.77	9	西南	北京	25.03	25	华北
浙江	40.18	10	华东	安徽	22.01	26	华东
湖北	38.96	11	华中	黑龙江	20.74	27	东北
山西	38.45	12	华北	广西	20.72	28	华南
吉林	36.76	13	东北	海南	15.30	29	华南
云南	35.09	14	西南	辽宁	13.34	30	东北
河北	34.94	15	华北	天津	5.47	31	华北
内蒙古	33.93	16	华北				

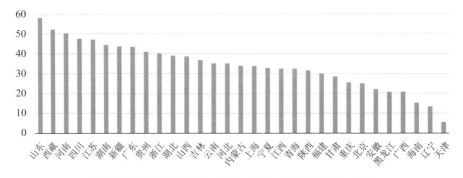

图 3.37 2017 年度各个省份 PPP 发展规模得分及排名

PPP 发展规模地区得分和排名如表 3.40 和图 3.38 所示。

表 3.40 2017 年度不同地区 PPP 发展规模得分及排名

排名	地区	本书涉及省份	平均得分
1	华中地区	河南、湖北、湖南	44.45
2	西南地区	四川、贵州、云南、重庆、西藏	40.18
3	华东地区	上海、江苏、浙江、安徽、福建、江西、山东	37.52
4	西北地区	陕西、甘肃、青海、宁夏、新疆	33.82
5	华北地区	北京、天津、山西、河北、内蒙古	27.56
6	华南地区	广东、广西、海南	26.45
7	东北地区	黑龙江、吉林、辽宁	23.61

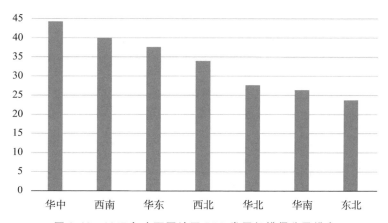

图 3.38 2017 年度不同地区 PPP 发展规模得分及排名

华中地区的 PPP 发展规模得分排名第 1，主要源于项目总投资、项目数量增速和项目总数量均为第 1 名，规模增长迅速；但项目资产寿命排名靠后，仍有进步空间。

西南地区的 PPP 发展规模得分排名第 2，主要源于项目投资增速为第 1 名，项目资产寿命排名同样靠前，为第 2 名；但项目总数量得分较低，应当控制规模、增加数量。

华东地区的 PPP 发展规模得分排名第 3，主要源于项目数量增速较高，为第2名；但项目总数量和项目资产寿命排名相对较低，有待改进。

西北地区的 PPP 发展规模得分排名第 4，主要源于项目资产寿命表现优秀，为第 1 名；虽然增速较好，但 GDP 修正后的项目总投资和数量存量得分过低，均为第 6 名，降低了整体排名。

华北地区的 PPP 发展规模得分排名第 5，主要源于项目总投资和项目数量增速表现尚好，项目数量增速为第 4 名；与西北地区情况相似，GDP 修正后的项目总投资和数量存量得分过低降低了整体排名，其余指标也有待加强。

华南地区的 PPP 发展规模得分排名第 6，主要源于项目数量增速表现尚好，但其余指标均排名较为靠后，有待加强。

东北地区的 PPP 发展规模得分排名第 7，虽然项目资产寿命较长对得分有所贡献，但项目投资增速、项目总数量、项目数量增速均为第 7 名，使整体排名降低。该地区排名落后，可能受经济环境影响，特别是有省份 PPP 发展规模出现了负增长，需要引起对 PPP 和经济发展工作的重视。

2. PPP 项目分布

PPP 项目分布由两个四级指标构成，分别为项目行业集中度和项目地区集中度，数据来自财政部 PPP 管理库 2017 年各省年报，旨在衡量通过 PPP 方式配置的资源的分布是否相对平均，从而促进 PPP 项目普惠发展。

其中，项目行业集中度反映了 PPP 项目是否广泛涉及各个行业领域，项目地区集中度则反映 PPP 项目是否惠及省级行政区下辖的各个地级行政区。指标计算借鉴经济学中集中度的计算方法，考虑到项目投资额与行业特点、地区经济财政能力有相关性，故使用项目数量而非投资额进行计算；考虑到项目落地标志着规划确定、开始实施，并且数据由各省年报直接提供，因此统计范围定为各省级行政区落地项目。具体的 PPP 项目指标体系构成如表 3.41 所示。

表 3.41　PPP 项目分布指标体系构成

三级指标	四级指标	经济含义	选择该指标的原因
PPP 项目分布	项目行业集中度	该省级行政区落地项目按照行业以数量统计，前三位的占比	负向指标。衡量 PPP 项目的行业分布，鼓励在各行各业而非单一领域开展 PPP 项目。考虑到不同行业融资规模特征不同，故统计项目数量而非投资额
	项目地区集中度	该省级行政区落地项目按照下辖地级行政区以数量统计，前三位的占比	负向指标。衡量 PPP 项目的行业分布，鼓励在省级行政区内各个而非单一地级行政区内开展 PPP 项目。考虑到不同地级行政区经济水平和融资能力不同，故统计项目数量而非投资额

PPP 项目分布分数排名如表 3.42 和图 3.39 所示。

表 3.42　2017 年度各个省份 PPP 项目分布得分及排名

省份	得分	排名	所属地区	省份	得分	排名	所属地区
河南	89.81	1	华中	西藏	56.67	17	西南
湖南	81.58	2	华中	北京	56.40	18	华北
新疆	80.91	3	西北	湖北	54.53	19	华中
山东	79.37	4	华东	甘肃	52.22	20	西北
江苏	71.02	5	华东	黑龙江	51.78	21	东北
浙江	70.61	6	华东	江西	49.96	22	华东
陕西	68.54	7	西北	辽宁	49.52	23	东北
贵州	67.64	8	西南	山西	46.75	24	华北
云南	66.47	9	西南	广东	45.33	25	华南
四川	66.06	10	西南	广西	44.22	26	华南
重庆	63.56	11	西南	宁夏	39.50	27	西北
福建	62.70	12	华东	吉林	37.12	28	东北

（续表）

省份	得分	排名	所属地区	省份	得分	排名	所属地区
内蒙古	62.49	13	华北	青海	28.32	29	西北
安徽	61.93	14	华东	海南	19.63	30	华南
河北	57.29	15	华北	天津	18.19	31	华北
上海	56.67	16	华东				

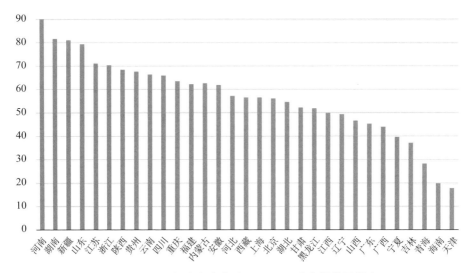

图 3.39　2017 年度各个省份 PPP 项目分布得分及排名

PPP 项目分布排前三名的省份为河南、湖南、新疆，分数分别为 89.81 分、81.58 分、80.91 分，第四名山东与前三名相差不大，为 79.37 分；排后三名的省份为青海、海南、天津，分数分别为 28.32 分、19.63 分、18.19 分。

天津排名第 31，主要受制于管理库项目总数较少，行业集中度过高（达到 90%），多集中于市政工程领域；地区集中度 60%，高于全国平均水平，与行政区划也有一定关联。

PPP 项目分布地区得分如表 3.43 和图 3.40 所示。

表 3.43 2017 年度不同地区 PPP 项目分布得分及排名

排名	地区	本书涉及省份	平均得分
1	华中地区	河南、湖北、湖南	75.31
2	华东地区	上海、江苏、浙江、安徽、福建、江西、山东	64.61
3	西南地区	四川、贵州、云南、重庆、西藏	64.08
4	西北地区	陕西、甘肃、青海、宁夏、新疆	53.90
5	华北地区	北京、天津、山西、河北、内蒙古	48.22
6	东北地区	黑龙江、吉林、辽宁	46.14
7	华南地区	广东、广西、海南	36.39

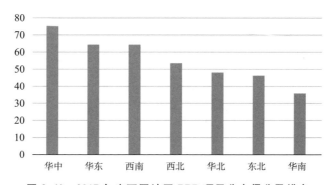

图 3.40 2017 年度不同地区 PPP 项目分布得分及排名

华中地区 PPP 项目分布得分排名第 1，主要源于其行业分布和地区分布均为第 1 名，PPP 资源分布较为均衡。

华东地区 PPP 项目分布得分排名第 2，主要源于行业分布较为均衡，得分为第 2 名，地区分布则稍显集中。

西南地区 PPP 项目分布得分排名第 3，主要源于地区分布较为均衡，得分为第 2 名，行业分布则稍显集中。

西北地区、华北地区 PPP 项目分布得分分别排名第 4 名、第 5 名，项目行业和地区分布都居于中间水平。

东北地区 PPP 项目分布得分排名第 6，主要源于项目地区集中度高，应多考虑向欠发达地区均衡分配 PPP 资源，为城市建设提供基础服务。

华南地区 PPP 项目分布得分排名第 7，主要源于项目行业集中度高，多集中于市政工程、交通运输等基础设施建设行业，应多向绿色环保、公共服务领域拓展 PPP 项目。

3. PPP 工作进展

PPP 工作进展由三项四级指标构成，包括各省级行政区 PPP 项目的落地率、开工率和移交率，从项目开始发起到运营完成，全阶段衡量各省级行政区 PPP 项目工作推进速度。落地率和开工率数据来自财政部 PPP 管理库 2017 年各省年报。PPP 项目落地率反映项目进入执行阶段、正式开始实施的进展情况；PPP 项目开工率反映项目正式开始工程建设的进展情况。二者均采用项目数量计算比例并排名。考察二者有助于督促 PPP 项目尽快落实投产，发挥效益，尽量避免拖延纠纷、简化准备流程。PPP 项目移交率衡量项目后期工作进展，目前由于尚无数据，仅为完善体系作为建议指标加入，不具有区分度。具体指标体系构成如表 3.44 所示。

表 3.44 PPP 工作进展指标体系构成

三级指标	四级指标	经济含义	选择该指标的原因
PPP 工作进展	项目落地率	该省份执行阶段的项目数占项目总数的百分比	衡量该省份 PPP 项目工作推进速度，鼓励项目尽快进入实际实施阶段。财政部对于落地率的定义：执行和移交两个阶段项目数之和与准备、采购、执行、移交四个阶段项目数之和的比值为项目落地率
	项目开工率	该省份开工（示范）项目数占落地（示范）项目数的百分比	衡量该省份 PPP 项目工作推进速度，督促项目尽快开工建设。考虑到数据可得性仅采用落地示范项目开工率
	项目移交率	该省份执行阶段的项目数占项目总数的百分比	标志着 PPP 项目顺利完成运营期。鉴于 PPP 项目周期较长，目前无项目已进入移交阶段，故将该指标作为未来的建议指标

PPP 工作进展分数排名如表 3.45 和图 3.41 所示。其中，排前三名的省份为安徽、上海、山东，分数分别为 65.06 分、53.63 分、46.16 分，第四名四川与前三名相差不大，为 45.64 分；排后三名的省份为内蒙古、贵州、西藏，分数分别为 19.19 分、13.56 分、0.00 分。西藏由于所有项目均尚未落地开工，故得分为零。

表 3.45　2017 年度各个省份 PPP 工作进展得分及排名

省份	得分	排名	所属地区	省份	得分	排名	所属地区
安徽	65.06	1	华东	江苏	27.76	17	华东
上海	53.63	2	华东	江西	27.44	18	华东
山东	46.16	3	华东	青海	27.05	19	西北
四川	45.64	4	西南	辽宁	25.92	20	东北
北京	40.45	5	华北	重庆	24.97	21	西南
吉林	38.09	6	东北	陕西	22.80	22	西北
河北	37.48	7	华北	湖南	22.25	23	华中
广东	34.35	8	华南	山西	21.05	24	华北
甘肃	34.02	9	西北	宁夏	20.72	25	西北
黑龙江	32.89	10	东北	广西	20.50	26	华南
福建	32.61	11	华东	河南	20.35	27	华中
浙江	31.22	12	华东	湖北	19.72	28	华中
海南	30.10	13	华南	内蒙古	19.19	29	华北
新疆	30.01	14	西北	贵州	13.56	30	西南
天津	29.79	15	华北	西藏	0.00	31	西南
云南	28.72	16	西南				

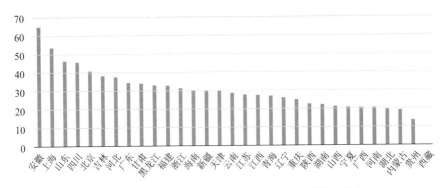

图 3.41　2017 年度各个省份 PPP 工作进展得分及排名

PPP 工作进展地区得分如表 3.46 和图 3.42 所示：

表 3.46　2017 年度不同地区 PPP 工作进展得分及排名

排名	地区	本书涉及省份	平均得分
1	华东地区	上海、江苏、浙江、安徽、福建、江西、山东	40.56
2	东北地区	黑龙江、吉林、辽宁	32.30
3	华北地区	北京、天津、山西、河北、内蒙古	29.59
4	华南地区	广东、广西、海南	28.31
5	西北地区	陕西、甘肃、青海、宁夏、新疆	26.92
6	西南地区	四川、贵州、云南、重庆、西藏	22.58
7	华中地区	河南、湖北、湖南	20.77

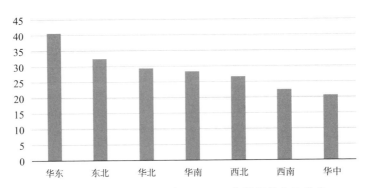

图 3.42　2017 年度不同地区 PPP 工作进展得分及排名

华东地区 PPP 工作进展得分排名第 1，主要源于项目落地率和项目开工率均为第 1 名，其中项目落地率得分远超其他省份，表现优秀。

东北地区 PPP 工作进展得分排名第 2，主要源于项目开工率高，为第 2 名，但项目落地率与第 1 名差距较大。

华北、华南、西北地区 PPP 工作进展得分排名分别为第 3 名、第 4 名、第 5 名，三个地区指标得分情况较为相似，项目落地率和项目开工率排名均较为居中。

西南地区 PPP 工作进展得分排名第 6，主要源于项目落地率低，为第 7 名，降低了整体排名；尽管落地项目开工率较高，仍需注意加快推进入库项目落地工作。

华中地区 PPP 工作进展得分排名第 7，主要源于项目落地率和项目开工率低，分别为第 6 名、第 7 名，该地区入库项目数量较多，故在发展规模的同时，还需要高度重视项目的建设和运营工作。

4. PPP 规范化程度

PPP 规范化程度由九项四级指标构成，分别为国家示范项目数、省级示范项目数、国家表彰市县数、完成物有所值评价比例、完成财政承受能力评价比例、物有所值报告定量比例、退示范退库及整改项目数、退示范退库及整改项目投资额、严重违法违规事件。这些指标从示范效应、流程合规、质量保证三方面，综合衡量了 PPP 项目是否规范，对表现优秀的项目加分表扬，对未达标准的项目扣分警示。

其中，国家示范项目数、省级示范项目数从各省份提交年报数据获得，国家表彰市县数则由国务院公开文件获得，综合评价示范效应。完成物有所值和财政承受能力评价项目数量占比，根据财政部 PPP 中心管理库项目数据统计获得；物有所值报告是否进行定量分析，由于数据暂不可得，作为建议指标加入，该三项综合评价项目流程是否合规。退示范退库及整改项目数和投资额，根据财政部 PPP 中心退库工作记录获得。严重违法违规事件目前尚未出现，但将保留该指标作为预防重大负面影响事件出现的警示。具体指标体系构成如表 3.47 所示。

表 3.47 PPP 规范化程度指标体系构成

三级指标	四级指标	经济含义	选择该指标的原因
PPP规范化程度	国家示范项目数	截至统计年度该省份入选所有批次国家示范项目的项目数总和	衡量该省份 PPP 项目在全国范围内的示范效应。国家示范项目评选涵盖了采购竞争性、社会资本真实性、运作合理性、交易结构适当性和财政持续性多个维度，综合反映该省份 PPP 工作水平，鼓励各省份开展质量优、可示范、可推广的 PPP 项目
	省级示范项目数	截至统计年度该省份入选该省份项目的项目数总和	衡量该省份 PPP 项目在该省范围内的示范效应。省级示范项目评选根据各省实际情况，评选出引导省内 PPP 项目健康发展的 PPP 项目
	国家表彰市县数	截至统计年度该省份国务院表扬推广 PPP 模式市、县数量总和	衡量该省份下辖区域 PPP 项目工作质量。国务院办公厅发文表扬推广 PPP 模式有力市县，被表扬者不仅积极开展 PPP 工作，而且 PPP 规范程度高、资源分布均衡，在医疗、环境等新领域外部效益好，具有示范作用。作为奖励，被表扬者将在以奖代补评审、来年专项补助等方面获得优先支持
	完成物有所值评价比例	该省份所有入库项目中完成物有所值评价的项目占总项目数的比例	衡量该省份 PPP 工作的前期论证质量和预期收益水平。物有所值评价拥有完善的评价体系和科学的评价方法，实行项目前开展论证，有利于识别优质项目，合理分配资源，最大化项目收益
	完成财政承受能力评价比例	该省份所有入库项目中完成财政承受能力论证的项目占总项目数的比例	衡量该省份 PPP 财政支出是否合规合适。财政承受能力论证能够有效防范和控制财政风险，规范和明确政府的支出责任，有利于PPP 项目中政府职能的发挥

（续表）

三级指标	四级指标	经济含义	选择该指标的原因
	物有所值报告定量比例	该省份所有入库项目中以定量方式进行物有所值评价的项目数占比	衡量该省份 PPP 前期论证工作的水平和质量。PPP 项目中成本估算、风险识别、权责分配都属于难以量化的部分，对相关部门的项目经验与工作能力都有要求。做好量化工作有利于合理预期和管理 PPP 项目风险和收益，该指标有助于促进定量分析的探索与开展
	退示范退库及整改项目数	该省份该年度被清退出国家级示范项目、被清退出 PPP 项目库、被要求整改的项目个数总和	依据《财政部关于进一步加强政府和社会资本合作（PPP）示范项目规范管理的通知》（财金〔2018〕54 号），当前部分 PPP 示范项目存在进展缓慢、执行走样等问题。问题类别主要有：①不再继续采用 PPP 模式实施（退出示范并出库）；②尚未完成社会资本方采购或项目实施发生重大变化（退出示范）；③运作模式不规范、采购程序不严谨、签约主体存在瑕疵（督促整改）。对存在问题的项目退库整改将起到警示作用
	退示范退库及整改项目投资额	该省份该年度被清退出国家级示范项目、被清退出 PPP 项目库、被要求整改的项目预计投资额总和	与数量指标作用类似，防止项目资金没有落实和虚报项目投资总额的问题发生
	严重违法违规事件	该省份认定为严重违法违规且造成重大负面影响的项目数	负向指标。对 PPP 项目运行中的严重违法违规事件进行严惩。目前无项目被认定为严重违法违规，该指标作为建议指标，起到警示作用

PPP规范化程度分数排名如表3.48和图3.43所示。其中，排前三名的省份为湖南、安徽、内蒙古，分数分别为87.54分、83.10分、76.35分；排后三名的省份为北京、辽宁、重庆，分数分别为47.80分、46.65分、45.55分。其中，北京、重庆由于省级示范项目和国家表彰市县区得分较低，完成物有所值评价比例和完成财政承受能力评价比例均低于全国平均，并且重庆该比例排全国最后一名，故二者在PPP规范化程度上排名落后。辽宁则主要由于退示范退库及整改项目数和投资额较多排名落后。

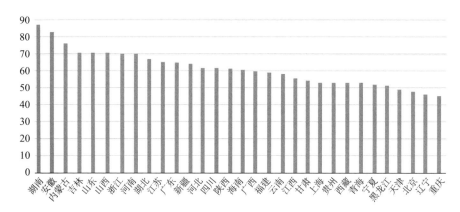

图3.43　2017年度各个省份PPP规范化程度得分及排名

表3.48　2017年度各个省份PPP规范化程度得分及排名

省份	得分	排名	所属地区	省份	得分	排名	所属地区
湖南	87.54	1	华中	广西	59.83	17	华南
安徽	83.10	2	华东	福建	59.48	18	华东
内蒙古	76.35	3	华北	云南	58.67	19	西南
吉林	71.26	4	东北	江西	56.35	20	华东
山东	71.05	5	华东	甘肃	54.65	21	西北
山西	70.74	6	华北	上海	53.60	22	华东
浙江	70.15	7	华东	贵州	53.48	23	西南
河南	70.01	8	华中	西藏	53.10	24	西南
湖北	67.50	9	华中	青海	53.06	25	西北

(续表)

省份	得分	排名	所属地区	省份	得分	排名	所属地区
江苏	65.81	10	华东	宁夏	52.44	26	西北
广东	65.33	11	华南	黑龙江	51.97	27	东北
新疆	64.78	12	西北	天津	49.15	28	华北
河北	62.31	13	华北	北京	47.80	29	华北
四川	61.93	14	西南	辽宁	46.65	30	东北
陕西	61.74	15	西北	重庆	45.55	31	西南
海南	60.95	16	华南				

PPP 规范化程度地区得分如表 3.49 和图 3.44 所示。

表 3.49 2017 年度不同地区 PPP 规范化程度得分及排名

排名	地区	本书涉及省份	平均得分
1	华中地区	河南、湖北、湖南	75.01
2	华东地区	上海、江苏、浙江、安徽、福建、江西、山东	65.65
3	华南地区	广东、广西、海南	62.04
4	华北地区	北京、天津、山西、河北、内蒙古	61.27
5	西北地区	陕西、甘肃、青海、宁夏、新疆	57.34
6	东北地区	黑龙江、吉林、辽宁	56.63
7	西南地区	四川、贵州、云南、重庆、西藏	54.55

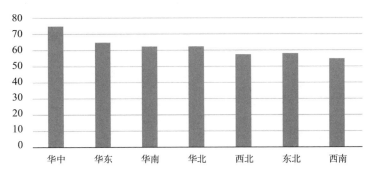

图 3.44 2017 年度不同地区 PPP 规范化程度得分及排名

华中地区 PPP 规范化程度得分排名第 1，主要源于项目示范效应突出，国家示范项目数、省级示范项目数、国家表彰市县数均为第 1 名，完成物有所值评价比例和完成财政承受能力评价比例则均为第 2 名。不足之处在于退示范项目虽然投资额小但数量过多，为第 7 名，可能存在小项目后期运营乏力或项目两极分化问题。

华东地区 PPP 规范化程度得分排名第 2，主要源于国家表彰市县数突出，国家示范项目数和国家表彰市县区数得分分别为第 2 名、第 3 名，且项目中完成物有所值评价比例和完成财政承受能力评价比例较高，被退库退示范及整改的比例也比较低。

华南地区 PPP 规范化程度得分排名第 3，主要源于项目合规程度高，完成物有所值评价比例和完成财政承受能力评价比例均为第 1 名，退示范退库项目数量和投资额也最少，排名均为第 1 名。但该地区项目示范效益很低，特别是省级示范项目、国家表彰市县区得分排名均仅为第 6 名，降低了整体排名，说明地方政府对项目的示范性、可推广性还需多做工作。

华北地区 PPP 规范化程度得分排名第 4，主要源于各项指标都居于中间位置，其中与示范效应相关的指标稍显弱势，仍有进步空间。

西北地区 PPP 规范化程度得分排名第 5，虽然国家表彰市县数和退示范退库项目得分较高，均进入前三，但国家示范项目得分较低，并且完成物有所值评价比例和完成财政承受能力评价均为第 7 名，对排名拖累明显，显示 PPP 项目的前期论证工作不到位，需要引起注意。

东北地区 PPP 规范化程度得分排名第 6，虽然退示范退库项目得分表现较好，但完成物有所值评价比例和完成财政承受能力评价的项目比例并不高，并且国家示范项目数和省级示范项目数得分过低，均为第 7 名，显示项目的示范效应弱，质量有待提高，需要更加重视 PPP 工作质量。

西南地区 PPP 规范化程度得分排名第 7，主要源于国家表彰市县数少，得分排名第 7 名，且退示范退库项目数和退示范退库项目投资额均过大，分别为第 6 名、第 7 名，其余指标表现也居中偏下，导致整体排名落后。

5. PPP 透明化程度

PPP 透明化程度由四项四级指标构成，分别为 PPP 信息公开率、PPP 市场透明度指数、PPP 政府网站信息公开、PPP 政府网站信息质量，数据分别来自荣邦瑞明数据库、《2017 中国 PPP 市场透明度报告》、各省级财政厅网站，衡量了政府 PPP 项目管理和运营工作是否公开透明，相关信息对于企业和公众而言是否简便易得，旨在促进 PPP 项目规范化、透明化程度提高，提升政策沟通、信息公示与公众监督水平。具体指标体系构成如表 3.50 所示。

表 3.50 PPP 透明化程度指标体系构成

三级指标	四级指标	经济含义	选择该指标的原因
PPP 透明化程度	PPP 信息公开率	该省份所有项目已公开文件总数占应公开文件总数的比例	衡量所有 PPP 项目相关文件公开水平。项目信息公开是 PPP 项目顺利运行的有力保障，信息公开水平越高，PPP 项目接受的监督越完善，风险越低，发展程度越好。考虑到数据在荣邦瑞明数据库中的可得性，我们认为省份 2017 每个项目应当公开的文件有可行性研究报告、实施方案附件、采购文件、PPP 项目合同附件共四项
	PPP 市场透明度指数	该省份 PPP 各责任主体对 PPP 项目信息公开的程度综合指数	综合衡量 PPP 项目透明度。该指数来源于《2017 中国 PPP 市场透明度报告》，从公开内容、时点和方式多角度，基于财政部 PPP 中心数据构建，反映该省份及时充分披露入库 PPP 项目的基本情况、实施方案、评价论证报告、采购文件、项目合同等关键信息的情况，确保 PPP 工作在阳光下开展
	PPP 政府网站信息公开	该省份财政厅网站有无 PPP 信息公开专栏	衡量政府是否积极为企业提供 PPP 政策信息，及时公开 PPP 工作规划和工作进展。该指标有助于政府和企业及时沟通政策与项目信息，并接受公众监督

（续表）

三级指标	四级指标	经济含义	选择该指标的原因
	PPP政府网站信息质量	该省份财政厅网站PPP公开信息是否内容充实、更新及时并经过归类整理	衡量政府信息公开工作是否积极到位，使企业和公众方便获得更有效及时的政策和项目信息，提高PPP工作效率和工作质量

其中，PPP 信息公开率统计了入库项目已公开文件数占应公开相关文件的比率；PPP 透明度指数引用《2017 中国 PPP 市场透明度报告》研究成果，该指数以财政部 PPP 项目管理库和储备库为统计范围，根据财政部对 PPP 项目不同阶段相应的信息公开要求，反映了各省份 PPP 项目的运营信息、项目文件等公开情况；PPP 政府网站信息公开和 PPP 政府网站信息质量两个指标，则对省级财政厅 PPP 政策和项目网上信息公开工作进行评价，促进相关工作进一步开展。

PPP 透明化程度分数排名如表 3.51 和图 3.45 所示。其中，排前三名的省份为安徽、吉林、河北，分数分别为 95.51 分、92.10 分、91.42 分；排后三名的省份为甘肃、西藏、重庆，分数分别为 21.33 分、16.85 分、5.75 分。重庆信息公开率和透明度指数得分都过低，且没有建立 PPP 信息公开平台，故透明化程度排名最后。

表 3.51　2017 年度各个省份 PPP 透明化程度得分及排名

省份	得分	排名	所属地区	省份	得分	排名	所属地区
安徽	95.51	1	华东	江苏	72.13	17	华东
吉林	92.10	2	东北	河南	70.40	18	华中
河北	91.42	3	华北	海南	68.83	19	华南
福建	89.50	4	华东	江西	65.06	20	华东
内蒙古	84.26	5	华北	北京	58.62	21	华北

（续表）

省份	得分	排名	所属地区	省份	得分	排名	所属地区
山东	83.09	6	华东	黑龙江	56.84	22	东北
宁夏	82.27	7	西北	贵州	50.47	23	西南
云南	79.61	8	西南	天津	44.49	24	华北
陕西	78.87	9	西北	上海	38.33	25	华东
湖北	78.81	10	华中	湖南	36.84	26	华中
四川	78.14	11	西南	广西	33.66	27	华南
山西	78.00	12	华北	辽宁	26.37	28	东北
浙江	76.78	13	华东	甘肃	21.33	29	西北
新疆	74.19	14	西北	西藏	16.85	30	西南
青海	73.46	15	西北	重庆	5.75	31	西南
广东	72.94	16	华南				

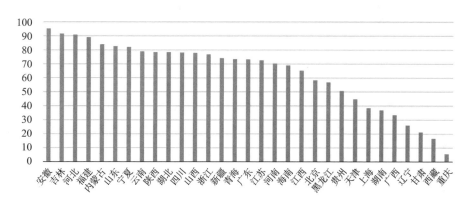

图 3.45　2017 年度各个省份 PPP 透明化程度得分及排名

PPP 透明化程度不同地区得分如表 3.52 和图 3.46 所示。

表 3.52　2017 年度不同地区 PPP 透明化程度得分及排名

排名	地区	本书涉及省份	平均得分
1	华东地区	上海、江苏、浙江、安徽、福建、江西、山东	74.34
2	华北地区	北京、天津、山西、河北、内蒙古	71.36

（续表）

排名	地区	本书涉及省份	平均得分
3	西北地区	陕西、甘肃、青海、宁夏、新疆	66.02
4	华中地区	河南、湖北、湖南	62.02
5	华南地区	广东、广西、海南	58.48
6	东北地区	黑龙江、吉林、辽宁	58.44
7	西南地区	四川、贵州、云南、重庆、西藏	46.17

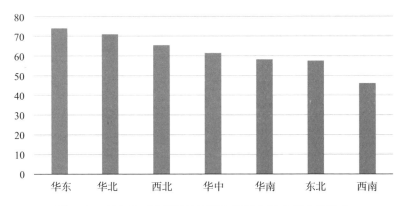

图 3.46 2017 年度不同地区 PPP 透明化程度得分及排名

华东地区 PPP 透明化程度排名第 1，主要源于 PPP 信息公开率、PPP 市场透明度指数得分均为第 1 名，说明项目相关信息及文件公开工作到位，尽管建立比例较高但 PPP 政府网站并未全部建立。

华北地区 PPP 透明化程度排名第 2，主要源于 PPP 政府网站信息公开及 PPP 政府网站信息质量得分均为第 1 名，该地区全部省份政府网站建立了 PPP 信息公开专栏，并且对信息进行了分类汇总；但该地区项目信息公开率较低，市场透明度还有进步空间，降低了排名。

西北地区 PPP 透明化程度排名第 3，主要源于 PPP 政府网站信息公开质量为第 2 名，虽未能实现所有省份建立 PPP 专栏，但已有专栏信息公开质量较好；该地区 PPP 信息公开率和 PPP 市场透明度指数较低，带低了排名。

华中地区PPP透明化程度排名第4，主要源于PPP市场透明度指数得分较高，为第2名；但PPP信息公开率则相对较低，并且由于该地区仅有三个省份，未实现所有省份建立PPP专栏，对评分影响较大。

华南地区PPP透明化程度排名第5，虽然PPP信息公开率得分较高，为第2名，但PPP市场透明度指数、PPP政府网站信息公开和PPP政府网站信息质量方面得分都居中游偏下，整体排名稍低。

东北地区PPP透明化程度排名第6，虽然PPP信息公开率和PPP市场透明度指数均为第3名，但其余项目稍弱，特别是PPP政府网站信息质量较低，没有及时更新整理，为第7名，降低了整体排名。

西南地区PPP透明化程度排名第7，主要源于PPP信息公开率、PPP市场透明度指数、PPP政府网站信息公开得分为均为第7名，该地区信息公开程度两极分化较大，未完善公开的省份还需要更加重视相关工作，从具体项目和政务公开两方面入手，提高PPP工作透明化程度。

6. PPP执行情况

PPP执行情况由六项四级指标构成，分别为公众满意度、项目建设进度符合性、项目质量符合性、项目造价符合性、社会资本或项目公司年度运营绩效、中期报告评估结果。具体指标体系构成如表3.53所示。

表3.53 PPP执行情况指标体系构成

三级指标	四级指标	经济含义	选择该指标的原因
PPP执行情况	公众满意度	该省份所有入库项目有公众评价机制的平均评价得分	衡量该省份PPP项目提供公共服务的实际效益。《关于在公共服务领域推广政府和社会资本合作模式指导意见的通知》（国办发〔2015〕42号）指出，应当建立政府、公众共同参与的综合性评价体系。在项目合同中纳入公众评价机制，有助于评价项目是否真正提供了公共服务，以区别于政府采购

（续表）

三级指标	四级指标	经济含义	选择该指标的原因
	项目建设进度符合性	该省份在财政部PPP中心公开报告并且建设经审查如期进展的项目数占执行阶段项目数的比重	衡量该省份PPP项目总体是否按约如期开工建设。财政部《政府和社会资本合作（PPP）综合信息平台信息公开管理暂行办法》（财金〔2017〕1号）要求实施机构或项目公司即时公开项目建设进度与PPP项目合同的符合性审查情况，监督项目按时按规划完成
	项目质量符合性	该省份在财政部PPP中心公开报告并符合项目质量检查标准的项目数占执行阶段项目数的比重	衡量该省份PPP项目平均工程质量是否达标。财政部《政府和社会资本合作（PPP）综合信息平台信息公开管理暂行办法》（财金〔2017〕1号）要求实施机构或项目公司即时公开项目质量与PPP项目合同的符合性审查情况，监督项目保证质量完成
	项目造价符合性	该省份在财政部PPP中心公开报告并符合项目造价检查标准的项目数占执行阶段项目数的比重	衡量该省份PPP项目平均造价是否按计划实现。财政部《政府和社会资本合作（PPP）综合信息平台信息公开管理暂行办法》（财金〔2017〕1号）要求实施机构或项目公司即时公开项目造价与PPP项目合同的符合性审查情况，监督项目按照合同以合适造价完成
	社会资本或项目公司年度运营绩效	该省份所有执行阶段项目披露的社会资本或项目公司资产回报率	衡量该省份PPP项目运营回报率。财政部《政府和社会资本合作（PPP）综合信息平台信息公开管理暂行办法》（财金〔2017〕1号）要求即时公开社会资本或项目公司财务状况和项目运营绩效，将绩效纳入考评能够反映PPP项目运营质量，改变PPP项目重建设现状，引导PPP工作重运营，体现PPP提供公共服务的本质特点
	中期报告评估结果	该省份在财政部PPP中心公开经审核达标中期评估报告的项目数占执行阶段项目数的比重	衡量该省份PPP项目公司平均运营状况。财政部《政府和社会资本合作（PPP）综合信息平台信息公开管理暂行办法》（财金〔2017〕1号）要求即时公开项目公司绩效监测报告、中期评估报告、项目重大变更或终止情况、项目定价及历次调价情况，其中，中期评估报告能够综合反映项目公司运营总体状况，监督项目公司健康稳定运转

上述指标对评估 PPP 执行效果很有价值，但数据暂不可得，故我们将其作为建议指标列出。针对当前 PPP 项目存在的"重建设、轻运营"、政府和企业运营能力弱的问题，PPP 执行情况从项目建设和运营成果、资源利用效率、专业和社会评估等方面，综合衡量 PPP 项目入库后的运营工作进展，有利于开展项目全生命周期监督和管理，实现 PPP 项目"运营"利用项目资产为社会公众持续提供公共服务、并依据公共服务的质量和数量获取报酬的本质特征。

7. PPP 移交情况

PPP 移交情况由两项四级指标构成，分别为项目设施移交标准达标检测结果、项目后评价结果。上述指标对评价 PPP 项目移交阶段成果很有价值，但数据暂不可得，故作为建议指标列出。PPP 项目移交标志着项目 PPP 合作的生命周期的结束，项目公司需将项目设施及相关权益以合同约定的条件和程序移交给政府或其他指定机构。虽然 PPP 项目在我国开展数年，但目前仍未有项目进入移交阶段。参考国外经验及研究结果，移交阶段时项目设施的价值评估及权益交割将成为该阶段能否顺利推进的关键。财政部 PPP 中心要求移交阶段项目公开项目设施移交标准达标检测和项目后评价结果，从而对价值评估和权益安排的合理性进行衡量和考核，保证 PPP 项目合作顺利结束。具体的指标体系构成如表 3.54 所示。

表 3.54 PPP 移交情况指标体系构成

三级指标	四级指标	经济含义	选择该指标的原因
PPP 移交情况	项目设施移交标准达标检测结果	该省份所有通过并公开移交标准达标检测结果的项目占移交项目总数的比重	衡量该省份 PPP 项目最终能否达到移交标准。PPP 项目在移交前需对项目设施移交时价值进行评估，需要达到权利、技术等多项标准，并且通过性能测试，才能符合移交要求。对移交标准进行达标检测，有助于保证项目资产质量，保障移交当事人的权益

(续表)

三级指标	四级指标	经济含义	选择该指标的原因
项目后评价结果		该省份平均所有移交阶段项目的项目移交后绩效评价得分	项目移交完成后,财政部门将组织有关部门对项目产出、成本效益、监管成效、可持续性、PPP模式应用等进行绩效评价,标志着一个PPP项目的生命周期正式结束。该评价结果可作为评价该PPP项目整体成果的综合指标

(三) PPP 风险收益评价

PPP风险收益衡量PPP项目在其生命周期中所能产生的内部与外部收益及潜在的风险,这些因素共同决定了PPP项目自身的价值。而只有PPP项目自身具有足够的价值,采用PPP模式进行项目投资才是有意义的,才能充分发挥PPP模式的优势,达到预期的效果。其中内部收益指项目本身带来的经济回报,外部收益指项目的社会意义、所具有的矫正正外部性的作用,而项目风险指可能造成项目失败的潜在因素。高的内外部收益和低的风险使得PPP项目拥有更高的创益能力和吸引力,代表更高的项目质量。

该指数由PPP项目收益、PPP项目风险、PPP外部效益三个三级指标构成。其中PPP项目收益包括全投资收益率、资本金收益率、合理利润率、物有所值(Value for Money,简称VFM)指数四个四级指标;PPP项目风险包括项目全部风险成本占比、风险隔离度两个四级指标;PPP外部效益包括PPP基础公共服务效益、PPP污染防治和绿色保护效益、PPP旅游文化发展效益、贫困县管理库总项目数、贫困县管理库项目总金额、贫困县覆盖率六个四级指标。指标体系如图3.47与表3.55所示。

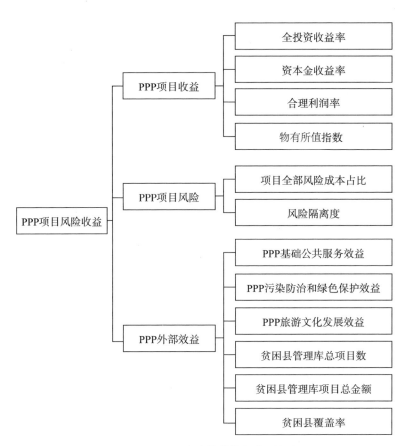

图 3.47　PPP 风险收益指标体系框架

表 3.55　PPP 风险收益指标体系构成

二级指标	三级指标	四级指标	指标的计算公式	选择该指标的原因
PPP项目风险收益	PPP项目收益	全投资收益率	该省份 PPP 项目全投资收益率的平均值	根据《建设项目经济评价方法与参数》[1] 的全投资现金流量模型测算的内部收益率，综合反映 PPP 项目给各参与方创造的整体投资效益

---

[1] 国家发展改革委、建设部：《建设项目经济评价方法与参数》。北京：中国计划出版社 2006 年版。

（续表）

二级指标	三级指标	四级指标	指标的计算公式	选择该指标的原因
		资本金收益率	该省份PPP项目资本金收益率的平均值	根据《建设项目经济评价方法与参数》的项目资本金现金流量模型测算的内部收益率，考虑了融资的杠杆因素，反映PPP项目给投资方创造的投资效益
		合理利润率	该省份PPP项目合理利润率的平均值	合理利润率用于政府根据项目建设成本、运营成本及利润水平合理确定运营补贴，应以商业银行中长期贷款利率水平为基准，充分考虑可用性付费、使用量付费、绩效付费的不同情景，结合风险等因素确定，不宜过高或过低
		物有所值指数	该省份PPP项目物有所值指数的平均值	反映了PPP模式与传统模式相比较，是否实现了物有所值及资源的最大化利用
PPP项目风险		项目全部风险成本占比	项目全部风险成本/项目总投资额，并计算各项目的平均值	项目全部风险成本是在充分考虑各项主要风险（在风险识别与分配环节确认）出现的概率及其后果后，对未来项目风险成本的度量，该比值反映了PPP项目风险成本的相对大小
		风险隔离度	成立项目公司特殊目的载体（Special Purpose Vehicle，简称SPV）的项目的比例	特殊目的载体能够实现PPP项目的有限追索，是风险隔离的重要载体，在管控项目风险、提高项目收益上发挥着重要作用
PPP外部效益	PPP基础公共服务效益	PPP基础公共服务效益	该省份入库项目中属于基本公共服务领域的项目数占比	基本公共服务领域包括文化、体育、医疗、养老、教育、旅游等，该指标体现PPP在基本公共服务领域的投入程度，引导政府发挥矫正外部性的作用

(续表)

二级指标	三级指标	四级指标	指标的计算公式	选择该指标的原因
		PPP污染防治和绿色保护效益	该省份入库项目中属于污染防治和绿色低碳领域的项目数占比	污染防治和绿色低碳领域包括公共交通、供排水、生态建设和环境保护、水利建设、可再生能源、林业、旅游等，该指标体现PPP在污染防治和绿色低碳领域的投入程度，引导政府发挥矫正外部性的作用
		PPP旅游文化发展效益	该省份入库项目中属于文化和旅游领域的项目数占比	旅游文化领域包括旅游和文化两个行业，该指标体现PPP在旅游文化领域的投入程度，引导政府发挥矫正外部性的作用
		贫困县管理库总项目数	直接引用数据	该指标反映PPP在贫困地区的总体实施情况，有助于发挥PPP助力贫困县脱贫的作用
		贫困县管理库项目总金额	直接引用数据	该指标反映PPP在贫困地区的总体实施情况，有助于发挥PPP助力贫困县脱贫的作用
		贫困县覆盖率	该省份有项目库项目的贫困县数占总贫困县数之比	该指标反映PPP在贫困地区的覆盖情况，有助于发挥PPP助力贫困县脱贫的作用，并鼓励贫困县推行PPP项目改善基础设施环境，发展经济

根据搜集的数据，我们计算得到31个省份的PPP风险收益指标得分，具体如表3.56和图3.48所示。

表3.56 2017年度各个省份PPP风险收益得分及排名

省份	得分	排名	所属地区	省份	得分	排名	所属地区
贵州	78.49	1	西南	山西	48.13	17	华北
山东	74.68	2	华东	吉林	44.35	18	东北

（续表）

省份	得分	排名	所属地区	省份	得分	排名	所属地区
河南	73.80	3	华中	宁夏	44.20	19	西北
内蒙古	69.91	4	华北	上海	43.67	20	华东
湖南	65.39	5	华中	海南	42.84	21	华南
新疆	64.89	6	西北	天津	42.10	22	华北
云南	62.14	7	西南	广东	41.95	23	华南
湖北	55.64	8	华中	黑龙江	40.96	24	东北
河北	55.46	9	华北	江西	40.34	25	华东
四川	55.27	10	西南	辽宁	39.61	26	东北
浙江	55.05	11	华东	西藏	38.59	27	西南
安徽	54.58	12	华东	甘肃	32.82	28	西北
江苏	54.18	13	华东	重庆	32.44	29	西南
福建	51.21	14	华东	青海	31.08	30	西北
广西	50.33	15	华南	北京	30.46	31	华北
陕西	49.98	16	西北				

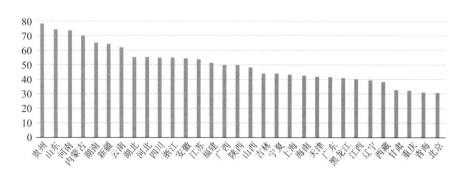

图 3.48　2017 年度各个省份 PPP 风险收益得分及排名

贵州排名第 1，主要源于 PPP 项目收益、PPP 项目风险、PPP 外部效益等状况较好，分别为第 6、4、2 名。尤其是在发展贫困县的 PPP 项目上，其贫困县项目总数与总金额均位列全国首位，且贫困县覆盖比例也位于高水平。

内蒙古排名第 4，主要源于 PPP 外部效益状况较好，为第 3 名；PPP 项目收益呈现相对中性影响，为第 19 名；但 PPP 项目风险拖累了其 PPP 风险收益指数，为第 24 名。内蒙古 PPP 项目的突出点是 PPP 外部效益高，在污染防治和绿色保护、文化旅游领域的项目方面投入力度大。

新疆排名第 6，主要源于 PPP 外部效益状况较好，为第 6 名；PPP 项目风险呈现相对中性影响，为第 18 名；但 PPP 项目收益拖累了其 PPP 风险收益指数，为第 24 名。与贵州、内蒙古一样，新疆注重 PPP 项目的外部效益，充分发挥了政府矫正外部性作用。

重庆排名第 29，主要源于 PPP 项目收益、PPP 项目风险、PPP 外部效益等相对较差，分别为第 26 名、第 27 名、第 27 名。其 PPP 项目全投资收益率及资本金收益率在全国处于较低水平，有待提高；此外，尚未有贫困县 PPP 项目进入财政部管理库，需要突破。

北京排名第 31，主要源于 PPP 项目风险、PPP 外部效益等相对较差，分别为第 31 名、第 28 名；不过项目收益状况较好，为第 3 名。PPP 项目风险方面，尤其是项目全部风险成本占比偏高，需要加以控制；PPP 外部效益上，反映出 PPP 模式在基础公共服务、旅游文化领域的运用较少。

我们同样选取不同地理地区作为整体，统计不同地区的平均得分，并进行排名，具体排名如表 3.57 和图 3.49 所示。

表 3.57　2017 年度不同地区 PPP 风险收益得分及排名

排名	地区	本书涉及省份	平均得分
1	华中地区	河南、湖北、湖南	64.94
2	华东地区	上海、江苏、浙江、安徽、福建、江西、山东	53.39
3	西南地区	四川、贵州、云南、重庆、西藏	53.39
4	华北地区	北京、天津、山西、河北、内蒙古	49.21
5	华南地区	广东、广西、海南	45.04
6	西北地区	陕西、甘肃、青海、宁夏、新疆	44.60
7	东北地区	黑龙江、吉林、辽宁	41.64

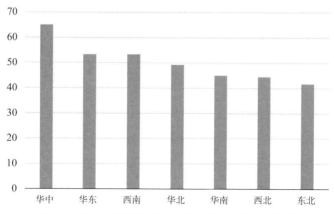

图 3.49　2017 年度不同地区 PPP 风险收益得分及排名

华中地区排名第 1，主要源于 PPP 外部效益状况较好，为第 1 名；PPP 项目收益呈现相对中性影响，为第 3 名；但 PPP 项目风险拖累了其 PPP 风险收益指数，为第 6 名。

华东地区排名第 2，主要源于 PPP 项目收益、PPP 项目风险等状况较好，分别为第 1 名、第 2 名；PPP 外部效益呈现相对中性影响，为第 3 名。

西南地区排名第 3，主要源于 PPP 项目收益、PPP 外部效益等状况较好，均为第 2 名；PPP 项目风险排名相对居中，为第 3 名。

华北地区排名第 4，PPP 项目收益、PPP 项目风险、PPP 外部效益等排名均相对居中，分别为第 5 名、第 5 名、第 4 名。

华南地区排名第 5，主要源于 PPP 项目风险状况较好，为第 1 名；但 PPP 项目收益、PPP 外部效益等相对较差，分别为第 7 名、第 6 名，对其 PPP 风险收益指数拖累较大。

西北地区排名第 6，主要源于 PPP 项目收益、PPP 项目风险等相对较差，分别为第 6 名、第 7 名；外部效益排名相对居中，为第 5 名。

东北地区排名第 7，主要源于 PPP 外部效益相对较差，为第 7 名；PPP 项目收益、PPP 项目风险等排名均相对居中，均为第 4 名。

（四）PPP 发展空间评价

PPP 模式指的是政府与社会资本合作参与公共基础设施建设，而 PPP

发展空间反映了一个地区尚未被满足的公共基础设施建设的需求。这部分需求越大，意味着未来开展 PPP 项目的机会越多，同时地方政府积极参与 PPP 以提升公共服务的意愿也更加强烈，形成对 PPP 模式推广发展的更强大的内在推动力。该指数是对地区未来 PPP 市场潜在规模的有力预示指标，指出了 PPP 模式将在何处能拥有更宽广的展示舞台。

该指数由基础设施现状、城镇化水平、基建投资潜力、储备项目规模 4 个三级指标构成。其中基础设施现状包括人均用电量、人均供水量、公路网密度等 17 个四级指标，反映地区基础设施水平；城镇化水平包括城镇化率 1 个四级指标；基建投资潜力包括基建投资增长率、基建投资额、基建投资占 GDP 比重 3 个四级指标，反映当前基建投资的表现；储备项目规模包括储备项目数、储备项目金额、储备项目数量增速、储备项目投资增速 4 个四级指标。指标体系如图 3.50 与表 3.58 所示。

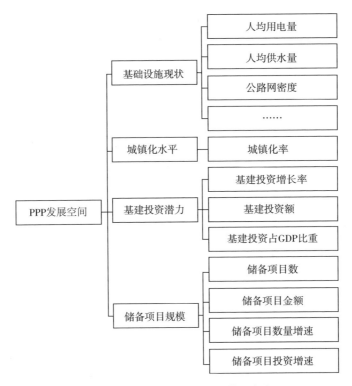

图 3.50　PPP 发展空间指标体系框架

表 3.58　PPP 发展空间指标体系构成

二级指标	三级指标	四级指标	指标的计算公式	选择该指标的原因
PPP发展空间	基础设施现状	人均用电量	全社会用电量/地区常住人口	是反映地区基础设施建设水平的指标之一，体现未来对 PPP 模式的潜在需求大小
		人均供水量	城市供水总量/地区常住人口	
		公路网密度	公路通车里程数/地区面积	
		排水管道密度	排水管道总长度/建成区面积	
		污水处理能力	污水处理厂和污水处理装置每昼夜处理污水量的设计能力	
		生活垃圾无害化处理率	生活垃圾无害化处理量/生活垃圾产生量	
		城市燃气普及率	使用燃气人口占总人口比率	
		互联网普及率	互联网用户数/地区常住人口	
		每万人拥有公共交通车辆	公共交通车辆运营数/地区常住人口×10 000	
		每万人拥有老年人服务床位数	老年人服务床位数/地区常住人口×10 000	
		每万人拥有公共图书馆建筑面积	公共图书馆建筑总面积/地区常住人口×10 000	
		每万在校生拥有中小学校数	中小学校数/中小学校在校学生数×10 000	
		每万人拥有卫生技术人员数	卫生技术人员数/地区常住人口×10 000	
		每万人医疗机构床位数	医疗卫生机构床位数/地区常住人口×10 000	

（续表）

二级指标	三级指标	四级指标	指标的计算公式	选择该指标的原因
		每万人拥有公共厕所数	公共厕所数/地区常住人口×10 000	
		城市绿化覆盖率	建成区绿化覆盖面积/建成区面积	
		人均公园绿地面积	公园绿地总面积/地区常住人口	
	城镇化水平	城镇化率	城镇人口/常住人口	城镇化的不断推进将对基础设施和公共服务产生持续、多样且庞大的需求，PPP都大有可为
	基建投资潜力	基建投资增长率	直接引用数据	较高的基建投资增长率表明基建投资需求的快速增长，体现出巨大的基建投资潜力，基建投资正是PPP的重要形式
		基建投资额	直接引用数据	基建投资额直接反映出地区基建投资的需求，基建投资是PPP的重要形式，能表现PPP的发展潜力
		基建投资占GDP比重	基建投资额/地区GDP	表现基建投资在经济中的比重及活跃程度，同样是刻画基建投资和PPP发展潜力的指标

(续表)

二级指标	三级指标	四级指标	指标的计算公式	选择该指标的原因
	储备项目规模	储备项目数	直接引用数据	储备库项目处于识别阶段，未来或成为新的PPP正式项目，其规模表现了未来可能的PPP项目规模。
		储备项目金额	直接引用数据	
		储备项目数量增速	直接引用数据	衡量储备项目规模的增长趋势
		储备项目投资增速	直接引用数据	

根据搜集的数据，我们计算得到31个省份的PPP发展空间指标得分，并根据PPP发展空间指标得分进行排名，具体如表3.59和图3.51所示。

表3.59　2017年度各个省份PPP发展空间得分及排名

省份	得分	排名	所属地区	省份	得分	排名	所属地区
贵州	63.85	1	西南	安徽	47.32	17	华东
新疆	59.15	2	西北	福建	47.07	18	华东
河南	58.61	3	华中	山东	46.70	19	华东
湖北	58.26	4	华中	山西	43.27	20	华北
云南	57.98	5	西南	广东	42.54	21	华南
西藏	57.34	6	西南	吉林	41.67	22	东北
四川	56.51	7	西南	重庆	41.63	23	西南
广西	52.47	8	华南	宁夏	38.82	24	西北
江西	50.32	9	华东	内蒙古	38.30	25	华北
陕西	49.67	10	西北	辽宁	37.61	26	东北

（续表）

省份	得分	排名	所属地区	省份	得分	排名	所属地区
河北	49.53	11	华北	天津	37.38	27	华北
湖南	48.88	12	华中	江苏	37.06	28	华东
甘肃	48.64	13	西北	浙江	36.78	29	华东
黑龙江	48.47	14	东北	上海	25.76	30	华东
海南	47.68	15	华南	北京	23.83	31	华北
青海	47.59	16	西北				

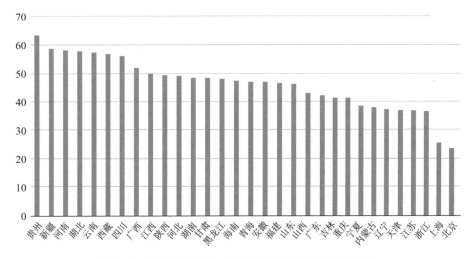

图 3.51　2017 年度各个省份 PPP 发展空间得分及排名

贵州排名第 1，主要源于基础设施现状、基建投资潜力、城镇化率、储备项目规模等状况均较好，分别为第 6 名、第 4 名、第 2 名、第 2 名。应当注意的是基础设施现状与城镇化率是负向指标，较薄弱的基础设施环境和较低的城镇化率意味着未来更广阔的建设空间、对 PPP 项目更大的需求。该省在这两项上相对落后的水平，以及其规模领先的储备项目量，能激起未来大量 PPP 项目的发展。

河南排名第 3，主要源于基础设施现状、基建投资潜力、城镇化率、储备项目规模等状况均较好，分别为第 7 名、第 7 名、第 7 名、第 5 名。该省属于经济较发达地区，但相对而言基础设施并不完善，农村人口占比高，此外较大的基建投资额和储备项目规模也创造了更多 PPP 发展的空间。

湖北排名第 4，主要源于基建投资潜力、储备项目规模等状况较好，分别为第 5 名、第 1 名；基础设施现状、城镇化率等呈现相对中性的影响，分别为第 19 名。该省属于较为发达地区，其基础设施环境较为良好，但近年来对基础设施建设的大量投资及储备项目快速增长的趋势使其排名靠前。

宁夏排名第 24，主要源于基础设施现状、基建投资潜力、储备项目规模等相对较差，分别为第 26 名、第 24 名、第 23 名；城镇化率排名相对居中，为第 17 名。该省处于西北偏远地区，但基础设施现状在全国达到较高标准，对基建投资的需求也较少。

上海排名第 30，主要源于基础设施现状、基建投资潜力、城镇化率等相对较差，分别为第 30 名、第 28 名、第 31 名；储备项目规模排名相对居中，为第 16 名。以上海为代表的发达地区，基础设施完善，基建投资占 GDP 比重小且增长空间小，PPP 储备项目往往也不会很多，导致 PPP 发展空间不如其他地区大。

我们同样选取不同地理地区作为整体，统计不同地区的平均得分，并进行排名，具体排名如表 3.60 和图 3.52 所示。

表 3.60　2017 年度不同地区 PPP 发展空间得分及排名

排名	地区	本书涉及省份	平均得分
1	西南地区	四川、贵州、云南、重庆、西藏	55.46
2	华中地区	河南、湖北、湖南	55.25
3	西北地区	陕西、甘肃、青海、宁夏、新疆	48.77
4	华南地区	广东、广西、海南	47.56

(续表)

排名	地区	本书涉及省份	平均得分
5	东北地区	黑龙江、吉林、辽宁	42.58
6	华东地区	上海、江苏、浙江、安徽、福建、江西、山东	41.57
7	华北地区	北京、天津、山西、河北、内蒙古	38.46

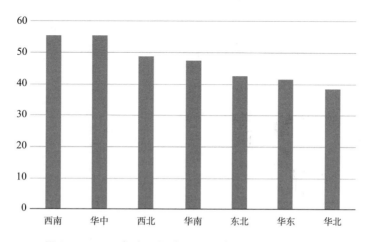

图 3.52　2017 年度不同地区 PPP 发展空间得分及排名

西南地区排名第 1，主要源于基础设施现状、基建投资潜力、城镇化率、储备项目规模等状况均较好，分别为第 1 名、第 2 名、第 1 名、第 2 名。

华中地区排名第 2，主要源于基建投资潜力、储备项目规模等状况较好，均为第 1 名；基础设施现状、城镇化率等呈现相对中性影响，均为第 3 名。

西北地区排名第 3，主要源于城镇化率状况较好，为第 2 名；基础设施现状、基建投资潜力、储备项目规模等排名均相对居中，分别为第 5 名、第 4 名、第 4 名。

华南地区排名第 4，主要源于基础设施现状较好，为第 2 名；基建投资潜力、城镇化率等排名均相对居中，分别为第 3 名、第 4 名；但储备项目规模相对较差,为第7名,对其PPP发展空间指数拖累较大。

东北地区排名第5,基础设施现状、城镇化率等排名均相对居中,分别为第4名、第5名;但基建投资潜力、储备项目规模等相对较差,分别为第7名、第6名,对其PPP发展空间指数拖累较大。

华东地区排名第6,主要源于基础设施现状、城镇化率等相对较差,均为第6名;基建投资潜力、储备项目规模等排名相对居中,均为第5名。

华北地区排名第7,主要源于基础设施现状、基建投资潜力、城镇化率等相对较差,分别为第7名、第6名、第7名;储备项目规模排名相对居中,为第3名。

第四章 政策建议

一、政府保障领域

(一) 从宏观和微观两个方面促进中部地区和北部地区省份 PPP 发展

2018 年 7 月 23 日，国务院总理李克强在国务院常务会议上指出："要有效保障在建项目资金需求。督促地方盘活财政存量资金，引导金融机构按照市场化原则保障融资平台公司合理融资需求，对必要的在建项目避免资金断供、工程烂尾。"在 PPP 项目的建设过程中，政府的财政资金是项目重要的资金来源和保障，因此，各省份的财政资金充裕水平对当地 PPP 项目的发展建设具有重要的影响。

根据 PPP 政府财政保障指数的计算结果，中部地区及北部地区数据显著落后于东南部地区，说明中部地区及北部地区经济发展水平、财政汲取能力都较为落后。这与 2017 年 GDP 的衡量结果相同。可见，较低水平的经济发展与政府财政非常不利于当地的 PPP 项目发展建设，不能做到与全国 PPP 项目协同发展。

本书中项目运行指数的相关数据表明，地区经济水平发达程度与当地 PPP 项目的开工率和落地率基本呈正相关关系。

"PPP"是"政府与社会资本合作"的简称，如果政府财政能力不允许政府方在资金方面给予地方企业足够的支持，将会非常不利于政府方与社会资本方建立长期稳定的合作关系。由于政府财政资金不足、支出限额较低，提供给 PPP 项目的资金会相应减少，导致项目建设方面临资金短缺、周转困难的可能性大大增加，甚至更容易面临资金链断裂、项目烂尾的风险。

从微观层面看，PPP 项目的违约率、拖欠款项率会随着政府财政压力增大而提高，不利于当地政府的信誉提升及当地的 PPP 发展。社会资本进入前通常会考虑合作方（政府）的资金充足度和信誉良好情况。因此我们建议，经济落后地区政府根据其自身的发展情况制定 PPP 项目。例如，政府可以帮助贫困地区制订脱贫计划并适当给予资金支持，助其实施。

从宏观层面看，可以适当增加中央转移支付或减税，在有关省份资助兴建公共基础设施，完善教育和医疗服务保障等。金融投资方面，可以加强当地金融市场体制深化改革，设置投资优惠、鼓励和引入外资，给予目标地区的龙头企业相关税收与政策优惠等。企业与产业方面，应培植和扶持特色经济和骨干企业，加大对当地优势产业的扶持力度，扶持高新技术产业发展。应从多个维度有针对性地改变落后省份的市场环境，提升其财政汲取能力，降低债务水平，提高财政自给能力，为当地 PPP 发展提供良好的财政保障。

（二）建立健全 PPP 相关的法律法规，提升法治水平

2017 年，我国加强了 PPP 相关的法律法规建设。针对当地 PPP 项目在发展过程中出现的问题，各省份出台了相应的规范要求与指导意见。但是法律法规总量提升的同时其总体水平依然不高，各地区间法治水平的差异则是更为突出的问题。

华东地区与华南地区政府建设的体系较为完善，决策程序透明度高，有较强的意识通过法律保障 PPP 项目在当地的发展，这给其他地区起了很

好的示范作用。法治发展较为落后的地区亟须转变观念，强化针对 PPP 项目的立法与执法，积极制定政策措施。

城市之间的协同与带动作用同样不可忽视，地理区域临近的地区具有更多相似之处及更大的可比性，相对落后的省份要选好参照物，进行多维比较，积极探求 PPP 发展之道，因地制宜制定并出台切实有效的法律法规，发挥区域协同作用，提高地区发展的均衡度。

（三）各地政府需要进一步提升基金规模与项目规模的匹配度，完善基金内部结构设计、防控风险，促进区域间平衡发展

2016 年经国务院批准，财政部与多方社会资本成立了注册资本为 1 800 亿元的中国 PPP 基金，旨在为各地 PPP 项目的开展提供资金支持。同时，地方政府也积极研究 PPP 引导基金的设立方案，为当地 PPP 项目丰富资金可获得性。二者综合体现了政府在金融方面对 PPP 项目的保障力度。2017 年，中国 PPP 基金已在各地陆续提供融资帮助，省级政府也逐渐设立地方引导基金，政府在金融方面的保障力度有了很大的提升。

但是，基金的总体规模仍然不高，面对庞大的项目数量与规模，保障 PPP 项目的稳健运行仍需大量社会资本的投入。各地区基金规模的差异较大，基金规模与项目规模的不匹配问题也依然存在。同时基金未能很好地隔离与把控内部风险，故其安全性与保障能力仍待加强。

一方面，各地政府需要进一步提升基金规模与项目规模的匹配；另一方面，要完善基金内部结构设计，强化风险的隔离与掌控。财政部方面要统筹规划与安排，综合考虑地区 PPP 的发展情况，给予不同力度的支持，降低项目集中地区的违约风险，使区域间的发展更加平衡。

（四）进一步规范办事流程，提高办事效率，提升政府透明度，强化政府公信力程度

政府受公众信任的程度对 PPP 的发展有着更为基础性的影响。政府公

信力的建设与政府职能的践行及政府目标的实现关系十分密切。2017年，除了东北地区表现差强人意，我国各个地区政府公信力都表现较好，量化得分基本能够达到良好水平，各个地区的公信力水平也较为接近。

提升政府公信力可以从以下三个方面考虑：一是政府要更加合理、有效地履行其职能，进一步规范办事流程，提高办事效率；二是政府透明度有待提高，尤其在信息的公开领域、公开范围、公开时效方面，应当更多地考虑群众的所思所想所求；三要总结教训、吸取经验，对表现好的地区进行实地考察，对本地的民风民情展开实地探访。

PPP是政府与社会资本合作的模式，政府的公信程度直接影响社会资本方对项目的认可程度及出资意愿，一个受信任的政府能够更加有序高效地完成其目标，同时提高人民群众的获得感。

二、社会参与领域

（一）降低融资成本，提高社会资本总体参与度

随着财政部PPP项目管理库清理整顿行动接近尾声，以及中共中央政治局会议要求加大基础设施领域补短板的力度，银行等金融机构开始加大对基础设施建设领域的投资，部分企业感受到PPP项目融资难现象有好转迹象，但是要求进一步降低社会资本的参与难度，因此提高社会资本参与度仍然困难重重。

在政策层面上，中央对地方政府债务的态度进一步收紧，降低地方政府负债率、清理地方政府隐形债务的力度在逐渐增大，多地涉及政府债务或者隐形债务的项目被要求限期偿还，化解债务，这要求社会资本在基础设施建设领域扮演更为重要的角色，PPP等项目中社会资本出资额占比会逐渐提高；与之对应，社会资本将承担更多责任，社会资本方的融资压力也会逐渐增大。同时，货币信用环境发生了转折性变化，"资管新规"要

求降低金融体系杠杆率，改变过去泛滥的影子银行业务，市场资金收紧会导致社会资本的融资成本升高、融资难度逐渐提升，进而对社会资本参与 PPP 项目形成压力。

因此，在社会资本融资成本不断提升的背景下，需要通过政策引导降低银行等金融机构的 PPP 项目借贷利率，减轻 PPP 参与企业的融资压力。需要明确责任归属、提高项目透明度，在严控地方政府杠杆率的同时，防范地方政府将债务转移给企业，防范"明股实债"现象；在实行"资管新规"、防范系统性金融风险的同时，需要保证市场流动性，化解银行"惜贷"现象，为企业提供充足流动性。

（二）提高民营企业、港澳台企业及外资企业参与度

民间资本在 PPP 项目中遇到的最大难题是融资难。财政部 PPP 项目管理库清理整顿期间，银行对 PPP 项目放贷较为谨慎，对民营企业的 PPP 融资需求批准率较低。而在债券市场上两极化偏向也较为明显，投资者偏好国有企业，对民营企业比较谨慎，民营企业的公司债券认购额不足的现象普遍存在，即便是信用评级较高的民营企业，债券认购规模也仍然偏小。根据全国 PPP 综合信息平台项目管理库各省 2017 年年报，PPP 参与企业中民营企业占比大多在 50% 以下，仅少数省份民营企业占比超过 50%。因此，改善民营企业融资条件，为民营企业营造公平参与 PPP 项目的环境，才能切实提高民营企业的参与度。

具体措施方面，第一，要营造公平公正的招投标环境，杜绝"跑关系、走后门"现象，减少地域歧视，减少对民营企业的不公平对待，确保真正有实力、有经验的企业能赢得项目；第二，为 PPP 参与企业营造相对宽松的营商环境，精准降低税费，引导社会资本积极参与 PPP 项目，促进 PPP 模式良性循环，增强社会资本方项目运作经验；第三，引导金融机构降低对 PPP 参与企业的融资门槛，降低企业资金负担，保证企业有充足的流动性用于多个项目的开展。

此外，港澳台及外资企业参与 PPP 项目的积极性也亟待提升。根据全国 PPP 综合信息平台项目管理库各省 2017 年年报，多数省份签约港澳台及外资企业比例低于 10%，相当数量省份的 PPP 项目没有港澳台及外资企业的身影。相比民营企业，外资企业融资条件较为宽松，但其对投资我国的 PPP 项目热情不高，与政府的沟通理解不够深入，造成其对 PPP 项目可持续性、投资回报率和风险存在疑惑，导致 PPP 参与度较低。因此加强政府与港澳台及外资企业的沟通交流，降低企业对 PPP 项目的担忧，引导港澳台及外资企业认识到 PPP 项目的价值，才能激发它们的参与热情，从源头提高港澳台及外资企业的参与热情。

（三）建立健全有关社会资本退出方式的法律法规，完善中国 PPP 市场建设

规范的社会资本退出方式有利于提高社会资本方对 PPP 项目的信任度，有利于 PPP 市场的良好发展。近年来，我国大规模开展 PPP 项目，大量项目投入运营。其中，仅有少数项目到期，进入社会资本退出阶段。因而，关于社会资本退出的操作方式，我国尚需普适性的规范文件。社会资本退出的操作方式可以分为到期移交、股权回购、售后回租、IPO 上市、资产证券化、PPP 交易所等。社会资本退出的灵活性将会极大影响社会资本是否进入 PPP 项目的决策，同时它也是衡量一个地区 PPP 市场完善程度的标志之一。

三、项目运行领域

（一）优化资源配置

优化行业资源配置。2017 年，各省份分行业项目数量前三位占比普遍较高，多数在 60%—80% 不等，高者可达 90%。PPP 资源集中于市政工

程、交通运输、生态建设和环境保护、城镇综合开发领域，主要原因是这些领域 PPP 运营模式较为成熟，并且我国基础设施需求空间仍然很大，但地方政府财政空间较为紧张。然而，资源过度集中于同一领域易产生过度竞争、发展不平衡等问题，地区除依赖投资发展经济外，也需要提升城乡建设水平，特别需要供给更优质的公共服务，改善城镇居民生活。PPP 可应用领域有 18 个之多，国务院也多次出台文件，提倡将 PPP 应用于农业、医疗、养老、文化、旅游等多个领域。

应鼓励 PPP 项目多元化发展，积极探索多领域存量项目转为 PPP、新领域新建项目拓展 PPP，为社会资本广泛投资基础设施和公共事业提供合作渠道，保证资金收益，实现协调发展。为扩大 PPP 行业覆盖面，可实行负面清单管理，减少政府和社会资本在新行业开发项目的限制，为社会资本进入创造平等机会；为实现有效激励，可在示范项目评选中，将项目是否结合地区实际情况拓展新领域、新模式，是否属于产业政策支持领域纳入评价体系；为从整体出发配置资源，可在财政承受能力论证年度总结阶段加强对行业和领域均衡性评估，以协调资源、改进工作，调整次年不同行业和领域 PPP 支出规划。

优化地区资源配置。2017 年，全国各省份 PPP 项目平均地区集中度为 48%，省份间差异较大，高者为 70%—80%，低者为 20%—30%。PPP 项目可投资基础设施和公共服务领域，可助力保护环境和脱贫攻坚，应统筹规划财政资源，协助识别和开发各个地区的优质项目，建立不同级别行政区间项目信息沟通渠道，为社会资本获取多种项目信息提供便利，从而促进地方经济均衡发展，防止地区间差异进一步增大。

（二）加强规范管理

加强规范管理主要有以下措施：

1. 严格入库标准

2017 年全国入库项目总投资增速为 32%，总数量增速为 38%，各省份积极推进项目入库的同时,也暴露出一些突击审核、以次充好问题,库中项目落地率平均仅40%,公示物有所值评价和财政承受能力论证的项目数也刚刚过半。PPP项目库实行动态管理,入库本身并不像市场准入那样是一种行政许可行为。但从社会资本与金融机构的态度看,项目入库特别是示范库,意味着对项目质量的肯定。

因此,一方面,入库工作要严格控制质量,依据《财政部办公厅关于规范政府和社会资本合作(PPP)综合信息平台项目库管理的通知》(财办金〔2017〕92号)规定,对存在三类问题(不适宜采用PPP模式实施、前期准备工作不到位、未建立按效付费机制)的PPP项目严格禁止入库;要提高入库项目通过物有所值评价、财政承受能力论证的审查标准,重视项目的量化分析和测算,确保项目工程设计和融资安排可行性,注重项目的真实性、合理性审查。另一方面,要求政府在协商与合同中明确向合作方说明,项目入库并不代表任何来自政府的财政承诺,并不代表项目的建设运营不存在风险。PPP项目入示范项目库,同样旨在对发挥PPP项目的示范效应,不能改变PPP项目本身性质。

2. 推进清退工作

截至2017年,已退库退示范174个项目,总投资超过6 000亿元,清退出库的主要原因为不再采用PPP模式,清退出示范库的主要原因为尚未落地。依据《财政部办公厅关于规范政府和社会资本合作(PPP)综合信息平台项目库管理的通知》(财办金〔2017〕92号)列出的五类不符合要求的PPP项目,清退整改工作仍在持续推进。入库的PPP项目应当在全生命周期都符合PPP实施条件,因此,应建立针对PPP入库项目常态化、制度化的质量审查、督促整改、组织清退的标准和办法,重视PPP项目的运营质量考核,将未通过考核项目的清退、整改情况纳入政府绩效考评,使项目清退、整改成本远大于项目入库收益,从而督促政府在PPP项目申报时谨慎开展论证、加快落地实施,以长期制度约束保证PPP工作质量。

同时，需配套跟进 PPP 项目清退、整改后续工作，对退示范项目，落实 PPP 的继续履约情况；对退库项目，处理好项目合同变更乃至解除的问题，明确政府和社会资本的责任分摊；对整改项目，及时跟进整改情况，督促其期内整改到位。

3. 推进信用管理

公平合理的合同建立后，按照合同履行约定的职责，其中政府方能否为资源整合创造条件，是当前社会资本最关心的问题。由于当前政府缺乏公开信用记录，政府违约成本不高，政府换届对合同能否继续并履约的影响非常大，故政府方的信用风险高，发生违约后社会资本方损失大。同样，社会资本和金融机构违约也将直接给项目带来建设运营停止、资金链断裂问题，导致项目流产。因而，应建立政府信用系统，综合各方信用信息对 PPP 项目进行信用评估，将信用信息公开，可降低各方信息不对称，增强 PPP 参与意愿。同时，应完善合同违约后追责赔偿机制，谁违约谁负担责任，以降低其余参与方的损失。

4. 加强信息公开

根据财政部要求，PPP 项目库需公开基础信息和多项文件，但各省份信息公开率（统计可行性研究报告、实施方案附件、采购文件、PPP 合同）平均不到 25%，物有所值评价和财政承受能力论证公开率也刚过 50%。因此，第一，应督促地方政府及时提交或补交项目库要求公开的文件。第二，应进一步明确 PPP 项目信息公开的重点内容，将信息公开覆盖到 PPP 项目全生命周期，针对 PPP 项目从发起准备、招标采购、建设管理、运营、移交等各环节，围绕物有所值的实现，制定各领域的信息公开清单、共享的办法、异议的处置程序等。第三，应当鼓励报送量化数据，促进项目前期量化分析，加强项目运行质量考核。第四，地方政府应加强地方 PPP 信息公开平台建设，及时发布地方规范性文件、PPP 工作进展、PPP 项目信息等，做到有条理、有时效、易获取、能反馈，防止空有平台、管理不善等情况，确保平台信息充实可用，为公众、社会资本方、金融机构各方的使用和监督提供服务。第五，由于 PPP 项目的公共性质，可将 PPP 信息公开工作与推进社会公益事业建设领域政府信息公开工作配合进行，实现信息对接共享，资源有效利用。

（三）保障 PPP 项目收益，防范收益不足风险

收益不足风险是指项目运营后的收益不能收回投资或达到其预期收益而产生的风险。虽然物有所值是 PPP 模式追求的重要目标，但过低的收益水平势必将降低项目的吸引力，打击社会资本方参与的积极性，甚至导致 PPP 项目的经济可行性缺失，成为项目失败的导火索。

例如，杭州湾跨海大桥项目采用了"建设—经营—转让"（Build-Operate-Transfer，简称 BOT）模式，社会资本方民营企业拥有 30 年的收费权限，但项目通车初始，实际车流量比预期少 30% 以上，即使在经营了四五年后，实际车流量仍不及预期，在通行费作为项目唯一收入来源的情况下，项目资本金很可能难以收回，此外，周边新建大桥、通道等进一步分散了项目的现金流，面临较大的收益不足风险，将导致项目被提前收回，以失败告终。

由此可见，项目收益率对项目成败有举足轻重的影响。在现金流无法保障的情况下，项目的可融资性也将受到影响，并增加自身的投资压力、融资成本、财务压力等，为将来项目执行埋下很大的隐患。此外，资本总是追逐高盈利的领域，而 PPP 项目前期投入大却收益偏低，自然缺乏强烈的吸引力，使得该领域竞争不足，甚至发生后期采购环节流标，造成成本损失。

为此，首先，政府应合理化设置招标条件和回报条件，采用技术手段遏制非理性的投标行为，避免恶性竞争和不合理的低价中标，规避风险。这其中，要选取界定清晰、准确适合的项目收益率指标，提高投资项目决策评估的公平性、可比性。而在预估项目收益时，政府应监督社会资本方保持合理、中性，采取科学、系统的方法流程，避免对预期收益估计过于

乐观或者估计不足。其次，对部分基层政府不舍得将"含金量"高、收益率好的项目拿来做 PPP 模式的心理，也应加以调整引导，政府要能公平对待社会资本，保障项目质量。

此外，要注意保障合理收益不等同于承诺固定回报。要坚持地方政府不得在 PPP 项目中承诺固定回报的原则。合理收益的取得要取决于社会资本项目融资、建设、运营管理的水平，对其用绩效考核和违约追责方式进行制约。

（四）重视风险识别分配机制，加强风险防控

PPP 项目风险来源多种多样，原因在于 PPP 项目参与方众多，机制较为复杂，建设周期长，在实际执行过程中不确定性因素多，难免遭遇一些障碍和困难。为保证项目的顺利进行，风险识别和分配工作就十分关键。

首先，地方政府应加强自身的风险管理意识，地方政府的 PPP 管理人员应将风险管理贯彻于 PPP 项目的整个生命周期中，搭建统一的 PPP 管理平台，对所有 PPP 项目按照项目性质、周期、所涉参与方进行分类管理，实现共性风险与特性风险分离。引进人才队伍针对不同类型项目有效地识别风险，规避风险。

其次，要建立有效的风险分担及灵活变更机制。明确 PPP 项目运行的风险分担原则，建立有效的风险分担机制，将 PPP 项目风险通过科学机制进行平衡、转移和分担，坚持最适宜原则，即根据 PPP 项目风险的种类不同，由应对和控制该风险能力强的最适宜的一方承担。因此，地方政府应根据风险的程度和合理的比例原则将属于公共部门承担的风险分给公共部门，属于私人部门的风险由私人部门承担，应当由公共部门和私人部门共同承担的风险交给双方去共同承担。

在项目执行过程中，还要形成有效的监管机制。各主管部门要相互沟通，明确 PPP 项目监管目标，确定监管主体、客体，明确监管内容，规范监管程序，整合监管方式，共同制定统一完整的监管制度体系。

最后，应当坚持项目风险和投资人风险隔离的交易结构，这是防止投

资人经营风险向 PPP 项目扩散的有效途径。无论是国际还是国内的 PPP 市场，基本都采用了设立特殊目的载体来实施项目的普遍交易模式。特殊目的载体的存在可以使得 PPP 项目的独立性大大加强，有效降低社会资本自身对项目的风险冲击，即当社会资本方因各种原因无法继续经营 PPP 项目时，该项目可以快速被处置或接管，为新的投资人进入创造一个相对有利的法律基础。如果 PPP 项目没有相对独立的风险隔离体系，势必会陷入资产处置的困境而难以脱身。

第五章 北京大学中国 PPP 指数应用

一、PPP 指数

　　从政府保障、社会参与、项目运行三个方面构造的 PPP 指数全面衡量了各省份的 PPP 发展情况与发展前景，因此，当社会资本方考虑投资 PPP 项目时，从多个维度构造的 PPP 指数的排名结果可以给予他们重要的参考。在有相关投资需求的情况下，综合各项考量指标，投资人将会更倾向于在得分靠前的省份投资建设 PPP 项目。

　　现在我国 PPP 项目处于快速发展、"野蛮生长"的阶段，虽然现阶段还存在一定乱象，例如政策朝令夕改、政企两方缺乏契约精神、投资回报机制不明确等问题，但随着国家对 PPP 模式的重视，服务保障、法律法规政策不断出台，我国的 PPP 项目建设将会愈发规范化。随着 PPP 模式的不断完善，这种模式将会在政府兴建公共基础设施等项目中占据更大的市场份额、发挥更加重要的作用。因此，各省级行政区政府应重视当地 PPP 发展环境的完善。从"政府、社会、项目"三个维度构建的 PPP 指数有利于排名不甚理想的省份及时查缺补漏、完善自身 PPP 发展环境，以便吸引外部投资，与本地政府方共同参与 PPP 项目。

二、政府保障指数

　　政府保障指数不仅可以衡量各省份对 PPP 项目建设的资金保障能力，

还可以对各省份政府综合财力起到一定的评价作用。这部分指数中充分考虑了衡量省份财政能力及可用资金余额的指标如财政收入、债务余额、财政自给率等，可以在一定程度上反映地区的经济发展程度与财政资金充裕水平，衡量在该地投资的适宜程度。

此外，在衡量政府关于其他类型项目的财政保障能力中，该财政保障指数的建立框架也具有很高的参考价值。测评政府关于其他项目的财政保障能力时，可以参考 PPP 政府保障指数的建立框架，并在其中加入其他相关指标。

三、社会参与指数

（一）衡量民间资本活跃度，推动地方政府提高民间资本占比

PPP 强调社会资本参与公共基础设施建设，提高项目运行效益，降低财政压力。"PPP 企业多样性"衡量民营企业、港澳台及外资企业的参与度，考察民间资本真正被调动的程度。长期以来，地方政府在 PPP 项目招投标过程中对国有企业有一定偏好，在报价、资金实力等相同的情况下，更乐于选择国有企业，而没有真正让民营企业、港澳台及外资企业参与 PPP 项目，无法真正调动民间资本投资 PPP 项目。因此 PPP 企业多样性通过计算民营企业、港澳台及外资企业占总企业数的比例，衡量民营企业、港澳台企业及外资企业的活跃度，考察各省份调动民间资本参与 PPP 项目的程度。

进一步，该项指标可以推动地方政府提高民间资本参与比例，提高 PPP 参与企业中民营企业、港澳台及外资企业的比例，推动民间资本更好地参与 PPP 项目。

（二）衡量社会资本活跃度，推动地方政府提高社会资本占比

"PPP 社会资本规模"衡量各省企业的社会资本总体实力，该指标从社会资本投资规模、入库项目社会资本出资比例、参与企业上市率等维度考察各省的社会资本规模实力及项目的社会资本投资占比。PPP 项目需要社会资本的广泛参与，社会资本方的投资实力、出资占比均是衡量企业参与的深度与广度的科学指标。

此外，该指标可激励各省级行政区政府采取措施，引进综合实力较强的社会资本投资方，提高社会资本出资比例，促进企业更加深入地融入项目，充分调动社会资本参与 PPP 项目建设，保证项目建设运营等环节高效、可持续发展。

四、项目运行指数

（一）用于评估地区 PPP 模式的发展潜力

北京大学中国 PPP 指数体系的二级指标"PPP 发展空间"衡量地区未来的 PPP 市场可发掘潜力的大小，这主要取决于地区的基础设施现状、城镇化水平、当前基建投资表现和储备项目规模等。该二级指标可用以分析不同方面对地区 PPP 发展潜力的贡献程度，以及相对优势和弱势。例如，北京的 PPP 发展空间得分为 23.83 分，排名第 31，这是由于其基础设施已经比较完善，基建水平的提升空间（第 31 名）、基建投资的增长空间（第 25 名）都比较小，此外，北京储备项目也很少（第 28 名），这些因素导致北京 PPP 发展空间较为不足。

（二）用于评估地区 PPP 项目的总体效益

北京大学中国 PPP 指数体系的二级指标"PPP 风险收益"从 PPP 项

目收益、PPP 项目风险、PPP 外部效益三方面评估地区 PPP 项目的综合效益，能用以指导地区在 PPP 效益不同方面的表现和相对优势及弱势。例如，北京的 PPP 风险收益得分为 30.46 分，排名第 31，其中北京的优势在于 PPP 项目收益整体平均水平较高（第 3 名），但由于 PPP 项目风险暴露较高（第 31 名），PPP 外部效益较小（第 28 名），使得北京 PPP 项目总体效益仍较为落后。

附录　北京大学中国PPP指数计算说明

一、北京大学中国PPP指数指标的确定

北京大学中国PPP指数以系统性、客观性、科学性、可操作性和可比性为基本原则，采用主观评价和客观评价相结合的评价体系，综合分析各个省份PPP市场发展现状。本书分析基于宏观经济的相关理论，综合运用专家法和层次分析法对各个省份PPP市场进行分析研究。

该指数争取能够达到以下四个目的：一是衡量当地政府保障水平，以期当地政府能够为PPP项目的运行提供更好的保障；二是反映PPP市场整体的运行状态，引导社会资金进入，给机构投资者提供参考；三是规范参与PPP市场的社会参与方的行为，使得PPP市场健康有序地运行；四是通过PPP发展空间评估不同省份的发展机会。

北京大学中国PPP指数指标体系属于客观指标体系，该指标体系包括政府保障指数、项目运行指数、社会参与指数三个一级指标，分别从三个不同维度全面衡量各个省份PPP的发展情况。该指标体系由3个一级指标、14个二级指标、40个三级指标和123个四级指标构成。考虑细分性与全面性，同时考虑数据的可获得性，各层级指标间通过加权计算来逐级合成。

二、北京大学中国 PPP 指数的构建步骤

第一步，中国 PPP 指数指标体系设计。指标均来自中华人民共和国财政部、中华人民共和国国家统计局、各省政府官方网站等权威机构，数据不漏不多，完全采用客观数据，确保构建完善的中国 PPP 指数指标体系。

第二步，数据采集处理。通过财政部及各政府部门公布的统计数据，如全国 PPP 综合信息平台项目管理库各省 2017 年年报（财政部）、各省国民经济和社会发展统计公报、各省 2017 年预算执行情况及 2018 年预算草案的报告、荣邦瑞明数据库、Wind 数据库等多个渠道收集的数据，完成数据采集工作。

北京大学中国 PPP 指数指标充分考虑数据来源的稳定性、数据的连续性和规范性及口径统一等原则，使数据易于比较和计算，评价指标含义明确。同时强调对数据的科学处理，辅之以权重体系进行计算，避免指数的灰色性、模糊性和不可追溯性，力求分析方法客观、指数可复制。

第三步，数据校验处理。通过专家、教授反复论证及对数据多方位对比监测，同步标准化处理相关的指标数据。

第四步，指数建模计算。在前期理论研究基础上，结合相应的问题及相关的数据，建立中国 PPP 指数模型，代入数据并计算出 2017 年度指数结果。

北京大学中国 PPP 指数指标体系的设计经多次专家、教授意见征集，和专家教授委员会座谈确定，各指标间具有互补性且相关性较低，避免特征上交叉重叠，同时避免了遗漏空缺。指标间相辅相成，综合涵盖 PPP 市场发展的各个方面，指标具有代表性和可比性，相差悬殊的指标不在同一类别比较。北京大学中国 PPP 指数的权重体系经过多轮教授专家的意见征集和考量，具有权威性和科学性。

三、对原始数据的处理

对原始数据的处理主要包括数据正向化和无量纲化处理。由于不同指标的原始数据量纲不同，指标间存在不可公度性，因此构建指数需排除量纲差异对计算结果的影响，即对数据进行无量纲化处理，使数值大小能反映指标的变化。本书通过采取初始化变换对数据进行无量纲化处理。

四级指标包括规模、数量、比率等多种类型指标，其单位、含义各不相同，需要进行去量纲操作使指标数据标准化、可比化。在进行指标去量纲化时，以指标变动幅度为基准，用相对化处理法对四级指标进行去量纲操作。

设第 k 项指标的最大值为 M，最小值为 m（其中 $k = 1, 2, \cdots, n$），原始数据为 X_k，根据指标的正逆性不同，指标的初始化处理如下：

当指标 X_k 为正向指标时，初始化变换的指标数据为 $x_k = \dfrac{X_k - m}{M - m}$；

当指标 X_k 为逆向指标时，初始化变换的指标数据为 $x_k = \dfrac{M - X_k}{M - m}$；

通过上述变换，得到无量纲化的指标数据。

四、北京大学中国 PPP 指数的计算

在指标体系确立的基础上，进而确定各指标的权重，按照权重将各子指标进行线性加权，并加总构成整体的北京大学中国 PPP 指数。指标权重的设定对北京大学中国 PPP 指数的最终结果具有重要影响，目前学术界有客观赋权法和主观赋权法两大类权重设定方法。客观赋权法依赖各指标的原始数据，在一定的统计标准下计算原始数据的指标权重。该方法完全不依赖于人的主观判断，因而具有较强的客观性，但缺陷是忽略指标的具体

经济意义分析。从方法论的角度看，该方法完全依赖历史数据，其本质上体现的是历史的、后看的信息价值，无法契合PPP发展的前瞻性特征。因此，为更好地满足促进PPP发展的导向性需求，该指数以主观赋权法的专家法为主，并辅之以层次分析法最终确定指标权重。具体而言，专家法通过业内专家座谈研讨方式，根据每位专家出具的权重意见及其理由，综合整理构建权重体系；权重值层次分析法如下表所示，采用两两比较的方法判断重要性不同的指标的权重值，即比较判断各指标间的相对重要性，最后综合给出各指标的权重。

权重值层次分析法比较表

指标对比	权重值比较
同等重要	相同
较强重要	较大
非常重要	最大

后 记

《北京大学中国 PPP 指数报告》由北京大学 PPP 研究中心第一次推出。本书通过对中国 PPP 市场发展情况进行研究和评估，从政府保障、项目运行和社会参与三个角度出发，构造出中国 PPP 指数，力图较为全面、准确地反映中国各省份的 PPP 发展状况。同时，在研究、评价我国各省份 PPP 指数得分的基础上，我们给出促进我国 PPP 市场发展的相关思考与政策建议，期望能为中国 PPP 市场健康、稳定、迅速发展略尽绵薄之力。

中国 PPP 指数及其报告能够顺利推出，我们需要感谢财政部政府和社会资本合作（PPP）中心，财政部 PPP 中心提供了大量与 PPP 相关的数据，为本指数的计算提供了坚实的数据基础。北京荣邦瑞明投资管理有限责任公司也为中国 PPP 指数的计算提供了部分数据支持。

在北京大学中国 PPP 指数报告撰写过程中，我们得到了许多专家的支持，他们提供了诸多具有建设性的专业意见，在此对各位专家的支持表示衷心的感谢，尤其需要感谢的是：焦小平（财政部 PPP 中心）、孙祁祥（北京大学 PPP 研究中心）、韩斌（财政部 PPP 中心）、邓冰（北京大学 PPP 研究中心）、谢飞（财政部 PPP 中心）、夏颖哲（财政部 PPP 中心）、赵芙卿（财政部 PPP 中心）、张戈（财政部 PPP 中心）、李博雅（北京大学 PPP 研究中心）、张汉（北京方程财达咨询有限公司）、彭松（北京荣邦瑞明投资管理有限责任公司）、孙进瑜（东方园林股份有限公司战略研究院）、孙梦凡（国寿投资控股有限公司）和任博（中信信托有限责任公司）等。

课题组负责人为北京大学经济学院金融学系主任王一鸣教授，课题组其他成员有王立夫、董婧延、梁月、刘蔚绮、邵锐成、张奇琦、朱彤和宋巢娜。

中国PPP指数是对我国自2014年大力发展PPP以来，全国PPP发展成果的总结与评价，也包含了对未来发展的建议与期许。由于时间与课题组成员精力所限，再加上信息披露与数据获取中存在的困难，中国PPP指数还存在一定的考虑不周之处，恳请广大读者进行批评指正，以便后续逐步修改完善，共同为中国PPP市场健康有序发展做出贡献。

北京大学PPP指数课题组

Executive summary

Since 2014, the Ministry of Finance and other departments have promoted PPP reform in the field of public services, and established a "five-in-one" system integrating relevant laws, policies, guidelines, contracts, and standards to promote the development of PPP in China in accordance with the arrangements of the Central Committee of the Communist Party of China and the State Council inorder to promote Chinese PPP into a systewatic and institutionalized stage.

However, the development of PPP in various provinces and cities is not balanced. By the end of 2017, the top three in projects quantity the National PPP Overall Information Platform established by the Ministry of Finance were Shandong Province (692), Henan Province (646), and Hunan Province (528), accounting for 26.1% of the total recovded projects altogether. The top three in amount invested according to database: Guizhou Province (845.3 billion yuan), Hunan Province (825.1 billion yuan), Henan Province (787 billion yuan), accounting for 22% of the total investment recorded projects altogether. The number of PPP projects, the total investment amount and development status of each province are different.[1]

---

[1] The data of this book is as of December 31, 2017, the same applies to below. All analyese in this book are based on statisitics for Chinese mainland only (excluding Hong Kong, Macao and Taiwan regions).

In order to evaluate the development of Chinese PPP comprehensively and objectively, Peking University tried to construct a set of indices that reflect the development of PPP in various provinces, municipalities and autonomous regions from a macro perspective. The index has four roles: The first is to measure the level of local government's guarantee and hope that the local government can provide better protection for the operation of PPP projects; The second is to reflect the overall operational status of the PPP market, to guide the entry of private funds, to provide reference for institutional investors; The third is to standardize the behavior of private participants in the PPP market, so that the PPP market operates in a healthy and orderly manner; The fourth is to assess the development opportunities of different provinces through the indicator of PPP development protential.

Based on the collected data, PKU · China PPP Index and first-grade indicators are calculated. According to scores and ranking, we divide 31 provinces into 3 tiers: First tier: Beijing, Guangdong, Henan, Jiangsu, Shandong, Zhejiang; Second tier: Anhui, Fujian, Guizhou, Hainan, Hebei, Hubei, Hunan, Jiangxi, Shaanxi, Shanghai, Sichuan, Xinjiang, Yunnan; Third tier: Chongqing, Gansu, Guangxi, Heilongjiang, Jilin, Liaoning, Inner Mongolia, Ningxia, Qinghai, Shanxi, Tianjin, Tibet. Provinces are listed by the order of the first letter, regardless of PPP index scores.

Considering the economic and demographic factors, the 2017 National PPP index scores are obtained by calculating the weighted average score of the 31 provinces, municipalities, with the assigned weight being the product of the population and GDP of the respective districts The thusly obtained PKU. China PPP index score was 73.62. The government guarantee index score was 76.93 points, the private participation index score was 64.02 points, and the project operation index score was 78.33 points in 2017.

Through the evaluation of the PPP index of each province, the following six conclusions are drawn:

The first condusion is in regards to the ranking of the PPP index in each province. Provinces in Central China and East China generally rank figher, while Northwest and Northeast provinces have seen lower ranking. Beijing (80.34), which ranked first in the PPP index, scored 21.94 points higher than the last Liaoning (58.40), and about 80% of the provincial PPP index scores were concentrated between 75.60 and 64.19.

The PPP index of Central China (73.33) and East China (72.94) scored more than 70 points. The scores of South China (69.09), Southwest China (69.04) and North China (68.63) were similar, and the Northwest and Northeast regions scored the lowest.

The second is the government's score in various provinces, and the government guarantee work in East China is the best. Among which, the most outstanding is Beijing, whose government guarantee index is the only city with more than 90 points, which scores 39.54 points higher than the last of the rank. Shandong, Jiangsu, Guangdong and Fujian scores between 80 to 90 points, and 16 provinces with 70 to 80 points. The remaining 10 provinces have a government guarantee index score of 70 or less.

The score of the government guarantee index in East China (79.84) is higher than the score in South China of 6.23, which mainly owing to the high rank of Shandong, Jiangsu, Fujian and Zhejiang, ranking 2, 3, 5 and 6 respectively. Government support scores in South China, Central China, North China, Southwest China, and Northwest China are similar, ranging from 71.24 to 73.18.

The third is that the level of private participation in the PPP industry is generally low at this stage, and the level of private participation in the Northwest is the lowest. Except the better performance of nine provinces including Beijing,

Guangdong, Zhejiang and Jiangsu, the remaining 22 provinces such as Xinjiang, Fujian and Jilin have a private participation index of less than 60 points. (Note: The level of private participation in this book refers to the participation of registered enterprises in the national PPP market.)

East China, Central China, South China and North China scored between 61.22 points and 59.92 points. Among them, East China has the highest level of private participation, and the lowest private participation level is in the Northwest, 51.06 points.

Fourth, the overall project operation index of the central and western provinces is higher than that of the developed areas in the east, and the projects operation in Central China is the best. The project operation index of the central and western provinces such as Henan, Xinjiang, Guizhou, Sichuan, and Anhui is ranked higher: ranking 1, 3, 4, 5, and 6 respectively. The four municipalities with relatively highly developed economic status are ranked very low, ranking at 5 the bottom.

The Central China project operation has an index of 82.87, Which is 5.99 points higher than East China. It is the only region with more than 80 points. This is mainly due to the higher ranking of Henan, Hubei and Hunan in Central China, which is 1, 8, 9 relatively. Other regions scored between 76.88 points and 70.15 points.

The fifth is that the level of PPP development varies greatly among provinces, and the level of PPP development in East China and Central China is relatively high. Shandong Province and Anhui Province score 25 points higher than the PPP development level of Chongqing and Tianjin.

The PPP development level scores in East China and Central China were 67.45 and 66.62 respectively, and the PPP development scores in the remaining regions were concentrated between 58.03 and 61.35.

Sixth, the development potential of PPP varies greatly from province to province, and the development potential of relatively underdeveloped area is relatively large. Guizhou Province, which has the highest PPP development potential score, is 40 points higher than the lowest Beijing. The infrastructure of economically underdeveloped provinces is relatively lacking, and it is necessary to introduce social capital to participate in the construction. The PPP development potential in Southwest China and Central China is the largest, with 55.46 points and 55.25 points respectively. The PPP development potential in North China is the smallest, which is 38.46 points.

Based on the results of the PPP index evaluation, this book proposes policy recommendations in three areas. First of all, in the field of government guarantee: to promote the development of PPP in the central and northern regions from both macro and micro aspects; to establish and improve PPP-related laws and regulations and raise the rule of law; local governments need to further improve the matching between fund size and project size; to improve the internal structure design of the fund, prevent and control risks, and to promote balanced development between regions; to further standardize the process of handling, improve the efficiency of work, enhance the transparency of the government, and strengthen the credibility of the government.

Secondly, in the field of private participation: to reduce financing costs, increase the overall participation of social capital and the participation of private enterprises, Hongkong, Macao and Taiwan enterprises and foreign-funded enterprises; to establish laws and regulations for the withdrawal of social capital, and improve the construction of Chinese PPP market.

Finally, in the field of project operation: to optimize resource allocation, strengthen standardized management, guarantee PPP project revenue, prevent risk of insufficient income; to attach importance to risk identification and distribution mechanism, strengthen risk prevention and control.

Although in the process of writing this book, we strive to build the PKU · China PPP Index as scientificly, comprehensively and objectively as possible. Due to the complexity and diversity of Chinese PPP industry, and the difficulty in obtaining some of the lastest data this book is inevitably as a phased research result, and we hope readers to offer generously their criticisms and suggestions.

contents

Chapter 1 Construction of PKU · China PPP Index 153
    1.1 Compilation Background of PKU · China PPP Index 153
    1.2 Description of PKU · China PPP Index 154
    1.3 Principles and Methods of Calculating Indicators 156

Chapter 2 PKU · China PPP Index Overall Evaluation 159
    2.1 Ranking: PPP Market in Provinces of China 160
    2.2 Ranking: PPP Market of Regions of China 164

Chapter 3 PKU · China PPP Index Sub-item Evaluation 168
    3.1 Ranking: Government Guarantee Index 168
    3.2 Ranking: Private Participation 195
    3.3 Ranking: Project Operation 228

Chapter 4 Policy Suggestions 286
    4.1 Government Guarantee Area 286
    4.2 Private Participation Area 290

4.3　Project Operation Area　……………………………………… 294

Chapter 5　Application for PKU · China PPP Index …………… 302
　　5.1　PPP Index: Evaluate the Development of PPP among Provinces to Provide Reference for Investors　……………………… 302
　　5.2　Government Guarantee Index: Assess Government Fiscal capacity　……………………………………………………… 303
　　5.3　Private Participation Index　………………………………… 303
　　5.4　Project Operation Index　…………………………………… 304

Appendix: Calculation of PKU · China PPP Index ……………… 306
　　1. Determination of Indicators of PKU · China PPP Index …… 306
　　2. Procedure of Constructing PKU · China PPP Index ………… 307
　　3. Raw Data Processing　………………………………………… 308
　　4. Calculation of PKU · China PPP Index ……………………… 309

Postscript ……………………………………………………………… 311

Figure Content

Figure 1.1	Indicator System Framework of PKU · China PPP Index	155
Figure 2.1	PKU · China PPP Index Framework	161
Figure 2.2	PKU · China PPP Index's First-grade Indicators Weight Distribution	162
Figure 2.3	PPP Index and First-grade Indicators in 2017 (region level)	166
Figure 3.1	Framework of the Government Guarantee Index Indicator System	170
Figure 3.2	Scores and Rankings of Government Guarantee Indexes for Each Province in 2017	170
Figure 3.3	Scores and Rankings of Government Guarantee Indexes in Different Regions in 2017	173
Figure 3.4	Framework of the Government Fiscal Support Indicator System	176
Figure 3.5	Scores and Rankings of Government Fiscal Support Indexes for Each Province in 2017	178
Figure 3.6	Scores and Rankings of Government Fiscal Support of Different Regions in 2017	180

Figure 3.7	Scores and Rankings of Government Service Support for Each Province in 2017	183
Figure 3.8	Scores and Rankings of Government Service Support in Different Regions	184
Figure 3.9	Local Government Legal and Policy Protection Scores and Rankings in 2017	187
Figure 3.10	Government Financial Security Scores and Rankings in 2017	191
Figure 3.11	Government Credibility Index Scores and Rankings in 2017	195
Figure 3.12	Private Participation Index Framework	197
Figure 3.13	Score and Rankings for Private Participation Index in 2017	199
Figure 3.14	Private Participation Index of 7 Regions in 2017	200
Figure 3.15	Business Participation Index Framework	204
Figure 3.16	Score and Rankings of PPP Business Participation in 2017	205
Figure 3.17	PPP Business Participation Index of 7 Regions in 2017	206
Figure 3.18	Business Credibility Index of 7 Regions in 2017	209
Figure 3.19	Private Fund Framework	210
Figure 3.20	Scores and Rankings of Private Fund in 2017 (province level)	212
Figure 3.21	Scores and Rankings of Private Fund in 2017 (region level)	214
Figure 3.22	Framework of Financial Service	215
Figure 3.23	Scores and Rankings of Financial Service in 2017 (province level)	217
Figure 3.24	Scores and Rankings of Financial Service in 2017 (region level)	218

Figure 3.25	Legal Service Framework	219
Figure 3.26	Scores and Rankings of Legal Service in 2017 (province-level)	220
Figure 3.27	Scores and Rankings of Legal Service in 2017 (region level)	222
Figure 3.28	Consulting Service Framework	223
Figure 3.29	Scores and Rankings of Consulting Service (province level)	225
Figure 3.30	Scores and Rankings of Consulting in 2017 (region-level)	227
Figure 3.31	Project Operation Indicator Framework	229
Figure 3.32	Scores and Rankings of Project Operation in 2017	231
Figure 3.33	Project Operation and Second-grade Indicators of 7 Regions in 2017	233
Figure 3.34	PPP Development Level Indicators Framework	235
Figure 3.35	2017 PPP Development Level Scores and Rankings	236
Figure 3.36	2017 PPP Development Level Scores and Rankings of 7 Regions	238
Figure 3.37	2017 PPP Development Scale Scores and Rankings	242
Figure 3.38	2017 PPP Development Scale Scores and Ranking of 7 Regions	243
Figure 3.39	2017 PPP Projects Distribution Scores and Rankings	246
Figure 3.40	2017 PPP Projects Distribution Scores and Rankings of 7 Regions	247
Figure 3.41	2017 PPP Work Progress Scores and Rankings	250
Figure 3.42	2017 PPP Work Progress Scores and Rankings of 7 Regions	251

Figure 3.43　2017 PPP Regulated Level Scores and Rankings ·············· 256
Figure 3.44　2017 PPP Regulated Level Scores and Rankings
　　　　　　 of 7 Regions ··· 257
Figure 3.45　PPP Transparency Scores and Rankings in 2017 ············ 262
Figure 3.46　PPP Transparency Scores and Rankings in 2017 ············ 263
Figure 3.47　PPP Risk & Revenue Indicator Framework ··················· 272
Figure 3.48　Scores and Rankings of PPP Risk & Revenue in 2017 ······ 274
Figure 3.49　PPP Risk & Revenue of 7 Regions in 2017 ···················· 275
Figure 3.50　PPP Development Potential Indicator Framework ·········· 277
Figure 3.51　Scores and Rankings of PPP Development Potential
　　　　　　 in 2017 ·· 282
Figure 3.52　PPP Development Potential of 7 Regions in 2017 ············ 284

Table Content

Table 1.1	Analytic Hierarchy Method	158
Table 2.1	Scores of PPP Index in 2017	162
Table 2.2	Chinese Geographic Demarcation	165
Table 2.3	Scores and Rankings of PPP Index in 2017 (region level)	165
Table 3.1	Scores and Rankings of Government Guarantee Indexes for Each Province in 2017	171
Table 3.2	Scores and Rankings of Government Guarantee Indexes in Different Regions in 2017	173
Table 3.3	Composition of Government Fiscal Support Indicator System	176
Table 3.4	Scores and Rankings of Government Fiscal Support for Each Province in 2017	178
Table 3.5	Scores and Rankings of Government Fiscal Support of Different Regions in 2017	179
Table 3.6	Composition of Government Service Support Indicator System	181
Table 3.7	Scores and Rankings of Government Service Support for Each Province in 2017	182

Table 3.8	Scores and Rankings of Government Service Support in Different Regions	184
Table 3.9	Government Legal and Policy Guarantee Index System	186
Table 3.10	Local Government Legal and Policy Protection Scores and Rankings in 2017	186
Table 3.11	The Government Financial Security Indicator System	189
Table 3.12	Government Financial Security Scores and Rankings in 2017	190
Table 3.13	Government Credibility Index Indicator System	192
Table 3.14	Government Credibility Index Scores and Rankings in 2017	193
Table 3.15	Scores and Rankings for Private Participation Index in 2017	198
Table 3.16	Private Participation Index of 7 Regions in 2017	199
Table 3.17	Component of Private Participation Index	202
Table 3.18	Scores and Rankings of PPP Business Participation in 2017	205
Table 3.19	PPP Business Participation Index of 7 Regions in 2017	206
Table 3.20	Component of Business Credibility	208
Table 3.21	Business Credibility Index of 7 Regions in 2017	208
Table 3.22	Private Fund Framework	210
Table 3.23	Scores and Rankings of Private Fund in 2017 (province level)	211
Table 3.24	Scores and Rankings of Private Fund in 2017 (region level)	213
Table 3.25	Framework of Financial Service	215
Table 3.26	Scores and Rankings of Financial Services in 2017	216
Table 3.27	Scores and Rankings of Financial Service in 2017 (region level)	218

Table 3.28	Legal Service Framework	219
Table 3.29	Scores and Rankings of Legal Service in 2017 (province-level)	220
Table 3.30	Scores and Rankings of Legal Service in 2017 (region-level)	221
Table 3.31	Consulting Service Framework	223
Table 3.32	Scores and Rankings of Consulting Service (province level)	225
Table 3.33	Scores and Rankings of Consulting Service in 2017 (region-level)	227
Table 3.34	Scores and Rankings of Project Operation in 2017	230
Table 3.35	Scores and Rankings of Project Operation of 7 Regions in 2017	233
Table 3.36	2017 PPP Development Level Scores and Rankings of Provinces	235
Table 3.37	2017 PPP Development Level Scores and Rankings of 7 Regions	237
Table 3.38	PPP Development Scale Indicators System	240
Table 3.39	2017 PPP Development Scale Scores and Rankings	241
Table 3.40	2017 PPP Development Scale Scores and Rankings of 7 Regions	242
Table 3.41	PPP Projects Distribution Indicators System	244
Table 3.42	2017 PPP Projects Distribution Scores and Rankings	245
Table 3.43	2017 PPP Projects Distribution Scores and Rankings of 7 Regions	247
Table 3.44	PPP Work Progress Indicators System	249
Table 3.45	2017 PPP Work Progress Scores and Rankings	250

Table 3.46	2017 PPP Work Progress Scores and Rankings of 7 Regions	251
Table 3.47	PPP Regulated Level Indicators System	253
Table 3.48	2017 PPP Regulated Level Scores and Rankings	255
Table 3.49	2017 PPP Regulated Level Scores and Rankings of 7 Regions	257
Table 3.50	The Degree of PPP Transparency Indicator System	259
Table 3.51	PPP Transparency Scores and Rankings in 2017	261
Table 3.52	PPP Transparency Scores and Rankings in 2017	262
Table 3.53	Composition of PPP Implementation Indicator System	264
Table 3.54	Composition of the PPP Handover Indicator System	267
Table 3.55	Composition and Explanation of PPP Risk & Revenue	269
Table 3.56	Scores and Rankings of PPP Risk & Revenue in 2017	273
Table 3.57	Scores and Rankings of PPP Risk & Revenue of 7 Regions in 2017	275
Table 3.58	Composition and Explanation of PPP Development Potential	278
Table 3.59	Scores and Rankings of PPP Development Potential in 2017	281
Table 3.60	Scores and Rankings of PPP Development Potential of 7 Regions in 2017	283

Chapter 1   Construction of PKU · China PPP Index

1.1   Compilation Background of PKU · China PPP Index

Document "Notice of the Ministry of Finance on issues related to the promotion of PPP" No. 76 published by the Ministry of Finance in 2014 defines PPP as follows: The public and private participation mode is a long-term cooperative relationship established in the field of infrastructure and public services. The usual mode is that social capital undertakes most of the work of designing, building, operating, and maintaining infrastructure, and obtains a reasonable return on investment through "user pays" and necessary "government payments"; government departments are responsible for infrastructure, public service prices and quality supervision to ensure that the public interest is maximized.

The "Decision of the Central Committee of the Communist Party of China on Several Major Issues Concerning Comprehensively Deepening Reforms" adopted by the Third Plenary Session of the 18th Party in 2013 puts forward "the decisive role of the market in resource allocation". Since 2014, the central government, the Ministry of Finance, and the National Development and Reform Commission have continuously introduced new policies to encourage PPP. At the 4th China PPP Financing Forum in 2018 Jiao Xiaoping, the director of the Ministry of Finance China Public Private Partnerships Center, pointed out that PPP reform is a system and mechanism reform to promote the modernization of state governance and the five-year reform has achieved remarkable results; PPP business cannot be stable and far-reaching without standard development and strict risk control; it is necessary to actively promote and increase the supply of diversified and multi-level high-quality public services.

PPP has entered a new stage of development. As of the end of December 2017, the national PPP integrated information platform project database has included 14 424 PPP projects with a total investment of 18.2 trillion yuan; among them, there are 7 137 projects in the preparation, procurement, implementation and transfer phases, with an investment of 10.8 trillion yuan, covering 31 provinces (autonomous regions, municipalities directly under the Central Government) and Xinjiang Production and Construction Corps, including 19 industry sectors.

In order to evaluate the development of Chinese PPP comprehensively and objectively, we tried to construct a set of indices that reflect the development of PPP in various provinces, municipalities and autonomous regions from a macro perspective. The index has four roles: The first is to measure the level of local government guarantee and hope that the local government can provide better protection for the operation of PPP projects; The second is to reflect the overall operational status of the PPP market, to guide the entry of private funds, to provide reference for institutional investors; The third is to standardize the behavior of private participants participating in the PPP market, so that the PPP market operates in a healthy and orderly manner; The fourth is to assess the development opportunities of different provinces through the indicator of PPP development protential.

1.2 Description of PKU · China PPP Index

PPP (Public-Private Partnership) can be translated into government and social capital cooperation in China. We will establish corresponding index from the capitaldemand side (Public), the capital supply side (Private), and the project (Partnership). The specific index structure is shown in Figure 1.1.

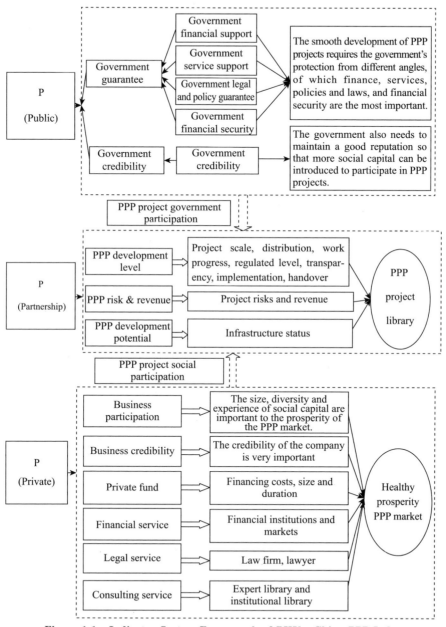

Figure 1.1 Indicator System Framework of PKU · China PPP Index

1.3 Principles and Methods of Calculating Indicators

The calculation of PKU · China PPP Index is based on data as of the end of 2017. These data are mainly from the China Public-Private Partnerships Center. Some of the data are derived from the statistical bulletins of the national economic and social development of different provinces, the National Bureau of Statistics and the wind database.

The design of PKU · China PPP Index System complies with the following principles:

First, being systemic. It is emphasized that each indicator of PKU · China PPP Index System should reflect the main characteristics of Chinese PPP market, and reflect the development status of PPP market in each province of China from as many aspects as possible. The future research will be flexible, amendment, supplement and improvement will be made according to social feedback and suggestions.

Second, being objective. It is emphasized that data has been processed scientifically, supplemented by the weight system for calculation, avoiding the ambiguity and non-retroactivity of the indicators. It is made sure that the analysis is objective and the procedure can be replicated.

Third, being scientific. The design of PKU · China PPP Index System has been advised and confirmed by experts and professors for many times. The indicators are complementary and less relevant, avoiding both overlapping and missing features. They complement each other and comprehensively cover all aspects of PPP market development. They are representative and comparable, and indicators with sharp difference are in different categories. PKU · China PPP Index System becomes convincingly authoritative and scientific after several rounds of advice and examination by experts and professors.

Fourth, being operable. PKU · China PPP Index System fully considers the data sources' stability, continuity, formalization and uniformity of calibration, making the data comparable and easy to calculate and indicators' meanings clear.

Fifth, being comparable. The design of PKU·China PPP Index System requires a cross-sectional comparison of PPP development in each province, i.e. the indicator system should observe the comparability principle.

In conclusion, the principle of PKU·China PPP Index composes of systematicness, objectivity, scientificalness, operability and comparability. It adopts an evaluation system combining both subjective and objective methods, analysing the development of PPP markets in each province comprehensively. Based on macroeconomic theories, the expert method and Analytic Hierarchy Process method, this book analyses the PPP market in each province in detail.

PKU·China PPP Index is classified as an objective indicator system. The three first-level indicators including government guarantee, private participation and project operation measure the PPP development in each province from three dimensions.

On the basis of the establishment of the index system, the weights of each indicator are determined, and the sub-indicators are linearly weighted according to the weights level by level, leading to the final result of PKU·China PPP Index. Obviously, the setting of index weights plays an important role in the final result. At present, there are two major types of weight setting methods academically: objective weighting method and subjective weighting method. The objective weighting method relies on the raw data and calculates the index weight of each indicator under certain statistical standards. This method is completely independent of humans' subjective judgment and therefore has strong objectivity, but the shortcoming is that it ignores the economic significance analysis of the indicators. From the perspective of methodology, this method relies entirely on historical data, which essentially reflects the historical and post-viewing information and cannot conform to the forward-looking characteristics of PPP development. Therefore, in order to better guide the promotion of PPP development, this book mainly adopts the expert method which endows weights subjectively, supplemented by the indicator quantity method and the analytic hierarchy process to determine the final index weights. Specifically, under the expert method, experts are invited to participate in seminars and express opinions on determining weights with corresponding reasons provided. Then the weight system is constructed after overall consideration. The analytic hierarchy method is shown in Table 1.1. It determines the relative weight between indictors by pairwise comparison at first, which represent relative importance between different indicators, then gives the weight of each indicator eventually in a comprehensive way.

Table 1.1　Analytic Hierarchy Method

Indicator comparison	Weight comparison
Equally important	Equal
More important	Larger
Most important	Maximum

Chapter 2 PKU · China PPP Index Overall Evaluation

PPP (Public-Private Partnership) emphasizes cooperation between government and private sectors, especially private sectors' operation of projects. Therefore, PPP has following advantages. First, PPP manages to reach higher economic efficiency by allowing for better allocation of revenue and risk between public and private entities, which effectively reduces overall cost of projects. PPP contributes to realize value for investment. Second, PPP arrangements promotes efficiency, because the time required to finish a project with PPP contracts is significantly shorter than that with traditional modes. Third, PPP increases investment on infrastructure, since private sectors contribute a larger part of fund, it releases government's financial budget pressure. Fourth, PPP improves quality of infrastructure and public service, owing to the fact that private sectors are better equipped with rich experience and skill.

PPP mode increases both economic and time efficiency, and can offer more public service with better quality. However, as mentioned in Chapter 1, PPP fails to act properly on a series of problems and issues on current Chinese PPP market. Aiming to deal with such situation, Ministry of Finance issues the Notice on Further Strengthening Standard Management of Public-Private Partnership (PPP) Example Projects. It announces that 173 example projects verified to be problematic are categorized and then disposed of. The announcement claims that local financial departments should take a warning, enhance projects' normative management, practically strengthen information disclosure and accept social supervision.

Under the guidance of China PPP center, we select corresponding indicators based on problems arising in the process of PPP development, build PKU · China PPP Index, quantitatively measure magnitude of PPP market health in provinces of China, and rank the indexes. PKU · China PPP Index serves as a reference for investors, and take the responsibility of facilitating sustained and sound development of Chinese PPP market.

2.1 Ranking: PPP Market in Provinces of China

PKU · China PPP Index aims to measure the condition of PPP market development in provinces of China, in order to serve as a reference for all walks of life in society. The higher the number is, the more developed the local PPP market is. Our research focuses on province-level rather than city-level, since it is a macroeconomic index which aims to depict PPP market development of various provinces. Basically, there are 34 province-level administrative areas in total. But in the database of China PPP Center, there are no project records of Taiwan, Hong Kong and Macau. Therefore, the 3 regions will not be scored or ranked in this book.

PKU · China PPP Index is composed of 3 first-grade indicators, including Government guarantee, Private participation and Project operation. PPP market is depicted from 3 dimensions: the higher the Government guarantee indicator is, the better the government behaves in PPP market; the higher the Private participation indicator is, the more actively private sectors act in PPP market, and the better financial service, legal service and consulting service are; the higher Operation projectindicator is, the better projects operate and develop in PPP market.

Besides, each first-grade indicator is composed of several second-grade indicators. Government guarantee contains 5 second-grade indicators, including Government fiscal support, Government service support, Government legal and policy guarantee, Government financial security and Government credibility index. Private participation includes 6 second-grade indicators, which are Business participation, Business credibility, Private fund, Financial service, Legal service, Consulting service. Project operation comprises 3 second-grade indicators. They are PPP development level, PPP risk & revenue, PPP development potential. Specifically, PKU · China PPP Index System is shown in Figure 2.1.

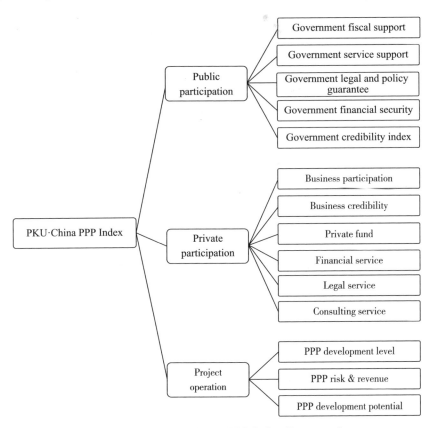

Figure 2.1　PKU · China PPP Index Framework

According to expertise, 3 first-grade indicators account for different weights. Government guarantee accounts for 30%, Private participation accounts for 30%, and Project operation accounts for 40% (see Figure 2.2).

Based on the collected data, PKU · China PPP Index and first-grade indicators are calculated, on the level of provinces, like Beijing, Tianjin and Hebei. There are 31 entries in total. For simplicity, PKU · China PPP Index is denoted as PPP Index below. Besides, 20 points are added as basic points to PPP Index

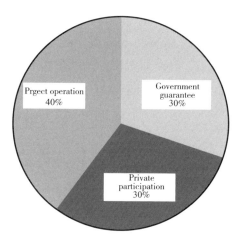

Figure 2.2　PKU · China PPP Index's First-grade Indicators Weight Distribution

and 3 first-grade indicators separately, i.e. to plus 20 to original scores. All indicators inferior to first-grade are original.

According to scores and ranking, we divide 31 provinces into 3 tiers (see Table 2.1):

First tier: Beijing, Guangdong, Henan, Jiangsu, Shandong, Zhejiang.

Second tier: Anhui, Fujian, Guizhou, Hainan, Hebei, Hubei, Hunan, Jiangxi, Shaanxi, Shanghai, Sichuan, Xinjiang, Yunnan.

Third tier: Chongqing, Gansu, Guangxi, Heilongjiang, Jilin, Liaoning, Inner Mongolia, Ningxia, Qinghai, Shanxi, Tianjin, Tibet.

Table 2.1　Scores of PPP Index in 2017

Tier	Provinces	Government guarantee	Private participation	Project operation
First tier	Beijing	93.84	90.42	62.65
	Guangdong	80.33	73.35	73.75
	Henan	71.80	64.23	86.89
	Jiangsu	80.99	67.60	75.60
	Shandong	85.36	65.70	86.55
	Zhejiang	79.79	67.75	76.21

(continued)

Tier	Provinces	Government guarantee	Private participation	Project operation
Second tier	Anhui	76.24	54.36	82.71
	Fujian	80.23	59.25	77.32
	Guizhou	72.93	56.38	83.94
	Hainan	76.66	54.72	71.01
	Hebei	65.79	56.98	79.84
	Hubei	74.49	60.03	80.89
	Hunan	72.97	58.27	80.83
	Jiangxi	77.31	51.45	73.17
	Shaanxi	69.71	51.51	77.00
	Shanghai	75.91	62.43	66.57
	Sichuan	73.50	61.72	82.86
	Xinjiang	74.38	59.40	84.84
	Yunnan	78.06	55.63	82.27
Third tier	Chongqing	78.99	56.27	63.42
	Gansu	73.67	50.52	68.03
	Guangxi	62.54	54.15	72.12
	Heilongjiang	68.87	53.88	71.30
	Jilin	63.58	58.34	75.37
	Liaoning	54.30	55.33	63.77
	Inner Mongolia	64.57	52.27	79.03
	Ningxia	73.90	46.23	70.39
	Qinghai	64.54	47.65	69.68
	Shanxi	69.02	52.68	74.83
	Tianjin	70.59	47.26	63.94
	Tibet	60.07	46.14	70.73

Note: Provinces in each tier are listed by the order of the first letter, which is irrelevant to PPP index scores.

Among all provinces, Beijing is in the first tier. Both Government guarantee and Private participation have high scores (93.84 and 90.42 respectively). However, the score of Project operation is 62.65, which shows tremendous disadvantage to the score of PPP Index.

Shandong, lying in East China, ranks high and lies in the first tier. The main reason is high scores for both Government guarantee and Project operation (85.36 and 86.55 respectively). Private participation equals to 65.70, which is also a good grade. So, Shandong performs almost equally well in all three dimensions. Besides, Jiangsu and Zhejiang, which lie in East China as well, rank in the first tier. They all get good scores for PPP Index.

Xinjiang ranks in the second tier. It basically owes to the fact that Project operation has a high score (84.84). It implies that project operation runs well in Xinjiang. And Government guarantee and Private participation of Xinjiang, which are also superior to median, equal to 74.38 and 59.40 respectively. Besides, Guizhou is also in the second tier. Similarly, the main reason is that Project operation equals to 83.94, which is a high score.

Among three other municipalities except Beijing, Shanghai is in the second tier, both Chongqing and Tianjin are in the third tier. Basically, Project operation of municipalities is inferior to median: 66.57 for Shanghai, 63.94 for Tianjin, 63.42 for Chongqing and 62.65 for Beijing. So, though to divergent extent, it has a significantly negative effect on the score of PPP Index for all municipalities. Besides, Government guarantee and Private participation of Shanghai are scored 75.91 and 62.43 separately, both of which are in the middle band. Chongqing is similar. Government guarantee and Private participation of Chongqing are scored 78.99 and 56.27 separately. And both indicators of Tianjin have low scores (70.59 and 47.26 respectively).

2.2 Ranking: PPP Market of Regions of China

In the last part, scores and ranking of PPP Index are analyzed on province-level. But it's still difficult to recognize differences of PPP development among regions due to large numbers of provinces. Therefore, we categorize them by geographic demarcations of different provinces, to calculate an average score, then to compare and analyze.

Basically, there are two common methods: either to divide provinces into the East, the Middle and the West part of China, or to divide them into 7 geographic regions, such as East China, South China, Central China etc. According to the perspective of experts in PPP field, the latter is superior. Classification based on geographic regions can reflect more relevant information, since provinces in one region are similar to each other. As a result, we adopts the second approach. Specifically, the classification standard is shown in Table 2.2.

Table 2.2   Chinese Geographic Demarcation

No.	Regions	Provinces included
1	East China	Shanghai, Jiangsu, Zhejiang, Anhui, Fujian, Jiangxi, Shandong, Taiwan
2	South China	Guangdong, Guangxi, Hainan, Hong Kong, Macau
3	Central China	Henan, Hubei, Hunan
4	North China	Beijing, Tianjin, Shanxi, Hebei, Inner Mongolia
5	Southwest China	Sichuan, Guizhou, Yunnan, Chongqing, Tibet
6	Northwest China	Shaanxi, Gansu, Qinghai, Ningxia, Xinjiang
7	Northeast China	Heilongjiang, Jilin, Liaoning

Our book selects different geographical reginons, uses the average scores of each province in the region as the score of the geographical region, and rank them(as shown in Table 2.3 anad Figure 2.3):

Table 2.3   Scores and Rankings of PPP Index in 2017 (region level)

No.	Districts	PPP Index		Government guarantee		Private participation		Project operation	
		Score	Rank	Score	Rank	Score	Rank	Score	Rank
1	Central China	73.33	1	73.08	3	60.84	2	82.87	1
2	East China	72.94	2	79.41	1	61.22	1	76.88	2
3	South China	69.09	3	73.18	2	60.74	3	72.29	5
4	Southwest China	69.04	4	72.71	5	55.23	6	76.64	3

(continued)

No.	Districts	PPP Index		Government guarantee		Private participation		Project operation	
		Score	Rank	Score	Rank	Score	Rank	Score	Rank
5	North China	68.63	5	72.76	4	59.92	4	72.06	6
6	Northwest China	66.29	6	71.24	6	51.06	7	73.99	4
7	Northeast China	63.49	7	62.25	7	55.85	5	70.15	7

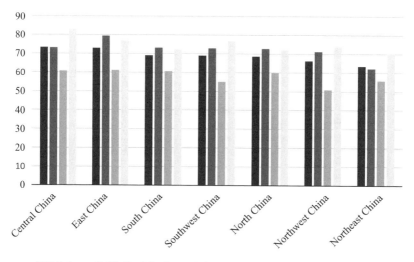

■ PPP Index ■ Public Participation ■ Private Paraticipation Project Operation

Figure 2.3 PPP Index and First-grade Indicators in 2017 (region level)

PPP Index of Central China ranks 1st, basically owing to the fact that Private participation and Project operation rank high, as 2nd and 1st separately, and that Government guarantee ranks in a medium place as 3rd.

PPP Index of East China ranks 2nd, basically because all of 3 first-grade indicators rank high. Government guarantee ranks 1st; Private participation ranks 1st and Project operation ranks 2nd.

PPP Index of South China ranks 3rd. Government guarantee ranks 2nd; Private participation ranks 3rd; Project operation ranks 5th.

As for Southwest China, PPP Index ranks 4th. Project operation ranks 3rd; Government guarantee ranks 5th; Private participation ranks 6th. Both Government guarantee and Private participation remain to be improved.

As for North China, PPP Index ranks 5th. Both Government guarantee and Private participation rank 4th, which is in a medium place. Project operation ranks in a lower place as 6th.

Northwest China's PPP Index ranks 6th. The reason lies in the fact that both Government guarantee and Private participation rank in a relatively lower place, as 6th and 7th separately. Project operation ranks 4th, which has a neutral effect on the PPP Index.

Northeast China's PPP Index ranks 7th. The reason lies in the fact that all 3 first-grade indicators are ranked in a low place. Government guarantee ranks 7th; Government guarantee ranks 5th; Project operation ranks 7th.

Chapter 3   PKU · China PPP Index Sub-item Evaluation

This chapter mainly analyzes the three secondary indicators of Government guarantee, Private participation and Project operation, and the third grade and fourth grade indicators after the that.

3.1   Ranking: Government Guarantee Index

3.1.1   The Overall Evaluation of Government Guarantee Index

The Government guarantee index mainly measures the ability of local governments to guarantee PPP projects from multiple dimensions. As the leading party in the PPP project, the government is also the setter of laws and regulations in this field and the provider of services such as project consulting, financing, and so on, which plays a vital role in the operation of PPP projects. The higher the local government's guarantee level for PPP, the better the development environment of PPP in this province, and the interests of private participants can also be guaranteed to the maximum extent.

On May 28, 2016, the National Development and Reform Commission and the Ministry of Finance jointly issued the Notice on Further Cooperating with related work of Public-Private Partnership (PPP) (Finance [2016] No. 32), requiring all localities to further strengthen inter-departmental coordination and cooperation, form a policy synergy, and actively promote the smooth implementation of Public-Private Partnership.

The Government guarantee index is mainly constructed from five aspects: Government fiscal support, Government service support, Government legal and policy guarantee, Government financial security and Government credibility index, which fully reflects the "hard power" and "soft power" of the ability of local government in developing PPP projects. "Hard power" mainly refers to the local economic development level and future potential; "soft power" mainly refers to the government's policy guarantees and preferential policies for PPP projects, and also government credibility. The former reflects the abundance of local fiscal funds, while the latter reflects the local government's emphasis on PPP and the determination to provide better services and guarantees. Both are important considerations for private capital to participate in investment. The indicator system framework of the Government guarantee index is shown in Figure 3.1.

When considering to attract social capital through the development of PPP projects, the local government proposes to consider the following four aspects: First, accelerate the development of the economy, increase fiscal revenue, and reduce liabilities; Second, improve the formulation of laws and regulations related to PPP; Third, increase the quantity and quality of financing services, and try best to solve the financing difficulties encountered by social capital in project development; Fourth, reduce the occurrence of illegal corruption and strengthen the credibility of the government. Only in these way can government select better and more suitable PPP projects and provide guarantee for the smooth completion of projects, so that the local PPP development environment will become better and achieve mutual benefit and win-win between the government and the social capital.

According to the collected data, we calculated and ranked the Government guarantee scores of 31 provinces. The specific scores and rankings are shown in Figure 3.2 and Table 3.1.

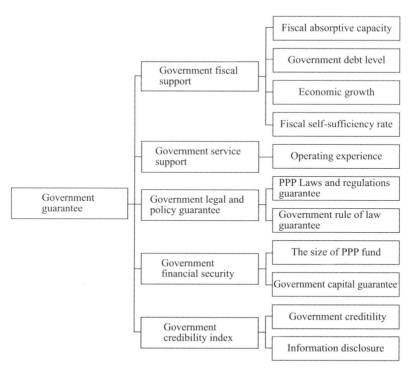

Figure 3.1　Framework of the Government Guarantee Index Indicator System

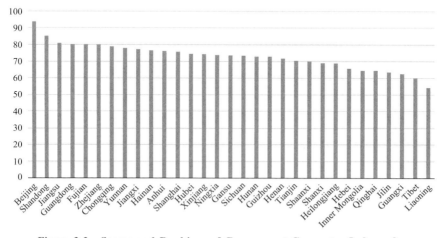

Figure 3.2　Scores and Rankings of Government Guarantee Indexes for Each Province in 2017

Table 3.1 Scores and Rankings of Government Guarantee Indexes for Each Province in 2017

Provinces	Score	Rank	Regions	Provinces	Score	Rank	Regions
Beijing	93.84	1	North	Sichuan	73.50	17	Southwest
Shandong	85.36	2	East	Hunan	72.97	18	Central
Jiangsu	80.99	3	East	Guizhou	72.93	19	Southwest
Guangdong	80.33	4	South	Henan	71.80	20	Central
Fujian	80.23	5	East	Tianjin	70.59	21	North
Zhejiang	79.79	6	East	Shaanxi	69.71	22	Northwest
Chongqing	78.99	7	Southeast	Shanxi	69.02	23	North
Yunnan	78.06	8	Southeast	Heilongjiang	68.87	24	Northeast
Jiangxi	77.31	9	East	Hebei	65.79	25	North
Hainan	76.66	10	South	Inner Mongolia	64.57	26	North
Anhui	76.24	11	East	Qinghai	64.54	27	Northwest
Shanghai	75.91	12	East	Jilin	63.58	28	Northeast
Hubei	74.49	13	Central	Guangxi	62.54	29	South
Xinjiang	74.38	14	Northwest	Tibet	60.07	30	Southwest
Ningxia	73.90	15	Northwest	Liaoning	54.30	31	Northeast
Gansu	73.67	16	Northwest				

Beijing, located in North China, gets 93.84 points in Government guarantee index, ranking the first. As the capital of China, Beijing's various secondary indicators rank top, indicating that Beijing has done a good job in the five dimensions of the index evaluation. Among them, the rank of Government fiscal support, Government financial security and Government credibility index are the top of all provinces, respectively the 1st, 2nd, and 2nd; the rankings of Government service support, Government legal and policy guarantee are relatively lower, respectively the 8th and the 6th place, slightly drags down the overall ranking of Beijing. It shows that Beijing still has room for improvement in service provision and the formulation of related laws and regulations.

In addition, in East China, the score of Government guarantee index of Shandong Province is also very high, which is 85.36 points, ranking the 2nd. The rankings of Shandong Government guarantee's secondary indicators are relatively high, especially the Government legal and policy guarantee, ranking the 2nd; Government fiscal support, Government service support and Government financial security are ranked 6th, and Government credibility index ranks 8th.

Xinjiang located in the northwest region scores 74.38, ranking 14th in the country. This is also a good result. The probable reason is that the rankings of Government service support and Government financial support of Xinjiang government are relatively high, ranking 3rd and 4th respectively. The Government fiscal support, Government legal and policy guarantee and Government credibility index are ranked lower, which are 22nd, 30th, and 25th respectively, dragging down the overall ranking of Xinjiang.

Tianjin, which ranks the lowest in the municipalities, scores 70.59 points, ranking 21st. The rankings of various secondary indicators of Tianjin are relatively moderate. The Government financial security and Government credibility index rank in the middle, respectively 12th and 11th; the rankings of Government fiscal support, Government service support and Government legal and policy guarantee are respectively 20th, 24th and 19th.

As discribed above, China can generally be divided into seven geographical regions, and there is a certain similarity between the provinces in the same geographical region. Therefore, our book selects different geographical regions as the whole, and counts the average scores of different regions and ranks them. The specific ranking of different regions is shown in Table 3.2 and Figure 3.3.

Table 3.2 Scores and Rankings of Government Guarantee Indexes in Different Regions in 2017

No.	Regions	Provinces involved in the calculation	Average score
1	East China	Shanghai, Jiangsu, Zhejiang, Anhui, Fujian, Jiangxi, Shandong	79.41
2	South China	Guangdong, Guangxi, Hainan	73.18
3	Central China	Henan, Hubei, Hunan	73.08
4	North China	Beijing, Tianjin, Shanxi, Hebei, Inner Mongolia	72.76
5	Southwest China	Sichuan, Guizhou, Yunnan, Chongqing, Tibet	72.71
6	Northwest China	Shaanxi, Gansu, Qinghai, Ningxia, Xinjiang	71.24
7	Northeast China	Heilongjiang, Jilin, Liaoning	62.25

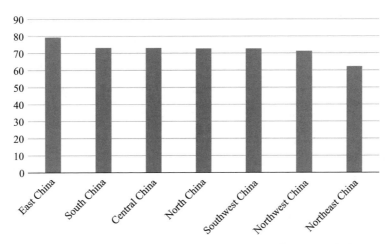

Figure 3.3 Scores and Rankings of Government Guarantee Indexes in Different Regions in 2017

The PPP Government guarantee index of East China ranks the 1st, with Government fiscal support, Government legal and policy guarantee and Government credibility index all ranking the 1st, and Government service support ranks the 2nd. Government financial security ranks the 5th, dragging down the overall ranking of the East China region.

The PPP Government guarantee index of South China ranks the 2nd, with Government fiscal support, Government service support and Government legal and policy guarantee ranking the 3rd, 3rd and 2nd respectively; Government financial security and Government credibility index ranks 6th and 4th respectively.

The PPP Government guarantee index of Central China ranks the 3rd, with Government fiscal support, Government legal and policy guarantee and Government credibility index ranking 2nd, 3rd, and 2nd respectively; Government financial security ranks in the middle, which is 4th; Government service support ranks 7th, dragging down the overall ranking of Central China.

The PPP Government guarantee index of North China ranks 4th, with the Government financial security ranking 2nd; the Government fiscal support and Government legal and policy guarantee ranks in the middle, which are both 4th; Government service support and Government credibility index are both in the 5th place.

The PPP Government guarantee index of Southwest China ranks 5th, with the Government financial security ranking at the top place, which is actually 3rd; Government service support ranks 4th. The rankings of Government fiscal support, Government legal and policy guarantee and Government credibility index are all in an inferior place, which are 5th, 5th, and 6th.

The PPP Government guarantee index of Northwest China ranks 6th, with the Government service support and Government financial security ranking at the top place, which are both the 1st; Government credibility index ranks the 3rd; Government fiscal support and Government legal and policy guarantee rank relatively lower, both are the 6th.

The PPP Government guarantee index of Northeast China ranks 7th, and the Government fiscal support, Government service support, Government legal and policy guarantee, Government financial security and Government credibility index are all ranked lower.

3.1.2 Evaluation of Second-grade Indicators of Government Guarantee Index

1. Government fiscal support

Government fiscal support mainly measures the ability of the local government to provide sufficient funds for PPP projects. The main indicators are fiscal absorptive capacity, government debt level, economic growth, etc. The level of local economic development, income and debt levels are all important factors affecting the government's allocation of funds to PPP projects, and the abundance of financial support directly affects the smooth progress of PPP projects. The more capital invested by the government, the smaller the funding pressure of the social capital side, and the lower the risk of project shutdown due to the break of the capital chain during the project development process. Therefore, the Government fiscal support is an important part of the overall government guarantee, and it is also a concern of the social capital side.

Government fiscal support includes four third-grade indicators: Fiscal absorptive capacity, Government debt level, Economic growth, and Fiscal self-sufficiency rate. These third-grade indicators also include fourth grade indicators. Fiscal absorptive capacity reflects the local government's total fiscal revenue, financial affordability, fiscal revenue growth and stability, and comprehensively measures the financial strength of local governments. Government debt level mainly measures the total amount of local government debt and debt repayment pressure. Combining with the Fiscal absorptive capacity, it could analyze the funds available of the local government. Economic growth is measured by GDP growth rates. The Fiscal self-sufficiency rate measures the degree to which local governments rely on central transfer payments. The Government fiscal support provides a good description of the government's ability to provide funding for PPP projects. The specific indicator system is shown in Figure 3.4 and Table 3.3.

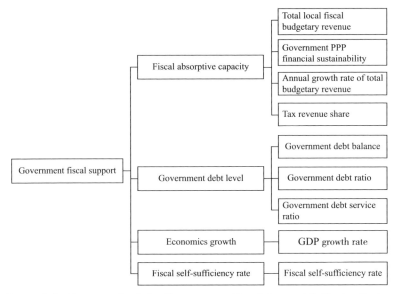

Figure 3.4　Framework of the Government Fiscal Support Indicator System

Table 3.3　Composition of Government Fiscal Support Indicator System

Second-grade indicators	Third-grade indicators	Fourth-grade indicators	Formula for calculating indicators	Reason for selecting this indicator
Government fiscal support	Fiscal absorptive capacity	Total local fiscal budgetary revenue	Local general public budget revenue + central transfer payment + government fund revenue	Total local fiscal budgetary revenue is the overall financial guarantee that the government can provide to PPP projects
		Financial sustainability	General public budget expenditure×10%	Central and provincial finances will conduct risk warnings for provinces that are close to or exceed the 10% red line
		Annual growth rate of total budgetary revenue	(The local government's fiscal revenue in the same year-the local government's fiscal revenue in the previous year) / the local government's fiscal revenue in the previous year	The faster the fiscal revenue grows, the faster the local economy is developing and the more likely it is to provide adequate financial security

(continued)

Second-grade indicators	Third-grade indicators	Fourth-grade indicators	Formula for calculating indicators	Reason for selecting this indicator
Government fiscal support		Tax revenue share	Tax revenue / local general public budget revenue	The higher the proportion of tax revenue in general public budget revenue, the more stable the local government fiscal revenue situation is, and the more reliable the financial protection of PPP projects
	Government debt level	Government debt balance	Get data directly	The greater the balance of local government debt, the greater the pressure on debt repayment, the more likely it is to default on PPP projects or lead to insufficient funds to invest in PPP projects
		Government debt ratio	Local government debt balance / local GDP	The greater the pressure on local governments to pay debts, the less funds are available to supply PPP projects
		Government debt service ratio	Local government debt balance / local general public budget revenue	The weaker the solvency of local governments, the greater the pressure on repayment of debt, and the less funds are available for PPP projects
	Economics growth	GDP growth rate	Get data directly	GDP growth rate reflects the growth rate of local economic. The faster the economic growth rate, the more favorable to the development of PPP projects
	Fiscal self-sufficiency rate	Fiscal self-sufficiency rate	Local general public budget revenue / local general public budget expenditure	The lower the fiscal self-sufficiency rate, the more serious the dependence of local finance on central transfer payments, and the more likely it is that only insufficient funds are available for PPP projects

According to the collected data, we calculated and ranked the Government fiscal support scores of 31 provinces in China. As shown in Figure 3.5 and Table 3.4.

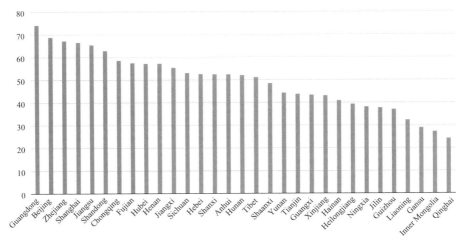

Figure 3.5 Scores and Rankings of Government Fiscal Support Indexes for Each Province in 2017

Table 3.4 Scores and Rankings of Government Fiscal Support for Each Province in 2017

Provinces	Score	Rank	Regions	Provinces	Score	Rank	Regions
Guangdong	74.13	1	South	Tibet	51.14	17	Southwest
Beijing	68.83	2	North	Shaanxi	48.51	18	Northwest
Zhejiang	67.25	3	East	Yunnan	44.29	19	Southwest
Shanghai	66.59	4	East	Tianjin	43.77	20	North
Jiangsu	65.47	5	East	Guangxi	43.36	21	South
Shandong	62.89	6	East	Xinjiang	43.08	22	Northwest
Chongqing	58.53	7	Southwest	Hainan	40.96	23	South
Fujian	57.43	8	East	Heilongjiang	39.33	24	Northeast
Hubei	57.15	9	Central	Ningxia	38.16	25	Northwest
Henan	57.14	10	Central	Jilin	37.73	26	Northeast

(continued)

Provinces	Score	Rank	Regions	Provinces	Score	Rank	Regions
Jiangxi	55.36	11	East	Guizhou	37.00	27	Southwest
Sichuan	53.06	12	Southwest	Liaoning	32.28	28	Northeast
Hebei	52.58	13	North	Gansu	28.91	29	Northwest
Shanxi	52.48	14	North	Inner Mongolia	27.22	30	North
Anhui	52.43	15	East	Qinghai	24.18	31	Northwest
Hunan	52.12	16	Central				

The top five scores of the Government fiscal support index are Guangdong, Beijing, Zhejiang, Shanghai, and Jiangsu, with scores of 74.13, 68.83, 67.25, 66.59, and 65.47, respectively. The last five scores are Guizhou, Liaoning, Gansu, Inner Mongolia and Qinghai, with scores of 37.00, 32.28, 28.91, 27.22 and 24.18 respectively. Overall, the Government fiscal support scores of the provincial governments have a significant positive correlation with the local economic development level. In economically developed provinces, the government has higher fiscal revenues and lower debt repayment pressures, so that the government has a better level of financial security and higher scores. In economically underdeveloped provinces, government revenues are lower and financial pressures are higher, government financial security is weaker, so their scores are lower.

The scores and ranking of Government fiscal support in different regions are shown in Table 3.5 and Figure 3.6.

Table 3.5　Scores and Rankings of Government Fiscal Support of Different Regions in 2017

No.	Regions	Provinces involved in the calculation	Average score
1	East China	Shanghai, Jiangsu, Zhejiang, Anhui, Fujian, Jiangxi, Shandong	61.06
2	Central China	Henan, Hubei, Hunan	55.47
3	South China	Guangdong, Guangxi, Hainan	52.81

(continued)

No.	Regions	Provinces involved in the calculation	Average score
4	North China	Beijing, Tianjin, Shanxi, Hebei, Inner Mongolia	48.98
5	Southwest China	Sichuan, Guizhou, Yunnan, Chongqing, Tibet	48.81
6	Northwest China	Shaanxi, Gansu, Qinghai, Ningxia, Xinjiang	36.57
7	Northeast China	Heilongjiang, Jilin, Liaoning	36.45

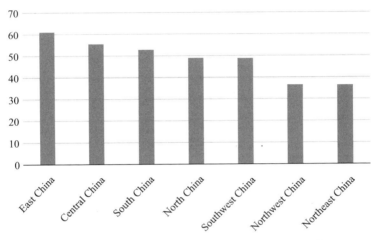

Figure 3.6 Scores and Rankings of Government Fiscal Support of Different Regions in 2017

Tables 3.5 and Figure 3.6 above show that the Government fiscal support in East China has the highest average score of 61.06 points, followed by Central China and South China, with 55.47 points and 52.81 points respectively. The region with the lowest Government fiscal support score is the Northeast region with a score of 36.45. The average score of Government fiscal support of the provinces in China is 49.46 points. East China, Central China and South China are above the average level, and North China, Southwest China, Northwest China and Northeast China are below the average level. Judging from the scoring results, the regional economic development has a significant positive impact on the Government fiscal support score. The economic development in East China and Central China has grown at a faster rate and higher levels, resulting in higher fiscal revenue levels and less financial pressure. In the Northeast and Northwest regions, economic growth has slowed down in recent years, and the debt ratio has been relatively high, which has had a certain negative impact on the Government fiscal support level.

2. Government service support

Government service support refers to the ability of the government to provide guarantees for various government services during the operation, which limited to the PPP project area. Our book selects the government's operating experience for PPP projects to represent the Government service support. Provinces with rich experience in project operation can provide guidance and guarantee for the operation of PPP projects in terms of project process, project supervision and project acceptance. Government service support indicator system is shown in Table 3.6.

Table 3.6 Composition of Government Service Support Indicator System

Second-grade indicators	Third-grade indicators	Fourth-grade indicators	Formula for calculating indicators	Reason for selecting this indicator
Government service support	Government timeliness	Project preparation speed	The average time area from the project initiation time to the procurement result: the contract signing time of PPP project of the province	Measure the pre-work speed of the PPP project in the provincial administrative area, urge the provinces and cities to speed up the examination and approval, simplify the procedures, shorten the preliminary review time of the PPP project, and put more energy into the actual construction of the project
	Government performance	Government performance evaluation	No information	The greater the government's performance, the more efficient it is when participating in a PPP project

(continued)

Second-grade indicators	Third-grade indicators	Fourth-grade indicators	Formula for calculating indicators	Reason for selecting this indicator
	Operating experience	Government operating experience	The number of PPP warehousing projects of the province/the total number of national PPP warehousing projects	The richer the government's operational experience with PPP projects, the more likely it is to provide guidance and assurance for the operation of PPP projects

According to the collected data, we calculated and ranked the Government service support scores of 31 provinces, municipalities and autonomous regions are calculated and ranked. In addition, the provinces are marked the region to which it belongs, as shown in Table 3.7 and Figure 3.7.

Table 3.7 Scores and Rankings of Government Service Support for Each Province in 2017

Provinces	Score	Rank	Regions	Provinces	Score	Rank	Regions
Chongqing	76.12	1	Southwest	Shanghai	48.46	17	East
Hainan	75.37	2	South	Jiangsu	48.19	18	East
Xinjiang	72.99	3	Northwest	Guizhou	48.04	19	Southwest
Ningxia	70.97	4	Northwest	Hebei	47.93	20	North
Jiangxi	64.26	5	East	Shaanxi	47.76	21	Northwest
Shandong	62.93	6	East	Inner Mongolia	47.33	22	North
Fujian	61.82	7	East	Tibet	47.22	23	Southwest
Beijing	59.07	8	North	Tianjin	45.32	24	North
Zhejiang	57.55	9	East	Yunnan	43.82	25	Southwest
Guangdong	54.05	10	South	Henan	42.49	26	Central
Shanxi	53.78	11	North	Hunan	42.46	27	Central

(continued)

Provinces	Score	Rank	Regions	Provinces	Score	Rank	Regions
Anhui	52.08	12	East	Qinghai	42.08	28	Northwest
Jilin	51.77	13	Northeast	Sichuan	39.44	29	Southwest
Hubei	50.72	14	Central	Liaoning	37.45	30	Northeast
Heilongjiang	50.16	15	Northeast	Guangxi	29.10	31	South
Gansu	49.41	16	Northwest				

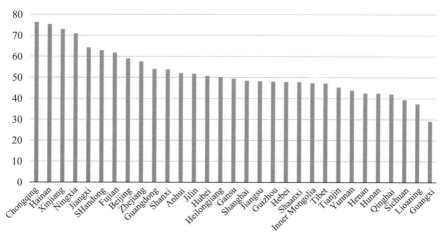

Figure 3.7 Scores and Rankings of Government Service Support for Each Province in 2017

The top five Government service support scores are Chongqing, Hainan, Xinjiang, Ningxia and Jiangxi, with 76.12 points, 75.37 points, 72.99 points, 70.97 points and 64.26 points respectively. The last five are Hunan, Qinghai, Sichuan, Liaoning and Guangxi, with 42.26 points, 42.08 points, 39.44 points, 37.45 points and 29.10 points respectively. Overall, Xinjiang, Guizhou and some other places have more PPP warehousing projects, and PPP operation experience is more abundant; Chongqing, Hainan, Xinjiang and some other places have faster preparation speeds and higher overall rankings. The economically developed provinces and cities such as Beijing and Shanghai are not prominent enough in these two terms, so they are ranked medium. They could accumulate relative experience and increase PPP service guarantee by increasing the undertaking of the PPP projects.

Through the calculation of the indicators, we get the scores and rankings of Government service support of different regions, The specific rankings of different regions are shown in Table 3.8 and Figure 3.8.

Table 3.8   Scores and Rankings of Government Service Support in Different Regions

No.	Regions	Provinces involved in the calculation	Average score
1	Northwest China	Shaanxi, Gansu, Qinghai, Ningxia, Xinjiang	56.64
2	East China	Shanghai, Jiangsu, Zhejiang, Anhui, Fujian, Jiangxi, Shandong	56.47
3	South China	Guangdong, Guangxi, Hainan	52.84
4	Southwest China	Sichuan, Guizhou, Yunnan, Chongqing, Tibet	50.93
5	North China	Beijing, Tianjin, Shanxi, Hebei, Inner Mongolia	50.69
6	Northeast China	Heilongjiang, Jilin, Liaoning	46.46
7	Central China	Henan, Hubei, Hunan	45.23

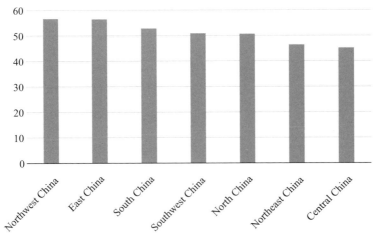

Figure 3.8   Scores and Rankings of Government Service Support in Different Regions

By analyzing Table 3.8 and Figure 3.8, we can easily find that the Northwest China ranks 1st with 56.64, and the East China region and South China region rank 2nd and 3rd with 56.47 points and 52.84 points respectively. The region with the lowest average score is Central China, with a score of 45.23. The proportion of warehousing projects in Guangdong, Guangxi and Hainan only slightly exceeds 1%. According to the situation of each province, the proportion of warehousing projects in Guizhou Province reaches 12.68%, while that in Tibet is only 0.03%. This shows that the distribution of warehousing projects varies greatly between provinces and regions.

On the one hand, the Government service support index can reflect the enthusiasm of the government to develop PPP projects, and on the other hand, it can also reflect the government's efforts to provide guarantees for the operation of PPP projects. The economic development of the central and western regions is relatively backward, and the government's willingness to develop PPP projects is stronger. The coastal cities in the southeastern part of the country are more developed, so they are not interested in the development of PPP very much.

3. Government legal and policy guarantee

Government legal and policy guarantee refers to the government providing guarantees for the operation of PPP projects through the formulation of laws and regulations and the introduction of relevant policies. This part portrays the government's protection through the number of local government laws and regulations on PPP and the government index of the rule of law. The number of laws and regulations on PPP directly reflects the government's measures to regulate the operation of PPP projects. The government index of rule of law more comprehensively reflects the level of rule of law construction of local governments.

The government legal and policy guarantee index system is shown in Table 3.9.

Table 3.9 Government Legal and Policy Guarantee Index System

Second-grade indicators	Third-grade indicators	Fourth-grade indicators	Formula for calculating indicators	Reason for selecting this indicator
Government legal and policy guarantee	Laws and regulations guarantee	Number of local government laws and regulations related to PPP	Number of PPP laws and regulations issued by provincial governments	The two are directly related. The local PPP regulations can further refine the PPP-related work requirements of each province. The more perfect the laws and regulations, the more the local PPP can be guaranteed
	Government rule of law guarantee	Law-based Government Index	The data is directly quoted from the "Annual Assessment Report on China's Law-based Government (2017)", and the indicator system includes 8 objective indicators and 1 subjective indicator	There is a positive correlation between the development of the rule of law and the development of the economy and society. The higher the level of construction of the local rule of law government, the more it can promote and improve the development of PPP

In terms of government legal and policy guarantees, the scores and rankings of each region is shown in Table 3.10 and Figure 3.9.

Table 3.10 Local Government Legal and Policy Protection Scores and Rankings in 2017

No.	Regions	Provinces involved in the calculation	Average score
1	East China	Shanghai, Jiangsu, Zhejiang, Anhui, Fujian, Jiangxi, Shandong	68.20
2	South China	Guangdong, Guangxi, Hainan	53.12
3	Central China	Henan, Hubei, Hunan	52.10
4	North China	Beijing, Tianjin, Shanxi, Hebei, Inner Mongolia	44.13

(continued)

No.	Regions	Provinces involved in the calculation	Average score
5	Southeast China	Sichuan, Guizhou, Yunnan, Chongqing, Tibet	43.79
6	Northeast China	Shaanxi, Gansu, Qinghai, Ningxia, Xinjiang	33.32
7	Northwest China	Heilongjiang, Jilin, Liaoning	33.02

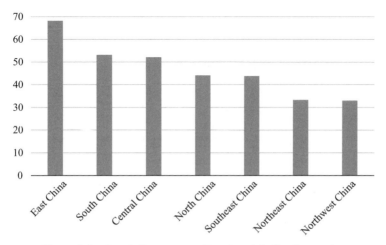

Figure 3.9　Local Government Legal and Policy Protection Scores and Rankings in 2017

The Government legal and policy guarantee score of East China ranked first. East China ranks 1st in terms of the number of Laws and regulations governing PPP, and ranks 2nd in the Law-based Government Index, and only one point away from the first.

South China's Government legal and policy guarantee score ranked second. South China performed poorly in terms of the number of Laws and regulations related to PPP, ranking fifth, and ranking first in the Law-based Government Index.

Central China's Government legal and policy guarantee score ranked third. Central China ranks 2nd in terms of the number of Laws and regulations on PPP and 3rd in the Law-based Government Index.

North China's Government legal and policy guarantee score ranked fourth.

North China ranks fourth in terms of the number of Laws and regulations on PPP and the government index of the rule of law, and the performance is relatively balanced.

Southwest China's Government legal and policy guarantee score ranked fifth. Southwest China ranks third in terms of the number of Laws and regulations related to PPP, and ranks sixth in the Law-based Government Index. The degree of Law-based Government needs to be improved.

Northwest China's Government legal and policy guarantee score ranked sixth. Northwest China ranked sixth in terms of the number of Laws and regulations related to PPP, and ranked seventh in the Law-based Government Index, which performed poorly.

Northeast China's Government legal and policy guarantee score ranked seventh. Northeast China ranks 7th in terms of the number of Laws and regulations related to PPP which needs to be targeted to improve, and ranking 5th in the Law-based Government Index.

From the perspective of specific scores, East China has performed better in terms of legal and policy guarantees, ranking first with a score of 68.20, and with a large difference from other regions. The scores in the northwest and northeast regions were low, only 33.32 and 33.02 respectively. In terms of the performance of the provinces, Jiangsu Province has issued the most Laws and regulations to guarantee the operation of PPP projects, and also has a high degree of law-based government, with a comprehensive score of 93.87 points. Xinjiang's performance in these two aspects is not satisfactory, the weighted average score is only 25.63 points.

The awareness of the rule of law is closely related to the level of economic development. The coastal areas in the southeastern region have achieved fruitful results inthe law-based government administration. The western region and the northeast region still need to be improved.

4. Government financial security

Government financial security refers to the government's financial assistance to PPP projects, which is directly reflected in the government's financial support for the project. The China PPP Fund (established with the approval of the State Council, with a registered capital of 180 billion yuan) and the local government PPP guidance fund can provide strong support for the project. The degree of government capital participation reflects the government guarantee from the perspective of project funding. The government financial security indicator system is shown in Table 3.11.

Table 3.11 The Government Financial Security Indicator System

Second-grade indicators	Third-grade indicators	Fourth-grade indicators	Formula for calculating indicators	Reason for selecting this indicator
Government financial security	Government fund guarantee	Number of investment projects of China PPP Fund by province	At the end of 2017, the number of projects that the Chinese PPP fund has decided	As a fund set up by the Ministry of Finance, China PPP Fund can provide strong financial support and guarantee for related projects
		PPP guidance fund scale of local government	The size of the PPP guidance fund that has been established by local government	PPP funds established by local government can support the development of PPP projects in the province in a more targeted manner
	Government capital guarantee	Government capital participation	PPP Center provides data: the amount of capital proposed by the government / (intended to introduce social capital quota + government proposed capital contribution)	Compared with social capital, government capital has stronger protection for the development of PPP projects

By valuing the data obtained, we get the scores and rankings of the regions in terms of government financial security, as shown in Table 3.12 and Figure 3.10.

Table 3.12 Government Financial Security Scores and Rankings in 2017

No.	Regions	Provinces involved in the calculation	Average score
1	Northeast China	Shaanxi, Gansu, Qinghai, Ningxia, Xinjiang	29.37
2	North China	Beijing, Tianjin, Shanxi, Hebei, Inner Mongolia	29.33
3	Southeast China	Sichuan, Guizhou, Yunnan, Chongqing, Tibet	22.52
4	Central China	Henan, Hubei, Hunan	15.76
5	East China	Shanghai, Jiangsu, Zhejiang, Anhui, Fujian, Jiangxi, Shandong	15.42
6	South China	Guangdong, Guangxi, Hainan	14.30
7	Northwest China	Heilongjiang, Jilin, Liaoning	12.81

The Northwest China Government's financial security score ranked first. The region ranked sixth in the number of China's PPP fund investment projects, with fewer investment projects, ranked first in terms of PPP guidance funds, and second in government capital participation.

The financial security score of the North China region ranked second. The region ranks third in the unmber of China's PPP fund investment projects, ranks fourth in terms of PPP guidance funds, ranks first in government capital participation, with a high level of government capital participation.

The Southwest China Government's financial security score ranked third. The region ranks second the number of China's PPP fund investment projects, and ranks sixth in terms of PPP guidance fund size, reflecting that the fund size needs to be improved. And the government's capital participation ranks third.

The Central China government's financial security score ranked fourth. The region ranks 1st in the number of China's PPP fund investment projects because of more investment projects, fifth in the size of PPP guidance funds, and sixth in terms of government capital participation.

The financial security score of the East China region ranked fifth. The region ranks 5th in the number of Chinese PPP fund investment projects, 3rd in terms of PPP guidance funds, and 4th in government capital participation.

South China's government financial security score ranked sixth. The region ranks 7th in the number of China's PPP fund investment projects, and ranks 7th in terms of PPP guidance fund size, reflecting the fund's ability to support projects needs to be improved. And the government's capital participation ranks 5th.

The Northeast China government's financial security score ranked seventh. The region ranks 2nd in the number of China's PPP fund investment projects, 4th in terms of PPP guidance fund size, and 7th in government capital participation.

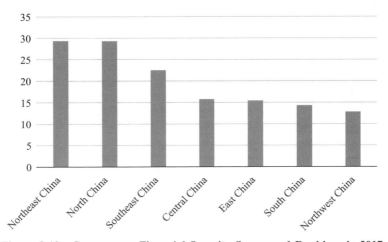

Figure 3.10 Government Financial Security Scores and Rankings in 2017

Overall, the performance of the government in terms of government financial security was poor, and the northwest region also made the first place in this category. The reason is mainly because the establishment of a large-scale PPP guidance fund in Xinjiang, which on the other hand reflects that the areas with relatively poor PPP development are actively taking measures to promote the development of related projects.

5. Government credibility index

Government credibility is the extent to which the government is trusted by the public. This paper selects several indicators such as the number of debt defaults, the number of company defaults, the number of administrative litigation case, duty crime rate and government transparency index to comprehensively reflect the credibility of a provincial government. The fact that the first four indicators are too high means that the efficiency and normativeness of government operations need to be questioned. The government transparency index more intuitively reflects the openness of its information and procedures, and is directly related to credibility(see Table 3.13).

Table 3.13 Government Credibility Index Indicator System

Second-grade indicators	Third-grade indicators	Fourth-grade indicators	Formula for calculating indicators	Reason for selecting this indicator
Government credibility index	Government credibility	Numbers of debt defaults	The number of bond defaults in a province was retrieved from the Wind Financial Terminal	A province's bond defaults, and the local government has not taken timely measures to help enterprises safeguard the interests of investors can reflects the government's credibility
		Number of company defaults	The number of bond defaulting companies in a province was retrieved from the Wind Financial Terminal	
		Number of administrative litigation cases	By conducting a search in the Chinese Judgment Document Network and setting the administrative case referee year to 2017, the number of cases in each province can be obtained	The more administrative litigation cases, the less reasonable the administrative system and the poor enforcement of the local government
		Rate of corruption**	N/A	More corruption means a more corrupt government

(continued)

Second-grade indicators	Third-grade indicators	Fourth-grade indicators	Formula for calculating indicators	Reason for choosing this indicator
		Duty crime rate	On the website of the Discipline Inspection Commission, statistics on the cadres of a certain province are subject to party and government affairs	The higher duty crime rate reflects the problems in the mechanism system of the local government and the unhealthy trend in the cadre team
	Information disclosure	Government transparency index	The data is directly selected from the "Annual Report on China Rule of Law No. 16 (2018)", in which the government transparency index consists of eight quantitative indicators	Higher government transparency is more able to meet the public's demand for information, thereby enhancing the government's credibility

In terms of the degree of government credibility, the overall scores of each region is shown in Table 3.14 and Figure 3.11.

Table 3.14 Government Credibility Index Scores and Rankings in 2017

No.	Regions	Provinces involved in the calculation	Average score
1	East China	Shanghai, Jiangsu, Zhejiang, Anhui, Fujian, Jiangxi, Shandong	82.13
2	Central China	Henan, Hubei, Hunan	82.02
3	Northeast China	Shaanxi, Gansu, Qinghai, Ningxia, Xinjiang	81.44
4	Southeast China	Sichuan, Guizhou, Yunnan, Chongqing, Tibet	81.08
5	South China	Guangdong, Guangxi, Hainan	77.16
6	North China	Beijing, Tianjin, Shanxi, Hebei, Inner Mongolia	77.11
7	Northwest China	Heilongjiang, Jilin, Liaoning	65.89

The East China Regional Government's credibility index scored the first place. East China ranks first in terms of the number of debt defaults, the first in debt defaulting companies, the sixth in administrative litigation, the third in terms of job crime rate, and the second in government transparency index.

The Central China Government's credibility index ranked second. Central China ranked first in terms of the number of debt defaults, the number of debt defaulting companies ranked first, and the number of administrative litigation cases ranked seventh, the rank of duty crimes was fifth, ranking first in government transparency index.

The Northwestern China Government's credibility index ranked third. Northwestern China ranks first in terms of the number of debt defaults, ranks first in debt defaulting companies, ranks first in administrative litigation, ranks first in duty crimes, and ranks first in government transparency index.

The Southwestern China Government's government credibility index ranked fourth. Southwestern China ranked sixth in terms of the number of debt defaults, fifth in debt defaulting companies, second in administrative litigation, second in duty crimes, and fourth in government transparency index.

South China's government credibility index scored the fifth. South China ranked fifth in terms of the number of debt defaults, seventh in debt defaulting companies, third in administrative litigation, sixth in job crimes, third in government transparency index which is better.

The North China government's credibility index score ranked sixth. North China ranks fourth in terms of the number of debt defaults, third in debt defaulting companies, fifth in administrative litigation, seventh in job crimes, and fifth in government transparency index.

The Northeastern China Government's government credibility index ranked seventh. Northeastern China ranked seventh in terms of the number of debt defaults, sixth in debt defaulting companies, fourth in administrative litigation cases, fourth in job crime rates, and seventh in government transparency index, with poor overall performance.

From the specific scores, the East China and Central China scored 82.13

and 82.02 respectively, ranking the top two. The third to 6th scores are relatively close, between 77-82 points. In contrast, the Northeast China performed poorly and only achieved a combined average of 65.89. According to the situation of each province, Yunnan Province and Guizhou Province have higher degree of public trust, and the comprehensive scores are all greater than 90; Liaoning Province scores only 34.24, which is far from the other provinces.

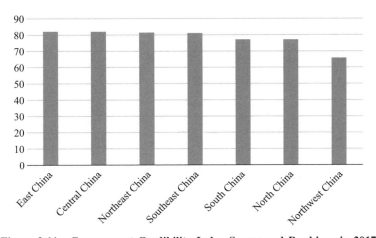

Figure 3.11 Government Credibility Index Scores and Rankings in 2017

It can be seen from the figure that except for the Northeast region, there is little gap in the credibility of the government. As the public is fully involved in all aspects of government governance, the public's trust in the government has been greatly enhanced. Northeast China should pay more attention to the concept of serving the people, further expand the content and decision-making procedures of government affairs, reduce the incidence of administrative litigation and the crime rate of duty, and create a more convenient environment for the development of PPP projects.

3.2 Ranking: Private Participation

3.2.1 The Overall Evaluation of Private Participation

The so-called "Private participation" refers to the ability of social forces, which is represented by enterprises, to participate in PPP projects. On one hand, "private participation" means the willingness to participate in PPP projects, on the other hand it measures enterprise's fund capacity, credit and professionalism. "Private participation", which relys on market power, effectively control financial deficit and promotes sound development of PPP. In the view of government financial resources, the limitation of fiscal fund prevents the implementation of governmental function while the development of society requires more high-quality public services for the public.

Realistic pressure of governmental finance means the construction of infrastructure requires more participation of social force. Historically, it is very common that the shortage of governmental fund discourage the implementation of public projects. Our country's fiscal revenue has been increasing steadily since entering the new era. However, high governmental leverage ratio, especially those of local governments, can by no means be ignored. Therefore, in order to prevent excessive fiscal deficit, it is nature to introduce social capital to public projects.

Great significance has been attached to private participation and a number of laws or regulations regarding social capital's participation in infrastructure and public utilities has been enacted. On December 11, 2001, the State Planning Commission issued a notice on "Several opinions on promoting and guiding private investment" ([2001] No. 2653), in order to encourage and guide social capital to participate in the construction of operational infrastructure and public welfare projects. On October 14, 2003, the Third Plenary Session of the 16th Central Committee passed "Decions of the CPC central committee on several issues concerning the improvement of socialist market economic system", allowing non-public capital to enter industries and fields of infrastructure, public utilities, etc, which are not prohibited by laws and regulations. In addition, the General Office of the State Council issued "Several opinions of General Office of the State Council on encouraging and guiding the healthy development of social capital" ([2010]No. 13) on May 7, 2010 and "Guidance by General Office of the State Council on government purchasing services from social forces" ([2013]No. 96) on Sep 30, 2013, indicating the importance of social capital.

In addition to participating in PPP projects directly, social capital also includes those institution that offer relative services, such as financial institution, law office and consulting companies. Since financing is vital to PPP, it will be discussed and measured specially. Our main emphasis is laid on the measurement of financial institutions and financial markets. Since these third-party participants as well as social capital are classified as non-public, we name the second first-class indicatorss after Private participation.

Private participation index is made up of six sub-indexes, including PPP business participation, business credibility, private fund, financial service, legal service and consulting service. Specially, Private Participation Index is shown in Figure 3.12.

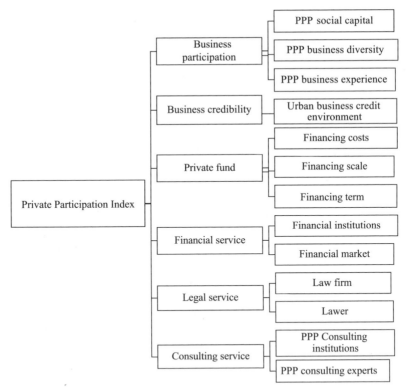

Figure 3.12 Private Participation Index Framework

Scores of Private participation index of 31 provinces are shown in Table 3.15 and Figure 3.13. The average score is 57.80. There are 13 entities above the average and 18 below the average, most of which range from 50 to 60. According to the distribution, define those above 55 points as Active PPP participation and define those below 55 points as Active PPP participation. Hence, 18 provinces, municipalities and autonomous regions are active PPP participation while 13 provinces, municipalities and autonomous regions are inactive PPP participation.

Table 3.15　Scores and Rankings for Private Participation Index in 2017

Provinces	Score	Rank	Regions	Provinces	Score	Rank	Regions
Beijing	90.42	1	North	Yunnan	55.63	17	Southwest
Guangdong	73.35	2	South	Liaoning	55.33	18	Northeast
Zhejiang	67.75	3	East	Hainan	54.72	19	South
Jiangsu	67.60	4	East	Anhui	54.36	20	East
Shandong	65.70	5	East	Guangxi	54.15	21	South
Henan	64.23	6	Central	Heilongjiang	53.88	22	Northeast
Shanghai	62.43	7	East	Shanxi	52.68	23	North
Sichuan	61.72	8	Southwest	Inner Mongolia	52.27	24	North
Hubei	60.03	9	Central	Shanxi	51.51	25	Northwest
Xinjiang	59.40	10	Northwest	Jiangxi	51.45	26	East
Fujian	59.25	11	East	Gansu	50.52	27	Northwest
Jilin	58.34	12	Northeast	Qinghai	47.65	28	Northwest
Hunan	58.27	13	Central	Tianjin	47.26	29	North
Hebei	56.98	14	North	Ningxia	46.23	30	Northwest
Guizhou	56.38	15	Southwest	Tibet	46.14	31	Southwest
Chongqing	56.27	16	Southwest				

Among all provinces, Beijing ranks 1st by 90.42. Guangdong, Zhejiang and Jiangsu rank right after Beijing. According to the scores, those performing well in Private participation are located mostly in developed areas, which indicates sufficient social capital, excellent business circumstance, high business credit and perfect financial and legal support. On the contrary, low-ranking provinces, autonomous regions and municipalities are primarily located in undeveloped areas, which have plenty of room for improvement in social capital, business environment and financial or legal support. It is noticeable that Xinjiang (exclude Xinjiang Production and Construction Corps) ranks 10th, the No.1 of Northwest ern areas. Xinjiang's performance is closely related to local governments's encouragement and different kinds of support for PPP.

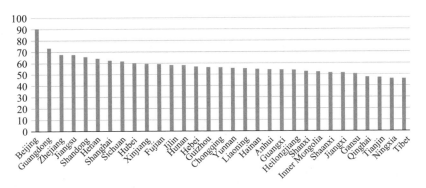

Figure 3.13 Score and Rankings for Private Participation Index in 2017

Provinces with active private participation are primarily in eastern, central and southern part of China while those with inactive private participation are mainly in northeastern, southwestern and northwestern part. Generally, entities within eachregion are in the same level of private participation. Jiangsu, Zhejiang and Shandong, all of which belong to East China, rank high among all the provinces. While most provinces in northwestern and southwestern part of China rank similarly to each other, which performs relatively unpleasantly. It is worth special attention that Beijing, Sichuan and Xinjiang rank among top ten, much better than adjacent provinces in the same region. Scores of private participation index for each region are shown in Table 3.16 and Figure 3.14.

Table 3.16 Private Participation Index of 7 Regions in 2017

No.	Regions	Provinces involved in the calculation	Average score
1	East China	Shanghai, Jiangsu, Zhejiang, Anhui, Fujian, Jiangxi, Shandong	61.22
2	Central China	Henan, Hubei, Hunan	60.84

(continued)

No.	Regions	Provinces involved in the calculation	Average score
3	South China	Guangdong, Guangxi, Hainan	60.74
4	North China	Beijing, Tianjin, Shanxi, Hebei, Inner Mongolia	59.92
5	Northeast China	Heilongjiang, Jilin, Liaoning	55.85
6	Southwest China	Sichuan, Guizhou, Yunnan, Chongqing, Tibet	55.23
7	Northwest China	Shaanxi, Gansu, Qinghai, Ningxia, Xinjiang	51.06

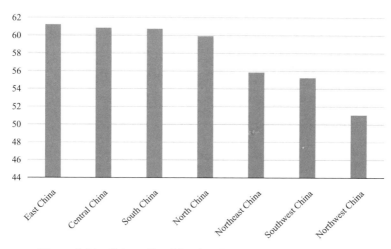

Figure 3.14　Private Participation Index of 7 Regions in 2017

Private participation index of East China ranks 1st, basically owing to the fact that Financial service, Legal service, Consulting service and Business participation rank in high places, as 1st, 1st, 2nd and 2nd separately. However Private fund ranks in a low place as 7th.

Private participation index of Central China ranks 2nd, basically owing to the fact that Business participation, Financial service, Legal service and Consulting service rank in high places, as 1st, 3rd, 3rd and 3rd separately. However, Private fund and Business credibility ranks in relatively low places, which have relatively negative effects on the index.

Private participation index of South China ranks 3rd, basically owing to the fact that Business credibility, Financial service and Legal service and Consulting service rank as 1st, 2nd and 2nd separately. Business participation, Private fund and Consulting service rank in a medium place, which remain to be improved.

Private participation index of North China ranks 4th. Consulting service and Business credibility rank in high places, as 1st and 3rd separately. However, Business participation and Private fund rank in relatively low places, which have relatively negative effects on the index.

Private participation index of Northeast China ranks 5th. Private fund and Business participation rank in high places, as 1st and 3rd separately. But Financial service, Legal service, Consulting service and Business credibility rank in relatively low places, which have relatively negative effects on the index.

Private participation index of Southwest China ranks 6th. Business credibility and Private fund rank in high places, both as 2nd. But Business participation, Financial service, Legal service rank in relatively low places, as 6th or 7th, which have relatively negative effects on the index.

Private participation index of Southwest China ranks 7th. Apart from the fact that Private fund rank in 3rd, other indicators rank in relatively low places, from 5th to 7th, which remains to be improved.

3.2.2 Evaluation of Second-grade Indicators of Private Participation Index

1. PPP business participation

PPP business participation index is constructed from three dimensions: PPP social capital, PPP business diversity and PPP business experience. PPP social capital focus on social capital investment, social capital contribution ratio, registered capital of PPP participating enterprises, and listing rate of PPP participating enterprises. PPP business diversity focuses on proportion of private enterprises, Hong Kong, Macao and Taiwan enterprises and foreign enterprises. PPP business experience concentrates on number of PPP projects by PPP participating enterprises.

Social capital's investment amount, listing rate of PPP participating enterprises, registered capital of PPP participating enterprises effectively reflect the abilities and willingness of social capital. Social capital contribution ratio reflects financial burden on social capital. PPP business diversity reflects the real degree to which non-public capital is used and whether social capital is active or not through measuring proportion of private enterprises, Hong Kong, Macao and Taiwan enterprises and foreign enterprises, in order to judge whether PPP projects illustrates "Public and Private Partnership" perfectly or not. PPP business experience functions as recessive capital, which promote PPP projects to operate more steady and smoothly. Enterprises with rich PPP experience tend to enjoy more experience during procedures of raising funds, construction and operation. They tend to handle the relationship with government better, further making landing rate, completion rate and yield higher. Scores of private participation index for each region is shown in Table 3.17 and Figure 3.15.

Table 3.17 Component of Private Participation Index

Third-grade Indicators	Fourth-grade Indicators	Formula	Reason for selecting the indicator
PPP social capital	Average social Capital Investment	$\sum \dfrac{\text{Social capital investment}}{\text{Number of all projects}}$	Average social capital investment measures average social capital for projects, further reflecting whether social capital engage in actively or not
	Sum of social capital Investment	$\sum \text{Social capital investment}$	Sum of social capital investment measure social capital employed of each province

(continued)

Third-grade Indicators	Fourth-grade Indicators	Formula	Reason for selecting the indicator
	Average social capital contribution ratio	$\sum \dfrac{\dfrac{\text{social capital of each project}}{\text{Total investment}}}{\text{Number of all projects}}$	Average social capital contribution ratio reflects the proportion of social capital
	Average registered capital ratio of social capital	$\sum \dfrac{\dfrac{\text{Social capital Investment}}{\text{Registered capital of PPP companies}}}{\text{Number of all projects}}$	Measurement of social capital, similar to average social capital contribution ratio
	Average registered capital of PPP participating companies	$\sum \dfrac{\text{Register capital of PPP companies}}{\text{Number of all projects}}$	Measurement of cashflow and assets to determine whether certaion enlerprise has sufficient fund
	Listing rate of PPP participating enterprises	$\sum \dfrac{\text{Listed companies among social capital}}{\text{Number of all social capital}}$	Listed companies generally have strouger economic strength and management capacity. Therefore, they tend to be better at operating PPP projects
PPP business diversity	Proportion of private companies	$\sum \dfrac{\text{Private companies among all investors}}{\text{Number of all social capital}}$	It measures the willingness of private companies
PPP business diversity	Proportion of Hong Kong& Macao&Taiwan and foreign enterprises	$\sum \dfrac{\text{Number of projetcs by these enterprises}}{\text{Number of all social capital}}$	Meansures of participation degree of foreign, Hong Kong& Macao&Taiwan reflects the attractiveness of PPP projects
Business experience	Average winning PPP projects	$\sum \dfrac{\text{Accumulative winning projects}}{\text{Number of social capital}}$	It measures experience of PPP participating enterprises, predicting landing rate and their payoff

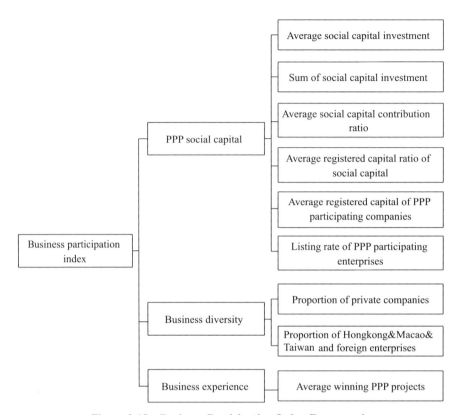

Figure 3.15　Business Participation Index Framework

Score of business participation index of 31 provinces, are shown in Table 3.18 and Figure 3.16. The average score is 38.50. There are 19 entities above the average and 12 below the average, most of which range from 30 to 45 points. According to the distribution, define those above 37.5 points as Active business participation and define those below 37.5 points as Inactive business participation. Hence, 19 provinces, municipalities and autonomous regions are active Business participation while 12 provinces, municipalities and autonomous regions are inactive Business participation.

It is remarkable that Xinjiang ranks 1st, largely owing to local governments' encouragement and all kinds of support for PPP. Meanwhile, four municipalities are all classified as Inactive Business participation, which is related to strong financial strength and well-developed city investment companies.

Table 3.18 Scores and Rankings of PPP Business Participation in 2017

Provinces	Score	Rank	Regions	Provinces	Score	Rank	Regions
Xinjiang	62.34	1	Northwest	Anhui	41.10	17	East
Henan	55.95	2	Central	Jiangxi	40.49	18	East
Shandong	51.77	3	East	Sichuan	38.60	19	Southwest
Jilin	48.70	4	Northeast	Guizhou	33.96	20	Southwest
Yunnan	47.91	5	Southwest	Qinghai	33.42	21	Northwest
Hunan	46.82	6	Central	Shaanxi	30.89	22	Northwest
Hubei	45.66	7	Central	Tibet	30.83	23	Southwest
Jiangsu	45.54	8	East	Gansu	29.30	24	Northwest
Shanxi	45.50	9	North	Hainan	27.72	25	South
Inner Mongolia	45.02	10	North	Beijing	27.07	26	North
Guangxi	43.26	11	South	Tianjin	26.38	27	North
Heilongjiang	42.40	12	Northeast	Liaoning	22.38	28	Northeast
Guangdong	42.03	13	South	Shanghai	22.15	29	East
Zhejiang	41.78	14	East	Chongqing	21.56	30	Southwest
Fujian	41.60	15	East	Ningxia	19.97	31	Northwest
Hebei	41.26	16	North				

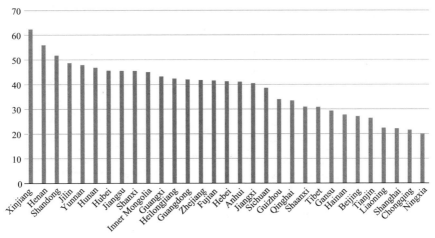

Figure 3.16 Score and Rankings of PPP Business Participation in 2017

Provinces with active Business participation are concentrated in East China, Central China and Northeast China, while provinces with relatively low Business participation are concentrated in North China, Southwest China and Northwest China. The score of business participation index of provinces in each region is basically in the same echelon. It is worth noting that Northeast China ranks high in business participation, in particular Jilin ranks 4th. Specific regional ranking is shown in Table 3.19 and Figure 3.17.

Table 3.19 PPP Business Participation Index of 7 Regions in 2017

No.	Regions	Provinces involved in the calculation	Average score
1	Central China	Henan, Hubei, Hunan	49.47
2	East China	Shanghai, Jiangsu, Zhejiang, Anhui, Fujian, Jiangxi, Shandong	40.63
3	Northeast China	Shaanxi, Gansu, Qinghai, Ningxia, Xinjiang	37.83
4	South China	Guangdong, Guangxi, Hainan	37.67
5	North China	Beijing, Tianjin, Shanxi, Hebei, Inner Mongolia	37.05
6	Northwest China	Shaanxi, Gansu, Qinghai, Ningxia, Xinjiang	35.19
7	Southeast China	Sichuan, Guizhou, Yunnan, Chongqing, Tibet	34.57

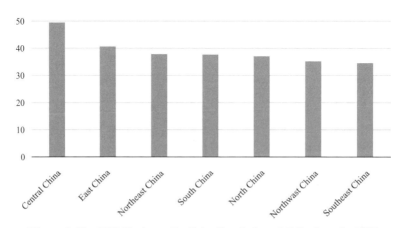

Figure 3.17 PPP Business Participation Index of 7 Regions in 2017

Business participation index of Central China ranks 1st, basically because PPP social capital and PPP business experience both rank 1st. PPP business diversity ranks 5th.

Business participation index of East China ranks 2nd, basically owing to the fact that PPP business experience ranks 2nd. PPP business experience and PPP social capital rank in medium place, both as 4th.

Business participation index of Northeast China ranks 3rd, basically owing to the fact that PPP business diversity ranks 2nd. PPP social capital and PPP business experience rank in relatively low place, as 5th and 7th separately.

Business participation index of South China ranks 4th, basically owing to the fact that PPP business diversity ranks 1st. PPP social capital and PPP business experience rank in relatively low place, both as 6th.

Business participation index of North China ranks 5th. PPP social capital ranks in high place as 3rd. PPP business experience ranks medium place as 4th and PPP business diversity ranks in relatively low place as 6th.

Business participation index of Northwest China ranks 6th. PPP business diversity ranks in high place as 3rd. PPP business experience and PPP social capital rank in relatively low place, as 5th and 7th separately.

Business participation index of Southwest China ranks 7th. PPP business experience and PPP business experience rank in high place, as 2nd and 3rd separately. However, PPP business diversity ranks in extremely low place, which has a negative effect on overall ranking.

2. Business credibility

Business credibility is measured from the dimension of commercial credit environment, which not only refers to the degree of integrity, but also pays more attention to the measurement of business environment and the possibility of stable business operation. It is divided into two fourth grade indicators, namely bad enterprises rate and urban commercial credit environment index, to measure the comprehensive credit level of enterprises in each province. If business credibility in certain province is better, then the awareness of observing disciplines and laws is stronger, and the possibility of breach of contract, violation of rules or laws is lower. Hence the quality and completion rate of PPP projects are guaranteed, which further contributes to better development of PPP projects and higher success rate (see Table 3.20).

Table 3.20　Component of Business Credibility

Second-grade indicator	Third-grade indicator	Fourth-grade indicator	Formula	Reason for selecting the indicator
Business credibility	Urban business credit environment	Bad Business Rate	$\dfrac{\sum \text{Number of bad business}}{\text{Number of all enterprises}}$	Bad business rate meansures operation performance of enterprises to reflect potential possibility of violating laws and regulations
		Urban commercial credit environment index	Cite China urban business credit environment index	Urban business credit environment index measures overall business environment in order to predict landing rate and operational benefits

Business credibility of each province in certain region enjoys somewhat similarities. Hence average score across different regions are calculated and listed in Table 3.21 and Figure 3.18.

Table 3.21　Business Credibility Index of 7 Regions in 2017

No.	Regions	Provinces involved in the calculation	Average score
1	South China	Guangdong, Guangxi, Hainan	52.29
2	Southwest China	Sichuan, Guizhou, Yunnan, Chongqing, Tibet	49.26
3	North China	Beijing, Tianjin, Shanxi, Hebei, Inner Mongolia	48.76
4	East China	Shanghai, Jiangsu, Zhejiang, Anhui, Fujian, Jiangxi, Shandong	46.18

(continued)

No.	Regions	Provinces involved in the calculation	Average score
5	Northwest China	Shaanxi, Gansu, Qinghai, Ningxia, Xinjiang	44.27
6	Central China	Henan, Hubei, Hunan	41.65
7	Northeast China	Heilongjiang, Jilin, Liaoning	41.05

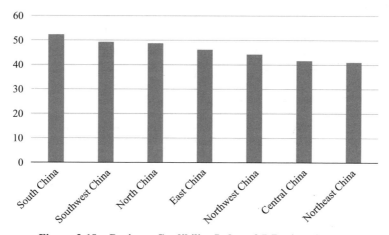

Figure 3.18　Business Credibility Index of 7 Regions in 2017

Business credibility index of South China ranks 1st. Bad business rate and Urban commercial credit environment index rank 1st and 3rd separately.

Business credibility index of Southwest China ranks 2nd. Bad business rate and Urban commercial credit environment index rank 2st and 4th separately.

Business credibility index of North China ranks 3rd. Bad business rate and Urban commercial credit environment index rank 7th and 1st separately.

Business credibility index of East China ranks 4th. Bad business rate and Urban commercial credit environment index rank 6th and 2nd separately.

Business credibility index of Northwest China ranks 5th. Bad business rate and Urban commercial credit environment index rank 3rd and 5th separately.

Business credibility index of Central China ranks 6th. Bad business rate and Urban commercial credit environment index rank 5th and 6th separately.

Business credibility index of Northeast China ranks 7th. Bad business rate and Urban commercial credit environment index rank 4th and 7th separately.

3. Private fund

Private fund refers to the difficulty of participation in financing PPP projects for private sectors. The fact that private sectors have problems in financing for PPP projects will dampen enterprises' enthusiasm to participate in PPP projects. It hinders the formation of a well-operated ambience. Private fund is composed of 3 third-grade indicators, which are Financing costs, Financing scale and Financing term. Respectively, they describe Private fund from 3 angles, which are interest rates, quantity and time. Furthermore, the third-grade indicators are described by one or two fourth-grade indicators. The framework is shown in Figure 3.19 and Table 3.22.

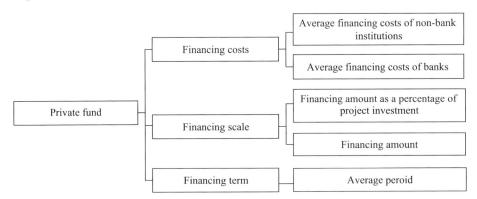

Figure 3.19 Private Fund Framework

Table 3.22 Private Fund Framework

Second-grade indicators	Third-grade indicators	Fourth-grade indicators	Formula	Reason for selecting this indicator
Private fund	Financing costs	Average financing costs of non-bank institutions	Direct reference	Average costs can measure the magnitude of difficulty in financing for PPP projects
		Average financing costs of banks	$[\sum(\text{Amount} \times \text{Costs})]/(\sum \text{Amount})$	Serve as a supplement for non-banks. Note: Only the interest rates of banks and policy lenders for exemplary projects in the first 3 batches are considered

(continued)

Second-grade indicators	Third-grade indicators	Fourth-grade indicators	Formula	Reason for selecting this indicator
	Financing scale	Financing amount as a percentage of project investment	Financing amount/Project investment	The percentage can measure the magnitude of fund security
		Financing amount	Direct reference	The amount directly measures financing scale
	Financing term	Average period	$[\sum(\text{Amount} \times \text{Period})]/(\sum \text{Amount})$	Financing term can measure the magnitude of continuity of the fund. The longer it is, the more secure projects are

According to the collected data, we calculate and rank Private fund scores for 31 provinces. Besides, regions those provinces belong to are shown in Table 3.23 and Figure 3.20.

Table 3.23　Scores and Rankings of Private Fund in 2017 (province level)

Provinces	Score	Rank	Regions	Provinces	Score	Rank	Regions
Beijing	76.01	1	North	Henan	48.95	17	Central
Jilin	70.04	2	Northeast	Qinghai	48.49	18	Northwest
Ningxia	69.15	3	Northwest	Hainan	47.54	19	South
Liaoning	64.98	4	Northeast	Tibet	46.98	20	Southwest
Chongqing	63.27	5	Southwest	Anhui	45.89	21	East
Jiangsu	60.86	6	East	Xinjiang	44.18	22	Northwest
Heilongjiang	58.86	7	Northeast	Hunan	43.91	23	Central
Guizhou	58.43	8	Southwest	Sichuan	43.55	24	Southwest
Gansu	58.06	9	Northwest	Hebei	42.44	25	North
Tianjin	57.20	10	North	Shaanxi	39.87	26	Northwest

(continued)

Provinces	Score	Rank	Regions	Provinces	Score	Rank	Regions
Hubei	56.58	11	Central	Shanghai	38.85	27	East
Zhejiang	55.77	12	East	Shanxi	38.08	28	North
Guangdong	55.16	13	South	Jiangxi	34.06	29	East
Fujian	54.66	14	East	Inner Mongolia	32.57	30	North
Guangxi	51.29	15	South	Shandong	28.84	31	East
Yunnan	50.37	16	Southwest				

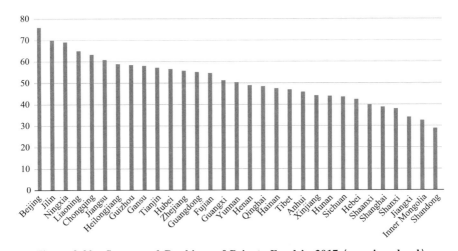

Figure 3.20　Scores and Rankings of Private Fund in 2017 (province level)

Jilin ranks 2nd, mainly owing to the fact that Financing costs, Financing scale and Financing term are high. Respectively, they are in the 7th, 3rd and 3rd places.

Ningxia ranks 3rd, mainly due to the fact that Financing costs, Financing scale and Financing term are in high places. Respectively, they are in the 9th, 8th and 2nd places. All of them have a positive effect on the indicator, Private fund.

Liaoning ranks 4th, mainly because Financing costs and Financing scale ranks high, at 1st and 6th respectively. Financing costs' rank is high, mainly because Average financing costs of banks is high (in the 3rd place). Besides, Financing term is in the middle place, which is at 20th.

Heilongjiang ranks 7th, mainly because Financing term ranks at 1st. Financing costs ranks in the middle place (11th), which has a relatively neutral influence on the indicator, Private fund. Financing scale ranks 28nd, relatively at a lower place, which has a negative effect on the ranking of Heilongjiang on this dimension.

Guizhou ranks 8th, mainly because both Financing scale and Financing term ranks at 5th. Financing costs ranks 22nd, relatively at a lower place, which has a negative effect on the ranking of Guizhou on this dimension.

Gansu ranks 9th, mainly owing to the fact that Financing costs ranks 5th, at a relatively high place. It has a consequently positive effect on the ranking of Gansu. However, Financing scale and Financing term ranks 20th and 12th respectively, which have a neutral effect on the ranking.

Shanghai ranks 27th, mainly because Financing costs ranks 30th, which has a harmful effect on the ranking. Financing scale and Financing term rank 15th and 7th respectively, which show a relatively neutral effect on the ranking.

Basically, there are a lot of similarities in private funds in one region. Scores and ranking of Private fund of 7 regions are shown in Table 3.24 and Figure 3.21.

Table 3.24 Scores and Rankings of Private Fund in 2017 (region level)

No.	Regions	Provinces involved in the calculation	Average score
1	Northeast	Heilongjiang, Jilin, Liaoning	64.63
2	Southwest	Sichuan, Guizhou, Yunnan, Chongqing, Tibet	52.52
3	Northwest	Shaanxi, Gansu, Qinghai, Ningxia, Xinjiang	51.95
4	South	Guangdong, Guangxi, Hainan	51.33
5	Central	Henan, Hubei, Hunan	49.82
6	North	Beijing, Tianjin, Shanxi, Hebei, Inner Mongolia	49.26
7	East	Shanghai, Jiangsu, Zhejiang, Anhui, Fujian, Jiangxi, Shandong	45.56

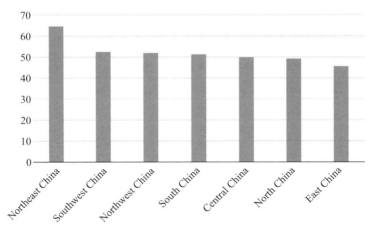

Figure 3.21 Scores and Rankings of Private Fund in 2017 (region level)

Northeast China ranks 1st. The score is significantly higher than other regions, mainly because Financing costs, Financing scale and Financing term are all in high places. They are at 1st, 2nd and 1st respectively.

Southwest China ranks 2nd, mainly because Financing scale and Financing term rank 1st and 2nd respectively, which have a positive effect on the ranking. Financing costs ranks 5th, which has a negative effect on the ranking.

Northwest China ranks 3rd, mainly because Financing costs and Financing term both rank 3rd, which has a relatively neutral effect on the ranking. Financing scale ranks 5th, which has a negative effect.

South China ranks 4th, mainly owing to the fact that Financing costs ranks 2nd. Financing scale and Financing term rank 7th and 5th respectively, which has a negative effect on the ranking.

Central China ranks 5th, mainly because Financing costs ranks 7th, which has a negative effect on the ranking. Financing scale and Financing term rank 7th and 5th respectively, which shows a negative effect on the ranking.

North China ranks 6th, mainly because Financing term ranks 6th, which has a negative influence. Financing costs and Financing scale rank 4th and 3rd respectively, which shows a neutral effect.

East China ranks 7th, Its score is significantly lower than others, mainly because Financing costs, Financing scale and Financing term are all relatively at lower places (6th, 6th and 7th respectively). This has a negative effect on the ranking.

4. Financial service

Financial service depicts thedevelopment level of local financial industry. One of reasons why we introduce this indicator is to know whether local financial industry operates well enough to offer prime service for PPP projects. Financial service is composed of two sub-indicators. Financial institutions and Financial market respectively. Further, Financial institutions is composed of Gross asset amount, Institutions' number, Employees' number. Financial market is depicted by the development level of financial industry. The framework is shown in Figure 3.22 and Table 3.25.

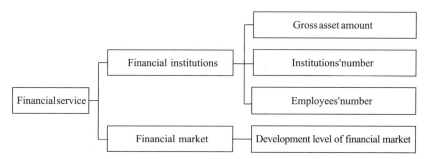

Figure 3.22 Framework of Financial Service

Table 3.25 Framework of Financial Service

Second-grade indicators	Third-grade indicators	Fourth-grade indicators	Formula	Reason for selecting this indicator
Financial service	Financial institutions	Gross asset amount	$\sum$ Financial institutions' asset	The larger asset amount is, the easier financing for PPP projects will be
		Institutions' number	Direct reference	A larger number of financial institutions will leave larger scope and morefreedom to financing for PPP projects

(continued)

Second-grade indicators	Third-grade indicators	Fourth-grade indicators	Formula	Reason for selecting this indicator
	Financial market	Employees' number	$\sum$ Employees' number	A larger number of financial employees will benefit financing for PPP projects
		Development level of financial market	Direct reference	A high-level financial market benefits financing for PPP projects

According to collected data, we calculate and rank Financial service's scores of 31 provinces. Scores and ranking of various provinces are shown in Table 3.26 and Figure 3.23.

Table 3.26　Scores and Rankings of Financial Services in 2017

Provinces	Score	Rank	Regions	Provinces	Score	Rank	Regions
Guangdong	86.30	1	South	Shanxi	33.45	17	North
Jiangsu	71.36	2	East	Guizhou	31.98	18	Southwest
Beijing	69.01	3	North	Jiangxi	31.30	19	East
Zhejiang	66.40	4	East	Tianjin	29.28	20	North
Shandong	63.29	5	East	Gansu	28.39	21	Northwest
Sichuan	56.76	6	Southwest	Chongqing	26.39	22	Southwest
Shanghai	53.38	7	East	Guangxi	26.33	23	South
Henan	50.13	8	Central	Jilin	26.22	24	Northeast
Liaoning	47.32	9	Northeast	Yunnan	25.77	25	Southwest
Hebei	46.72	10	North	Xinjiang	24.32	26	Northwest
Fujian	44.38	11	East	Heilongjiang	23.47	27	Northeast
Shaanxi	42.90	12	Northwest	Qinghai	23.11	28	Northwest
Hunan	40.91	13	Central	Inner Mongolia	15.52	29	North
Hainan	39.39	14	South	Ningxia	9.02	30	Northwest
Hubei	39.36	15	Central	Tibet	4.35	31	Southwest
Anhui	38.55	16	East				

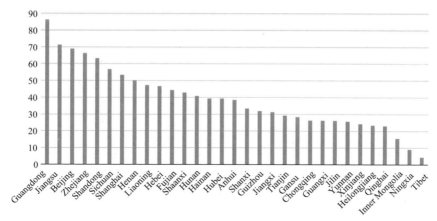

Figure 3.23 Scores and Rankings of Financial Service in 2017
(province level)

Liaoning ranks 9th, mainly because financial institutions and financial market rank 9th and 10th, in relatively high places. This has positive effect on the ranking.

Shaanxi ranks 12th, mainly because Financial market ranks 3rd, in a relatively high place, which has a positive effect on the ranking. Financial institutions rank 17th, in a middle place, which has a relatively neutral effect on the ranking.

Guizhou ranks 18th, mainly because Financial market ranks highly (8th), which has a positive effect on the ranking. But Financial institutions ranks 24th, which acts as a drag on the ranking.

Tianjin ranks 20th, mainly because Financial institutions ranks 27th, which acts as a drag on the ranking. But Financial market ranks highly (9th), which has a positive effect on the ranking.

Chongqing ranks 22nd, mainly because Financial institutions and Financial market both act as drags on the ranking (25th and 22nd respectively).

Basically, there are a lot of similarities in private funds in one region. Therefore, scores and ranking of Financial service in 7 regions are shown in the Table 3.27 and Figure 3.24.

Table 3.27 Scores and Rankings of Financial Service in 2017 (region level)

No.	Regions	Provinces involved in the calculation	Average score
1	East	Shanghai, Jiangsu, Zhejiang, Anhui, Fujian, Jiangxi, Shandong	52.67
2	South	Guangdong, Guangxi, Hainan	50.67
3	Central	Henan, Hubei, Hunan	43.47
4	North	Beijing, Tianjin, Shanxi, Hebei, Inner Mongolia	38.79
5	Northeast	Heilongjiang, Jilin, Liaoning	32.34
6	Southwest	Sichuan, Guizhou, Yunnan, Chongqing, Tibet	29.05
7	Northwest	Shaanxi, Gansu, Qinghai, Ningxia, Xinjiang	25.55

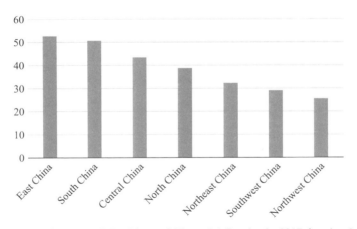

Figure 3.24 Scores and Rankings of Financial Service in 2017 (region level)

East China ranks 1st, mainly because Financial institutions ranks 1st and Financial market ranks 2nd. Both are in high places, which has a positive effect on the ranking.

South China ranks 2nd, mainly because Financial institutions ranks relatively in a high place (1st). However, Financial market ranks 4th, which has a negative effect on the ranking.

Central China ranks 3rd, mainly because Financial institutions ranks relatively in a middle place (3rd). Nevertheless, Financial market ranks 5th, which has a relatively negative effect on the ranking.

North China ranks 4th, mainly because both Financial institutions and Financial market rank in a middle place (4th and 3rd respectively), which has a relatively neutral effect on the ranking.

Northeast China ranks 5th, mainly because both Financial institutions and Financial market rank in a low place (5th and 7th respectively), which acts as a drag on the ranking.

Southwest China ranks 6th, mainly because both Financial institutions and Financial market rank 6th, which shows a negative effect on the ranking.

Northwest China ranks 7th, mainly because Financial institutions ranks 7th, which acts as a tremendous drag on the ranking, even though Financial market ranks 2nd.

5. Legal service

Legal service refers to service related to legal affairs. It is aimed to standardize PPP market and promote the market's efficiency by normalizing participants' behavior, flow path and relevant documents of PPP projects. Legal service is composed of Law firm and Lawyer (see Figure 3.25 and Table 3.28).

Figure 3.25　Legal Service Framework

Table 3.28　Legal Service Framework

Second-grade indicators	Third-grade indicators	Fourth-grade indicators	Formula	Reason for selecting this in dicator
Legal service	Law firm	Number of law firms	Direct reference	A larger number of law firms leave more choices for PPP projects, which promotes competence and then efficiency
	Lawyer	Number of lawyers	Direct reference	A larger number of lawyers offer a large pool of professionals to serve for PPP project

According to collected data, we calculate and rank scores of Legal service of 31 provinces (see Table 3.29 and Figure 3.26).

Table 3.29 Scores and Rankings of Legal Service in 2017 (province-level)

Provinces	Score	Rank	Regions	Provinces	Score	Rank	Regions
Guangdong	100.00	1	South	Tianjin	20.26	17	North
Beijing	88.89	2	North	Anhui	18.52	18	East
Shandong	65.36	3	East	Shaanxi	18.15	19	Northwest
Jiangsu	60.58	4	East	Inner Mongolia	15.55	20	North
Shanghai	58.32	5	East	Jiangxi	14.60	21	East
Henan	49.44	6	Central	Jilin	14.46	22	Northeast
Zhejiang	47.25	7	East	Guizhou	14.27	23	Southwest
Sichuan	44.49	8	Southwest	Xinjiang	13.34	24	Northwest
Liaoning	31.89	9	Northeast	Guangxi	12.52	25	South
Hunan	31.64	10	Central	Gansu	10.01	26	Northwest
Hebei	29.90	11	North	Shanxi	8.96	27	North
Hubei	27.91	12	Central	Ningxia	4.26	28	Northwest
Chongqing	25.66	13	Southwest	Qinghai	2.38	29	Northwest
Yunnan	23.84	14	Southwest	Hainan	1.26	30	South
Fujian	23.48	15	East	Tibet	0.00	31	Southwest
Heilongjiang	21.95	16	Northeast				

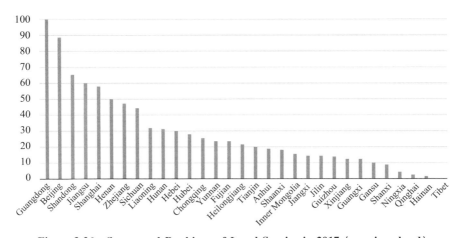

Figure 3.26 Scores and Rankings of Legal Service in 2017 (province-level)

Liaoning ranks 9th, mainly because Law firm ranks 9th and Lawyer ranks 10th, which has positive effect on the ranking.

Chongqing ranks 13th, mainly because Law firm ranks 12th and Lawyer ranks 13th, which has neutral effect on the ranking.

Yunnan ranks 14th, mainly because Law firm ranks 13th and Lawyer ranks 15th, which has neutral effect on the ranking.

Tianjin ranks 17th, mainly because Law firm ranks 17th and Lawyer ranks 18th, which has neutral effect on the ranking.

Shanxi ranks 27th, mainly because Law firm ranks 27th and Lawyer ranks 23rd, which acts as a drag on the ranking.

Ranking of regions are shown in Table 3.30 and Figure 3.27.

Table 3.30　Scores and Rankings of Legal Service in 2017 (region-level)

No.	Regions	Provinces involved in the calculation	Average score
1	East China	Shanghai, Jiangsu, Zhejiang, Anhui, Fujian, Jiangxi, Shandong	41.16
2	South China	Guangdong, Guangxi, Hainan	37.93
3	Central China	Henan, Hubei, Hunan	36.33
4	North China	Beijing, Tianjin, Shanxi, Hebei, Inner Mongolia	32.71
5	Northeast China	Heilongjiang, Jilin, Liaoning	22.77
6	Southwest China	Sichuan, Guizhou, Yunnan, Chongqing, Tibet	21.65
7	Northwest China	Shaanxi, Gansu, Qinghai, Ningxia, Xinjiang	9.63

East China ranks 1st, mainly because Law firm ranks 1st and Lawyer ranks 2nd, which has a relatively positive effect.

South China ranks 2nd, mainly because Law firm ranks 2nd, which has a positive effect. And Lawyer ranks 3rd, which has a relatively neutral effect.

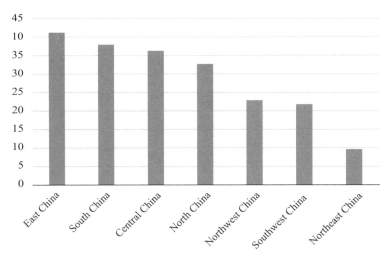

Figure 3.27 Scores and Rankings of Legal Service in 2017 (region level)

Central China ranks 3rd, mainly because Law firm ranks 1st, which has a positive effect. And Lawyer ranks 4th, which has a relatively neutral effect on the ranking.

North China ranks 4th, mainly because Law firm ranks 3rd and Lawyer ranks 4th, which has a relatively neutral effect on the ranking.

Northeast China ranks 5th, mainly because Law firm ranks 5th and Lawyer ranks 6th, which acts as a drag on the ranking.

Southwest China ranks 6th, mainly because Law firm ranks 6th and Lawyer ranks 5th, which acts as a drag on the ranking.

Northwest China ranks 7th, mainly because both Law firm and Lawyer rank 7th, which has a relatively negative effect.

6. Consulting service

Consulting service refers to a sort of services including combination of information and guidance of processing flow for PPP projects. Consulting service is beneficial to leading private fund to participate in PPP programs orderly, thus to promoting the standardization process of PPP projects. Consulting service is composed of PPP consulting institutions and PPP consulting experts. And PPP consulting institutions is composed of Institutions' number, Investment amount,

Projects' number, Average number of service categories and Price rate. PPP consulting experts is composed of Experts' number, Research ability, Experience of consulting and Experience of PPP (see Figure 3.28 and Table 3.31).

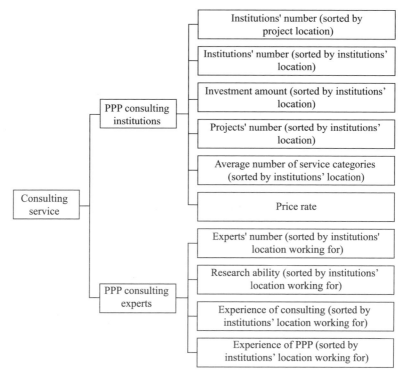

Figure 3.28　Consulting Service Framework

Table 3.31　Consulting Service Framework

Second-grade indicators	Third-grade indicators	Fourth-grade indicators	Formula	Reason for selecting this in dicator
Consulting service	PPP consulting institutions	Institutions' number (sorted by project location)	$\sum$ Institutions	A variety of consulting institutions could offer sufficient service relevant to PPP
		Institutions' number (sorted by institutions' location)	$\sum$ Institutions	

(continued)

Second-grade indicators	Third-grade indicators	Fourth-grade indicators	Formula	Reason for selecting this in dicator
		Investment amount (sorted by institutions' location)	$\sum$ Investment amount	A large amount of investment amount means consulting institutions offer sufficient service to some extent
		Projects' number (sorted by institutions' location)	$\sum$ Projects	A large number of consulting institutions means consulting institutions offer sufficient service to some extent
		Average number of service categories (sorted by institutions' location)	$\sum$ Service categories / $\sum$ Institutions	A large number of service categories means consulting institutions offer sufficient service to some extent
		Price rate	Direct reference	A low price rate means consulting institutions offer sufficient service to some extent
	PPP consulting experts	Experts' number (sorted by institutions' location working for)	$\sum$ Experts	A large number of experts means consulting institutions offer sufficient service to some extent
		Research ability (sorted by institutions' location working for)	$\sum$ Researchprojects	A large number of research projects meansexperts are strong at research ability, and that consulting institutions offer sufficient service to some extent
		Experience of consulting (sorted by institutions' location working for)	$\sum$ Consulting projects which experts have participated in	A large number of consulting projects means experts have rich research ability, and that consulting institutions offer sufficient service
		Experience of PPP (sorted by institutions' location working for)	$\sum$ PPP projects which experts have participated in	A large number of PPP projects means experts have rich experience, and that consulting institutions offer sufficient service

According to collected data, we calculate and rank scores of Consulting service of 31 provinces. Besides, the regions those provinces belong to are shown in the table (see Figure 3.29 and Table 3.32).

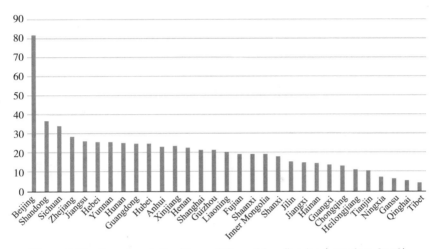

Figure 3.29　Scores and Rankings of Consulting Service (province level)

Table 3.32　Scores and Rankings of Consulting Service (province level)

Provinces	Score	Rank	Regions	Provinces	Score	Rank	Regions
Beijing	81.41	1	North	Fujian	19.93	17	East
Shandong	37.28	2	East	Shaanxi	19.72	18	Northwest
Sichuan	34.80	3	Southwest	Inner Mongolia	19.59	19	North
Zhejiang	29.17	4	East	Shanxi	18.61	20	North
Jiangsu	26.85	5	East	Jilin	16.17	21	Northeast
Hebei	26.40	6	North	Jiangxi	15.66	22	East
Yunnan	26.18	7	Southwest	Hainan	15.16	23	South
Hunan	26.02	8	Central	Guangxi	14.11	24	South
Guangdong	25.57	9	South	Chongqing	13.89	25	Southwest
Hubei	25.54	10	Central	Heilongjiang	11.75	26	Northeast
Anhui	24.18	11	East	Tianjin	11.02	27	North

(continued)

Provinces	Score	Rank	Regions	Provinces	Score	Rank	Regions
Xinjiang	23.87	12	Northwest	Ningxia	7.91	28	Northwest
Henan	23.33	13	Central	Gansu	7.24	29	Northwest
Shanghai	22.16	14	East	Qinghai	5.86	30	Northwest
Guizhou	21.82	15	Southwest	Tibet	4.86	31	Southwest
Liaoning	20.90	16	Northeast				

Yunnan ranks 7th, mainly because PPP consulting institutions ranks at a relatively higher place (7th), which has a relatively positive effect on the score and rank. PPP consulting experts ranks 11th, which has a relatively neutral effect on the ranking.

Xinjiang ranks 12th, mainly because PPP consulting institutions ranks 6th, which has a relatively higher place. And PPP consulting experts ranks 16th, which has a relatively neutral effect on the score.

Shanghai ranks 14th, mainly because PPP consulting experts ranks 2nd, which means many consulting institutions lie in Shanghai. PPP consulting institutions ranks 26th, which acts as a drag on the ranking.

Guizhou ranks 15th, mainly because both PPP consulting institutions and PPP consulting experts rank in a neutral effect.

Chongqing ranks 25th, mainly because PPP consulting institutions ranks in a relatively low place (25th), which acts as a drag on the ranking. The main reason lies in that Institutions' number (sorted by project location), Average number of service categories (sorted by institutions' location) and Projects' number (sorted by institutions' location) rank in a low place. PPP consulting experts ranks 6th, which is in a relatively high place.

Tianjin ranks 27th, mainly because PPP consulting institutions ranks in a relatively low place (27th), which acts as a drag on the score. The main cause lie in that Institutions' number, Investment amount, Projects' number and Average number of service categories are relatively small. PPP consulting experts ranks in a relatively neutral place (13th).

Consulting service has similarities in one region. Ranking of regions are shown in Table 3.33 and Figure 3.30.

Table 3.33   Scores and Rankings of Consulting Service in 2017 (region-level)

No.	Regions	Provinces involved in the calculation	Average score
1	North China	Beijing, Tianjin, Shanxi, Hebei, Inner Mongolia	31.41
2	East China	Shanghai, Jiangsu, Zhejiang, Anhui, Fujian, Jiangxi, Shandong	25.03
3	Central China	Henan, Hubei, Hunan	24.96
4	Southwest China	Sichuan, Guizhou, Yunnan, Chongqing, Tibet	20.31
5	South China	Guangdong, Guangxi, Hainan	18.28
6	Northeast China	Heilongjiang, Jilin, Liaoning	16.27
7	Northwest China	Shaanxi, Gansu, Qinghai, Ningxia, Xinjiang	12.92

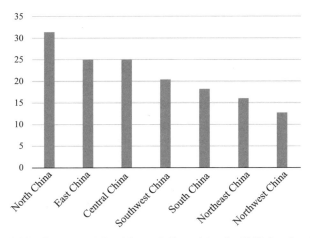

Figure 3.30   Scores and Rankings of Consulting in 2017 (region-level)

North China ranks 1st, mainly because both PPP consulting institutions and PPP consulting experts rank in a high place (2nd and 1st respectively), which has positive effect on the ranking.

East China ranks 2nd, mainly because PPP consulting institutions and PPP consulting experts rank in a high place (3rd and 2nd respectively), which has positive effect on the ranking.

Central China ranks 3rd, mainly because PPP consulting institutions ranks 1st, in a relatively high place; PPP consulting experts rank 4th, which has a relatively neutral effect on the score.

Southwest China ranks 4th, mainly because PPP consulting institutions and PPP consulting experts rank 4th and 3rd respectively, which has relatively neutral effect on the score.

South China ranks 5th, mainly because both PPP consulting institutions and PPP consulting experts rank 5th, which has a relatively negative effect on the score.

Northeast China ranks 6th, mainly because PPP consulting institutions and PPP consulting experts rank 6th, which has negative effect on the score.

Northwest China ranks 7th, mainly because PPP consulting institutions and PPP consulting experts rank in a relatively low place (at 7th), which has a negative effect on the score.

3.3 Ranking: Project Operation

3.3.1 Project Operation Overall Evaluation

The Project Operation indicator aims to measure the achievements, current situation and potential of regional PPP development comprehensively. Compared to Government guarantee and Private participation, it is based on PPP projects themselves and takes into account multiple dimensions such as scale, quality, regional distribution, implement, results and development potential. The goal is to evaluate the current and potential performance of regional PPP market comprehensively.

The indicator is composed of three second-grade indicators, including PPP development level, PPP risk & revenue, PPP development potential. Furthermore, PPP development level is composed of seven third-grade indicators. They are PPP development scale, PPP project distribution, PPP work progress, PPP regulated level, the degree of PPP transparency, PPP implementation, PPP handover, depicting the macroscopy view of regional PPP operation; PPP risk & revenue is composed of three third-grade indicators, including project revenue, project risk and external benefits, in order to evaluate the return and risk of PPP projects; PPP development potential is composed of four third-grade indicators, including infrastructure level, urbanization rate, infrastructure investment, reserve projects, to measure development potential of PPP market. The Project Operation indicator framework is shown in Figure 3.31.

Figure 3.31　Project Operation Indicator Framework

The three indicators describe three aspects of regional PPP market: the overall performance of PPP market, the revenue and risk, and the potential for future growth. Sound and thriving PPP market ought to have the characteristics of large scale, rapid growth, balanced distribution among industries and regions, high implement ratio, being normative and transparent——this is what PPP mode should highlight; Reasonable internal and external revenues and lower risks mean higher investment value of PPP projects, playing a crucial part in appealing participants; Higher growth potential means more opportunities in the future, providing sustaining driving force for PPP development. Therefore, it is comprehensive and optimal to choose these three indicators to score the performance and prospects of PPP market.

Based on the collected data, Project Operation indicators of 31 provinces are calculated. The magnitude and ranking of Project operation are shown in Table 3.34 and Figure 3.32.

Table 3.34 Scores and Rankings of Project Operation in 2017

No.	Provinces	Project operation		PPP development level		PPP risk & revenue		PPP development potential	
		Score	Rank	Score	Rank	Score	Rank	Score	Rank
1	Henan	86.89	1	89.10	4	93.80	3	78.61	3
2	Shandong	86.55	2	95.21	1	94.68	2	66.70	19
3	Xinjiang	84.84	3	88.23	6	84.89	6	79.15	2
4	Guizhou	83.94	4	78.18	23	98.49	1	83.85	1
5	Sichuan	82.86	5	89.70	3	75.27	10	76.51	7
6	Anhui	82.71	6	95.20	2	74.58	12	67.32	17
7	Yunnan	82.27	7	84.89	14	82.14	7	77.98	5
8	Hubei	80.89	8	84.58	15	75.64	8	78.26	4
9	Hunan	80.83	9	86.18	11	85.39	5	68.88	12
10	Hebei	79.84	10	87.77	8	75.46	9	69.53	11
11	Inner Mongolia	79.03	11	87.13	10	89.91	4	58.30	25
12	Fujian	77.32	12	85.92	12	71.21	14	67.07	18
13	Shaanxi	77.00	13	84.21	17	69.98	16	69.67	10
14	Zhejiang	76.21	14	88.32	5	75.05	11	56.78	29
15	Jiangsu	75.60	15	87.30	9	74.18	13	57.06	28
16	Jilin	75.37	16	88.01	7	64.35	18	61.67	22
17	Shanxi	74.83	17	84.45	16	68.13	17	63.27	20
18	Guangdong	73.75	18	85.19	13	61.95	23	62.54	21
19	Jiangxi	73.17	19	80.00	19	60.34	25	70.32	9
20	Guangxi	72.12	20	72.62	27	70.33	15	72.47	8
21	Heilongjiang	71.30	21	77.14	24	60.96	24	68.47	14
22	Hainan	71.01	22	76.29	25	62.84	21	67.68	15
23	Tibet	70.73	23	71.61	28	58.59	27	77.34	6
24	Ningxia	70.39	24	79.80	20	64.20	19	58.82	24

(continued)

No.	Provinces	Project operation		PPP development level		PPP risk & revenue		PPP development potential	
		Score	Rank	Score	Rank	Score	Rank	Score	Rank
25	Qinghai	69.68	25	78.38	22	51.08	30	67.59	16
26	Gansu	68.03	26	73.74	26	52.82	28	68.64	13
27	Shanghai	66.57	27	80.22	18	63.67	20	45.76	30
28	Tianjin	63.94	28	68.61	31	62.10	22	57.38	27
29	Liaoning	63.77	29	69.13	29	59.61	26	57.61	26
30	Chongqing	63.42	30	68.88	30	52.44	29	61.63	23
31	Beijing	62.65	31	78.82	21	50.46	31	43.83	31

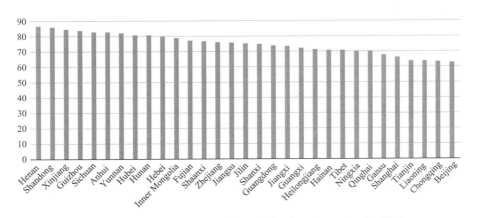

Figure 3.32 Scores and Rankings of Project Operation in 2017

Henan ranks 1st by 86.89, mainly due to the fact that PPP development level, PPP revenue & risk and PPP development potential show good status, ranking 4th, 3rd and 3rd separately. A majority of dimensions are quite satisfactory, especially the large PPP market size, balanced distribution of PPP projects and significant external benefits. What's more, there is great development potential in terms of infrastructure construction and scales of reserve projects.

Shandong ranks 2nd by 86.55. The main reason is that PPP development level and PPP revenue & risk are ranked in a high place as 1st and 2nd. PPP development potential which ranks 19th has a relatively neutral effect. Although PPP development potential is not outstanding as expected, the PPP development with high quality shows a tremendous advantage, such as being highly transparent and normative and creating great external benefits in public services, pollution treatment and environment protection.

Because of the good PPP development level, PPP revenue & risk and PPP development potential ranking 6th, 6th and 2nd separately, Xinjiang ranks 3rd. Actually, Xinjiang and other northwestern regions usually have great opportunities in infrastructure investment and PPP development. In addition, Xinjiang also attaches great importance to the existing PPP projects. The investment is widely distributed with large scale. External benefits in field of Pollution treatment and environment protection are remarkable.

Guizhou Province ranks 4th, basically owing to the fact that PPP revenue & risk and PPP development potential are ranked 1st both; but PPP development level ranking 23th incurs a negative impact. This province is characterized by a large amount of reserve projects with a rapid growth rate and an acute shortage in infrastructure causing huge demand for PPP development. Although backward in PPP development level, Guizhou has low risk in PPP projects and made good use of PPP mode in anti-poverty.

Beijing ranked 31st. It's obvious that PPP development level, PPP revenue & risk and PPP development potential rank low as 21st, 31st and 31st separately. Fundamentally, the demand for infrastructure investment is less in developed regions like Beijing, meaning less PPP development potential accordingly. It is necessary to improve the standard and transparency, lower operation risks and expand external benefits in the future. But it is remarkable that the implementation rate and operating rate in Beijing is high.

Based on the geographic demarcation, the average score of each region is calculated and ranked for comparison and analysis. The result is shown in Table 3.35 and Figure 3.33.

Table 3.35 Scores and Rankings of Project Operation of 7 Regions in 2017

No.	Regions	Project operation		PPP development level		PPP risk & revenue		PPP development potential	
		Score	Rank	Score	Rank	Score	Rank	Score	Rank
1	Central	82.87	1	66.62	2	64.94	1	55.25	2
2	East	76.88	2	67.45	1	53.39	2	41.57	6
3	Southwest	76.64	3	58.66	5	53.39	3	55.46	1
4	Northwest	73.99	4	60.87	4	44.60	6	48.77	3
5	South	72.29	5	58.03	7	45.04	5	47.56	4
6	North	72.06	6	61.35	3	49.21	4	38.46	7
7	Northeast	70.15	7	58.09	6	41.64	7	42.58	5

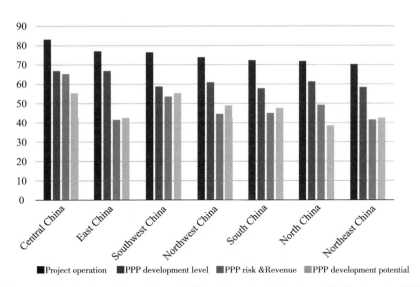

Figure 3.33 Project Operation and Second-grade Indicators of 7 Regions in 2017

Project operation of Central China ranks 1st, basically owing to the fact that PPP development level, PPP revenue & risk and PPP development potential rank in high places, as 2nd, 1st and 2nd separately.

Project operation of East China ranks 2nd, basically because of PPP development level and PPP revenue & risk rank in a high place as 1st and 2nd separately. But PPP development potential ranks 6th, remaining to be improved.

Project operation of Southwest China ranks 3rd, mainly due to PPP revenue & risk and PPP development potential ranking 2nd and 1st separately. PPP development level ranks 5th, which is in a medium place.

Project operation of Northwest China ranks 4th. PPP development level and PPP development potential rank 4th and 3rd, which is in a medium place. PPP revenue & risk ranks in a relatively lower place as 6th.

Project operation of South China ranks 5th. PPP revenue & risk ranks 5th; PPP development potential ranks 4th; PPP development level ranks 7th, remaining to be improved.

Project operation of North China ranks 6th. The reason lies in the fact that PPP development potential ranks in a relatively lower place as 7th. PPP development level and PPP revenue & risk rank 3rd and 4th, which has a relatively neutral effect on the Project operation indicator.

Project operation of Northeast China ranks 7th. The reason lies in the fact that PPP development level and PPP revenue & risk are ranked in a relatively lower place, as 6th and 7th separately. PPP development potential ranks in a medium place as 5th.

3.3.2 PPP Development Level

PPP development level aims to measure the overall operation status of PPP projects that every province has carried out. Thus it can reflect the progress and quality of every province's work on PPP, while provide positive motivation for high quality and a warning for weakness. This indicator can urge relevant departments to not only care about PPP's growth, but also its quality and managements, which in order to make the PPP market operate better and let PPP bring efficiency and benefit to the real economy.

This part is mainly constructed based on PPP projects' public information. From seven dimensions, including PPP development scale, PPP project distribution, PPP work progress, PPP regulated level, PPP transparency level, PPP implementation status and PPP transfer status, it makes overall evaluation on each province's all PPP projects(Figure 3.34). The data mainly uses quantitative ones like the total number and the gross investment of projects in order to maintain an objective and impartial manner, while use qualitative data as supplementary. Most of the data come from each province's annual report collected by China PPP Center established by Ministry of Finance, besides, some are from statistical information of projects management pool, websites of each province's department of finance, removed projects, 'PPP YouLi' database (RongBangRuiMing.corp) and China PPP Market Transparency Report 2017. When calculating, we use methods like (after adjusted by GDP) absolute value aggregation and calculating concentration .ratio, rank them by one-way or satisfactory level and score on each dimension, and then we calculate the weighted average of each dimension and get the overall score of the part PPP development level. Finally, by compare each province's score overall and on each dimension, we can give out some analysis and evaluation results (see Table 3.36 and Figure 3.35).

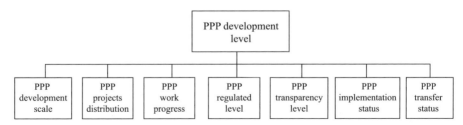

Figure 3.34 PPP Development Level Indicators Framework

Scores and ranking of PPP development level is shown in Table 3.36. The top three provinces are Shandong, Anhui and Sichuan, withs scores of 75.21, 75.29, 69.70. The last three provinces are Liaoning, Chongqing and Tianjin, with scores of 49.13, 48.88, 48.61.

Table 3.36 2017 PPP Development Level Scores and Rankings of Provinces

Provinces	Score	Rank	Regions	Provinces	Score	Rank	Regions
Shandong	75.21	1	East	Shaanxi	64.21	17	Northwest
Anhui	75.20	2	East	Shanghai	60.22	18	East
Sichuan	69.70	3	Southwest	Jiangxi	60.00	19	East

(continued)

Provinces	Score	Rank	Regions	Provinces	Score	Rank	Regions
Henan	69.10	4	Central	Ningxia	59.80	20	Northwest
Zhejiang	68.32	5	East	Beijing	58.82	21	North
Xinjiang	68.23	6	Northwest	Qinghai	58.38	22	Northwest
Jilin	68.01	7	Northeast	Guizhou	58.18	23	Southwest
Hebei	67.77	8	North	Heilongjiang	57.14	24	Northeast
Jiangsu	67.30	9	East	Hainan	56.29	25	South
Inner Mongolia	67.13	10	North	Gansu	53.74	26	Northwest
Hunan	66.18	11	Central	Guangxi	52.62	27	South
Fujian	65.92	12	East	Tibet	51.61	28	Southwest
Guangdong	65.19	13	South	Liaoning	49.13	29	Northeast
Yunnan	64.89	14	Southwest	Chongqing	48.88	30	Southwest
Hubei	64.58	15	Central	Tianjin	48.61	31	North
Shanxi	64.45	16	North				

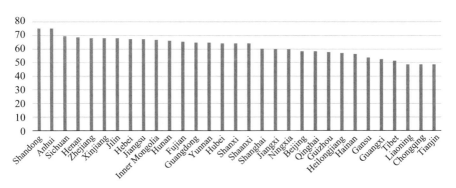

Figure 3.35 2017 PPP Development Level Scores and Rankings

Liaoning ranks the 29th. This is mainly because it ranks low as 30th on PPP development scale, which is due to its double negative growth of PPP in total number and gross investment. Also, its PPP regulated level and PPP transparency level rank 30th and 28th separately, which implies that the quality control and information publication is not in place to implement. Though its economy faces the pressure to descend, Liaoning still needs to attach greater importance to this work.

Chongqing ranks the 30th. This is mainly because its PPP regulated level and PPP transparency level ranks the 31st as the last that far behind other provinces. Though in other ways it ranks the middle course, this still makes Chongqing behave not well in this part. Chongqing should take investigation at early stage more seriously and strengthen projects' model effect to improve its PPP projects' quality, while establish a information publication column and public more operation information to improve the transparency.

Tianjin ranks the 31st. This is partly because of its administrative division that makes its projects low in amount and centralized in distribution, which let it rank 31st on PPP development scale and PPP projects distribution. In other dimensions, it is in a place higher than middle course in PPP work progress, however still shows weakness in PPP regulated level and PPP transparency level.

PPP development level score and ranking of 7 regions are shown in Table 3.37 and Figure 3.36.

Table 3.37　2017 PPP Development Level Scores and Rankings of 7 Regions

No.	Regions	Provinces reported	Average score
1	East China	Shanghai, Jiangsu, Zhejiang, Anhui, Fujian, Jiangxi, Shandong	67.45
2	Central China	Henan, Hubei, Hunan	66.62
3	North China	Beijing, Tianjin, Shanxi, Hebei, Inner Mongolia	61.35
4	Northwest China	Shaanxi, Gansu, Qinghai, Ningxia, Xinjiang	60.87
5	Southwest China	Sichuan, Guizhou, Yunnan, Chongqing, Tibet	58.66
6	Northeast China	Heilongjiang, Jilin, Liaoning	58.09
7	South China	Guangdong, Guangxi, Hainan	58.03

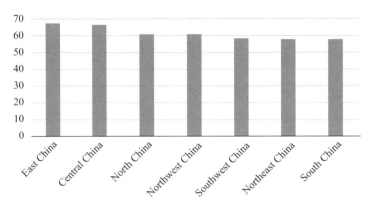

Figure 3.36 2017 PPP Development Level Scores and Rankings of 7 Regions

East China ranks 1st, mainly because it gets the highest score in PPP working progress and transparency level, and grades the second in both PPP projects distribution and PPP regulated level. PPP projects in this area grow fast and are well put into effect, and the development is comprehensive.

Central China ranks 2nd. Its PPP development scale, PPP project distribution and PPP regulated level are all ranked the first, but it ranks the last on PPP work progress and ranks only 4th on PPP transparency level. The low rate of capacity and imperfect information publication hold the grading back, and provinces in this zone should take actions to solve these problems specifically.

North China ranks 3rd. This is because it ranks relatively high on PPP work progress and PPP transparency level as 3rd, 2nd separately. However its development scale and project distribution ranks below the middle course, which leaves room for improvement.

Northwest China ranks 4th. It ranks relatively high on PPP transparency level as 3rd; relatively low on PPP regulated level as 5th; and all other dimensions are all ranked in middle course. This zone shows average performance in almost all aspects, though its PPP scale and quality remains to be improved.

Southwest China ranks 5th. Though it gets the 2nd, 3rd place separately on PPP development scale and PPP projects distribution, it ranks too low in other aspects, especially PPP regulated level and PPP transparency level that both rank 7th. This partly because of the special case Tibet. Besides, it shows the weakness this zone has on PPP implement, quality control and information publication, which should be taken more seriously.

Northeast China ranks 6th. This zone ranks 7th on PPP development scale, which lacks power of development; ranks 6th on projects PPP distribution, PPP regulated level and PPP transparency level, which falls behind overall. Though this zone's work on projects implementation is relatively fast, but it should pay more attention to the quality and information publication. Also, it needs to find more situations for PPP applications, and let the PPP help the zone's economy to keep growth.

South China ranks 7th. Though on PPP work progress, PPP regulated level and PPP transparency level, it behaves just well, but the 6th place on PPP development scale and especially the 7th place on PPP project distribution hold the overall rank back. This reflects the resource allocation problems in this zone. It should be motivated to find more space for PPP application, meanwhile, attach importance to distribute the PPP capital resource more equally in both industrial and spatial dimensions.

1. PPP development scale

PPP development scale consists of 5 fourth-grade indicators (see Table 3.38). The data are from annual reports collected by China PPP Center established by Ministry of Finance, and Asset Life is calculated with information from project management pool. This part measures each province's PPP project's amount, investment, duration, development potential at an aggregate level. For amount and investment, we consider its stock and increment separately to not only reflect the outcome in the past but also give incentives to promote the current work. And since the economic development levels are different among provinces, which will make their PPP demand and supply capability different, when score this two indicators, we adjust the score by each province's GDP. The duration indicator, otherwise, reflects PPP projects average period that they can be put into use in the future.

Table 3.38 PPP Development Scale Indicators System

Third-grade indicators	Fourth-grade indicators	Calculation	Reason for selecting this indicator
PPP development scale	Gross investment	Sum of investment of one province's projects stocked in PPP management pool	Measure PPP resource amount that is put in one province to reflect the development scale of all past PPP projects. The larger this indicator is, the finance capacity the province get from PPP is larger, which means that PPP contributions more to its economy
	Investment growth	Yearly growth rate of gross investment of one province's projects stocked in PPP management pool	Measure the growth speed of PPP in one province to reflect whether its work about PPP is active in the last year. This term scores increments to motivate provinces whose PPP stock is relatively lower to work on PPP
	Total number	Total number of one province's projects stocked in PPP management pool	Measure the number of PPP projects one province stocked to reflect the scale of all past PPP work. The larger this indicator is, the more experienced this province is in operating PPP
	Number growth	Yearly growth rate of total number of one province's projects stocked in PPP management pool	Measure the growth speed of number of projects stocked to reflect whether its work about PPP is active in the last year. This term scores increments to motivate provinces whose PPP stock is relatively lower to work on PPP
	Asset life	Asset value averaged by expected service time (operation) of one province's projects stocked in PPP management pool	Like the concept of duration, this term measures how long the PPP asset can serve the public. The larger this indicators is, the project scale is larger on time dimension, which means the time that they can be put into use is longer

PPP development scale score and ranking are shown in Table 3.39 and Figure 3.37. The top three provinces are Shandong, Tibet and Henan, with the score 57.84, 52.00 and 50.03 separately. The last three provinces are Hainan, Liaoning and Tianjin, with the score 15.30, 13.34 and 5.47 separately. As for Tibet, since its existing 2 PPP projects are all newly established in 2017, so the score on total number and investment growth are both 100, which makes its final score in this part become very high.

Table 3.39 2017 PPP Development Scale Scores and Rankings

Provinces	Score	Ranking	Regions	Provinces	Score	Ranking	Regions
Shandong	57.84	1	East	Shanghai	33.57	17	East
Tibet	52.00	2	Southwest	Ningxia	32.74	18	Northwest
Henan	50.03	3	Central	Jiangxi	32.40	19	East
Sichuan	47.62	4	Southwest	Qinghai	32.38	20	Northwest
Jiangsu	47.03	5	East	Shaanxi	31.68	21	Northwest
Hunan	44.36	6	Central	Fujian	29.60	22	East
Xinjiang	43.68	7	Northwest	Gansu	28.59	23	Northwest
Guangdong	43.32	8	South	Chongqing	25.40	24	Southwest
Guizhou	40.77	9	Southwest	Beijing	25.03	25	North
Zhejiang	40.18	10	East	Anhui	22.01	26	East
Hubei	38.96	11	Central	Heilongjiang	20.74	27	Northeast
Shanxi	38.45	12	North	Guangxi	20.72	28	South
Jilin	36.76	13	Northeast	Hainan	15.30	29	South
Yunnan	35.09	14	Southwest	Liaoning	13.34	30	Northeast
Hebei	34.94	15	North	Tianjin	5.47	31	North
Inner Mongolia	33.93	16	North				

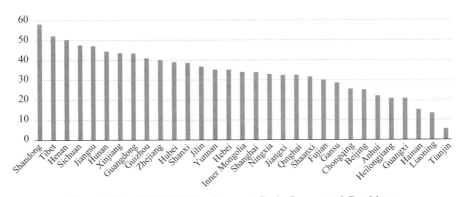

Figure 3.37 2017 PPP Development Scale Scores and Rankings

PPP development scale score and ranking of 7 regions are shown in Table 3.40 and Figure 3.38.

Table 3.40 2017 PPP Development Scale Scores and Rankings of 7 Regions

No.	Regions	Provinces involved in the calculation	Average score
1	Central China	Henan, Hubei, Hunan	44.45
2	Southwest China	Sichuan, Guizhou, Yunnan, Chongqing, Tibet	40.18
3	East China	Shanghai, Jiangsu, Zhejiang, Anhui, Fujian, Jiangxi, Shandong	37.52
4	Northwest China	Shaanxi, Gansu, Qinghai, Ningxia, Xinjiang	33.82
5	North China	Beijing, Tianjin, Shanxi, Hebei, Inner Mongolia	27.56
6	South China	Guangdong, Guangxi, Hainan	26.45
7	Northeast China	Heilongjiang, Jilin, Liaoning	23.61

Central China ranks 1st. This is due to its ranking 1st on Gross investment, Investment growth and Total number, showing its quickly growth of PPP scale. But this region ranks relatively low on Asset life so there remains space for improvement.

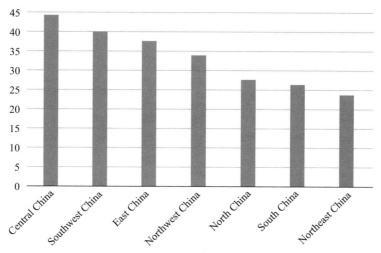

Figure 3.38　2017 PPP Development Scale Scores and Rankings of 7 Regions

Southwest China ranks 2nd. It ranks 1st on investment growth and 2nd on asset life. But its score on the Total number of projects is relatively low, so this region's provinces may try to introduce more projects into PPP pattern.

East China ranks 3rd. In this region projects' Total number's growth is fast and the score ranks 2nd. However its Total number stocked and Asset life ranks relatively low that can be further improved.

Northwest China ranks 4th. This is because it behaves good on Asset life part and ranks 1st. Though, its stocked investment and Total number of PPP projects are low-ranking as 6th, which brings down its total score.

North China ranks 5th. This is because it behaves not bad on investment and Total number, and get the 4th on the latter. Like Northwest China, this region's projects' stock is relatively low and brings down the score.

South China ranks 6th. Its projects' Total number growth is in the middle course but except this, the other indicators ranks relatively low and remains to be improved.

Northeast China ranks 7th. Though project' asset life contributes a little, on investment growth, Total number stocked and growth, it all ranks the 7th and lead to its ranking the last. This region scores low in this part, probably because of the effect of its economy downstream. Especially, some province faces descend in PPP scale and needs to make more effort for PPP and economic growth.

2. PPP project distribution

PPP project distribution consists of 2 fourth-grade indicators, project industrial concentration and project spatial concentration. The Data are from annual reports collected by China PPP Center established by Ministry of Finance. This part aims to promote the PPP's inclusive development through measure whether the PPP resource allocation is equal.

In this part, project industrial concentration reflects whether the PPP projects covers the various sections in economy, while spatial concentration reflects whether the PPP resource are used to benefit the subordinate prefectures and so on. The calculation uses the concentration concept in regional economics. Also, we use the total number instead of investment to score since the latter is more relative to one industry's characteristics and the fiscal capability of a zone; we set the statistical range as the implemented projects, because implementation means the project is more likely to succeed and the data can be directly get from the annual reports. More specific indicators are shown in Table 3.41.

Table 3.41 PPP Projects Distribution Indicators System

Third-grade indicators	Fourth-grade indicators	Calculation	Reason for selecting this indicator
PPP Projects distribution	Industrial concentration	One province's stocked PPP Projects, counted by industrial separately, take the percentage of the top three	Negative indicator. Measure the distribution of PPP resource among industries. This term encourages the province to apply PPP into different areas. Considering about the scales of capital are different among industries, this term counts the number instead of investment

(continued)

Third-grade indicators	Fourth-grade indicators	Calculation	Reason for selecting this indicator
	Spatial concentration	One province's stocked PPP Projects, counted by prefecture of this zone separately, take the percentage of the top three	Negative indicator. Measure the distribution of PPP resource among different zones. This term encourages the province to allocate the PPP capital and projects more equally among different prefectures. Considering about levels of economic development and finance capacity are different among zones, this term counts the number instead of investment

PPP projects distribution score and ranking are shown in Table 3.42 and Figure 3.39.

Table 3.42　2017 PPP Projects Distribution Scores and Rankings

Provinces	Score	Rank	Regions	Provinces	Score	Rank	Regions
Henan	89.81	1	Central	Tibet	56.67	17	Southwest
Hunan	81.58	2	Central	Beijing	56.40	18	North
Xinjiang	80.91	3	Northwest	Hubei	54.53	19	Central
Shandong	79.37	4	East	Gansu	52.22	20	Northwest
Jiangsu	71.02	5	East	Heilongjiang	51.78	21	Northeast
Zhejiang	70.61	6	East	Jiangxi	49.96	22	East
Shaanxi	68.54	7	Northwest	Liaoning	49.52	23	Northeast
Guizhou	67.64	8	Southwest	Shanxi	46.75	24	North
Yunnan	66.47	9	Southwest	Guangdong	45.33	25	South
Sichuan	66.06	10	Southwest	Guangxi	44.22	26	South
Chongqing	63.56	11	Southwest	Ningxia	39.50	27	Northwest

(continued)

Provinces	Score	Rank	Regions	Provinces	Score	Rank	Regions
Fujian	62.70	12	East	Jilin	37.12	28	Northeast
Inner Mongolia	62.49	13	North	Qinghai	28.32	29	Northwest
Anhui	61.93	14	East	Hainan	19.63	30	South
Hebei	57.29	15	North	Tianjin	18.19	31	North
Shanghai	56.67	16	East				

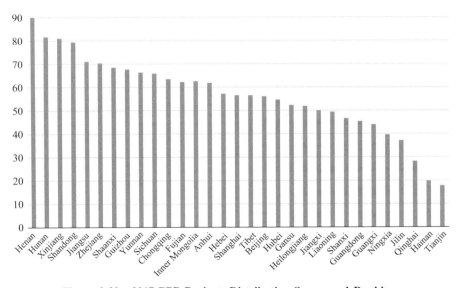

Figure 3.39　2017 PPP Projects Distribution Scores and Rankings

PPP projects distribution ranking is shown in Table 3.42. The top three provinces are Henan, Hunan and Xinjiang, with the score 89.81, 81.58 and 80.91 separately. The 4th place, Shandong, is close to them with a score of 79.37. The last three provinces are Qinghai, Hainan and Tianjin, with the score 28.32, 19.63 and 18.19 separately.

Tianjin ranks 31st, this is mainly because the number of its projects that are in the projects management pool of PPP Center is relatively small. This causes its industrial concentration to be higher than 90% with most of its projects are in public works area. And its project spatial concentration to be higher than 60% that is over the nationwide level, which is partly because of its administrative division.

PPP projects distribution score and ranking of 7 regions are shown in Table 3.43 and Figure 3.40.

Table 3.43 2017 PPP Projects Distribution Scores and Rankings of 7 Regions

No.	Regions	Provinces involoed in calculetion	Average score
1	Central China	Henan, Hubei, Hunan	75.31
2	East China	Shanghai, Jiangsu, Zhejiang, Anhui, Fujian, Jiangxi, Shandong	64.61
3	Southwest China	Sichuan, Guizhou, Yunnan, Chongqing, Tibet	64.08
4	Northwest China	Shaanxi, Gansu, Qinghai, Ningxia, Xinjiang	53.90
5	North China	Beijing, Tianjin, Shanxi, Hebei, Inner Mongolia	48.22
6	Northeast China	Heilongjiang, Jilin, Liaoning	46.14
7	South China	Guangdong, Guangxi, Hainan	36.39

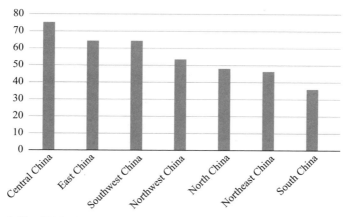

Figure 3.40 2017 PPP Projects Distribution Scores and Rankings of 7 Regions

Central China ranks 1st. It ranks both 1st on project industrial and spatial concentration, which shows that its PPP resource allocation is very balanced.

East China ranks 2nd. Its PPP resources are relatively balanced among industries and ranks 2nd, while the project spatial concentration isn't that much.

Southwest China ranks 3rd. Its PPP resources are relatively balanced among spaces and ranks 2nd, while the project industrial concentration isn't relatively higher.

Northwest and North China ranks 4th, 5th separately, in the middle course on both indicators.

Northeast China ranks 6th. This is because its spatial concentration is high, thus this region should consider to allocate more PPP resource to those less developed areas, to provide infrastructure for them.

South China ranks 7th. It behaves badly in concentration among industries. Most of its projects are in municipal works and transportation area, and we suggest the resource to be allocated more in environment protection and public service area.

3. PPP work progress

PPP work progress consists of 3 fourth-grade indicators, including each province's PPP projects implementation rate, operating rate and transferred rate. This part measures the speed provinces promote the work on PPP through its whole-of life cycle, starting from the preparation stage to the transferring stage. Data of implementation rate and operating rate are from annual reports collected by China PPP Center established by Ministry of Finance. The implementation rate reflects the status that projects are finished value of money and fiscal capacity argument and prepared to be executed. The operating rate reflects the status of the projects being put into construction. These two are all calculated by projects numbers' ratio and use this to rank. They are helpful to push the PPP projects into implementation as soon as possible and promote the efficiency, to avoid delay and force to simplify the procedures. While, PPP projects transferring rate is to measure the progress in the last stage. Since now there are still no projects in transfer stage, this indicator is added just for perfect the score system temporarily. More specific indicators are shown in Table 3.44.

Table 3.44　PPP Work Progress Indicators System

Third-grade indicators	Fourth-grade indicators	Calculation	Reason for selecting this indicator
PPP work progress	PPP implementation rate	Percentage of one province's projects that are after previous argument and be put into implementation	Measure the speed the one province implements its planned PPP projects, to encourage faster implementation. Ministry of Finance defines 'implementation rate' as the number of executed and transferred projects over the number of prepared, purchased, executed and transferred projects
	PPP operating rate	Percentage of one province's projects that are already under construction and operation (demonstration projects)	Measure the speed of one province's PPP construction and push the projects to start construction earlier. Considering about the availability of data, we only take demonstration projects into consideration
	PPP transferring rate	Percentage of one province's projects that finish the transfer procedure	Transfer procedure marks the finish of PPP projects. Since PPP projects have longer periods, now there is still no projects transferred, so this indicators is for suggestion and perfection

PPP work progress scores and ranking are shown in Table 3.45 and Figure 3.41. The top three provinces are Anhui, Shanghai and Shandong, with the score 65.06, 53.63 and 46.16 separately. The 4th place, Sichuan, is close to them with a score of 45.64. The last three provinces are Inner Mongolia, Guizhou and Tibet, with the score 19.19, 13.56 and 0.00 separately. Tibet, since its 2 projects are newly established and not in implementation or operation stage, so the score is 0.00.

Table 3.45 2017 PPP Work Progress Scores and Rankings

Provinces	Score	Rank	Regions	Provinces	Score	Rank	Regions
Anhui	65.06	1	East	Jiangsu	27.76	17	East
Shanghai	53.63	2	East	Jiangxi	27.44	18	East
Shandong	46.16	3	East	Qinghai	27.05	19	Northwest
Sichuan	45.64	4	Southwest	Liaoning	25.92	20	Northeast
Beijing	40.45	5	North	Chongqing	24.97	21	Southwest
Jilin	38.09	6	Northeast	Shaanxi	22.80	22	Northwest
Hebei	37.48	7	North	Hunan	22.25	23	Central
Guangdong	34.35	8	South	Shanxi	21.05	24	North
Gansu	34.02	9	Northwest	Ningxia	20.72	25	Northwest
Heilongjiang	32.89	10	Northeast	Guangxi	20.50	26	South
Fujian	32.61	11	East	Henan	20.35	27	Central
Zhejiang	31.22	12	East	Hubei	19.72	28	Central
Hainan	30.10	13	South	Inner Mongolia	19.19	29	North
Xinjiang	30.01	14	Northwest	Guizhou	13.56	30	Southwest
Tianjin	29.79	15	North	Tibet	0.00	31	Southwest
Yunnan	28.72	16	Southwest				

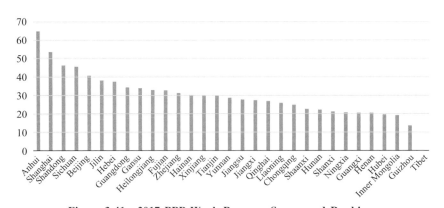

Figure 3.41 2017 PPP Work Progress Scores and Rankings

PPP work progress score and ranking of 7 zones are shown in Table 3.46 and Figure 3.42.

Table 3.46 2017 PPP Work Progress Scores and Rankings of 7 Regions

Ranking	Regions	Provinces involved in the calculation	Average score
1	East China	Shanghai, Jiangsu, Zhejiang, Anhui, Fujian, Jiangxi, Shandong	40.56
2	Northeast China	Heilongjiang, Jilin, Liaoning	32.30
3	North China	Beijing, Tianjin, Shanxi, Hebei, Inner Mongolia	29.59
4	South China	Guangdong, Guangxi, Hainan	28.31
5	Northwest China	Shaanxi, Gansu, Qinghai, Ningxia, Xinjiang	26.92
6	Southwest China	Sichuan, Guizhou, Yunnan, Chongqing, Tibet	22.58
7	Central China	Henan, Hubei, Hunan	20.77

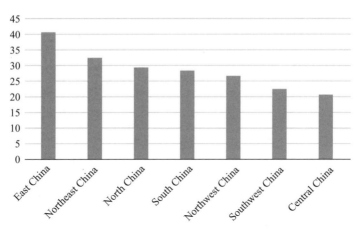

Figure 3.42 2017 PPP Work Progress Scores and Rankings of 7 Regions

East China ranks 1st. This is because it ranks 1st on both PPP implementation rate and PPP operating rate, and gets especially high score on implementation compared with other regions.

Northeast China ranks 2nd. On PPP operating rate it ranks 2nd but on implementation its gap with East China is relatively large.

North, South and Northwest China ranks 3rd, 4th and 5th separately. These three regions perform similarly in this part and form the middle course.

Southwest China ranks 6th. This is due to its 7th ranking on PPP implementation rate. Though for demonstration projects this region's PPP operating rate is relatively high, it should speed up its previous argument work and let more projects quickly be put into construction.

Central China ranks 7th. It ranks 6th and 7th separately on PPP implementation rate and PPP operating rate. This region holds a lot projects in PPP management pool, so at the same time when it expands its PPP scale, this region should also take the work to let planned projects be constructed and operated seriously.

4. PPP regulated level

PPP regulated level are consists of 9 fourth-grade indicators, including national demonstration, provincial demonstration, national honors, value of money evaluation completion rate, fiscal capacity evaluation completion rate, VFM report quantify ratio, total number of removed projects, gross investment of removed projects and serious irregulated or illegal events. This part comprehensively measures the regulated level of PPP through the demonstration effects, procedure compliance and quality guarantee three aspects. For projects with good performance, this part adds points to encourage them; for those that are not qualified, this part also creates demerits to alert them.

Among the indicators, data of national demonstration and provincial demonstration are collected from annual reports collected by China PPP Center established by Ministry of Finance; data of national honors is collected from publications of the State Council. For VFM and fiscal capacity evaluation passing rate, they are calculated by statistics in projects management pool. Whether the VFM report is quantified, since the statistics now is not available, so we add this indicators as a suggestion. These three together judges the compliance of projects. As for the total number and gross investment of removed projects, we get this from the record of this work done by Ministry of Finance. There is still no serious irregulated or illegal events happens in PPP area, but we keep this indicator in order to remain alert to large risks. More specific information about indicators is shown in Table 3.47.

Table 3.47　PPP Regulated Level Indicators System

Third-grade indicators	Fourth-grade indicators	Calculation	Reason for selecting this indicator
PPP regulated level	National demonstration	Sum of the number of one province's projects elected as national demonstration	Measure the demonstration effect of one province's PPP work among nationwide. The selection of national demonstration projects considers many dimensions including purchasing competitiveness, authenticity of social capital, project rationality, arrangement fitness, fiscal capacity and so on, reflects the quality of PPP projects comprehensively
	Provincial demonstration	Sum of the number of one province's projects elected as provincial demonstration	Measure the demonstration effect of one province's PPP work among provincial level. The selection of provincial demonstration projects considers the different situation of each province and select the projects that benefit much to the province. This reflects the PPP's help to one province's economy
	Nationally honored cities and counties	Sum of the number of one province's cities, regions or counties honored for PPP by the State Council	Measure the quality of PPP work of one province's prefectures. General Office of State Council public paper to honor the cities, regions and counties that actively promote their PPP work. Also, the honored ones' PPP projects is highly regulated and equally allocated, and has good external effects in areas like medication or environment. As reward, the honored ones can also get benefit on next year's subsidy or so on

(continued)

Third-grade indicators	Fourth-grade indicators	Calculation	Reason for selecting this indicator
	Value of money evaluation completion rate	Percentage of one province's projects that finish VFM evaluation among all projects	Measure one province's previous argument work and expected earnings. VFM evaluation system is comprehensive and reasonable. Evaluation before the implementation is helpful to distinguish the good projects and allocate resource for them, meanwhile find the risks ahead
	Fiscal capacity evaluation completion rate	Percentage of one province's projects that finish fiscal capacity evaluation among all projects	Measure whether one province's fiscal expenditure on PPP is suitable. Evaluation on fiscal capacity can help to control the risk of finance, making the expenditure duty of government more clear. That will be good for the government to play its own role in PPP
	VFM report quantify ratio	Percentage of one province's projects thatare evaluated under quantified methods	Measure the quality of one province's previous evaluation work on PPP. Thedifficult to quantified parts in PPP, including cost estimating, risk recognition and so on, all have requirements on experience and ability of related departments. Promoting the quantified work means a lot to make good expectation and management on benefits and risks
	Total number of removed projects	Sum of the number one province's projects that are removed form PPP management pool or national demonstrations, including those are rectified	According to No.54 [2018] from Ministry of Finance, now some PPP projects are slack in progress or irregulated when executed. Classifications mainly are: i). stop to use PPP pattern (removed from pool); ii). not complete the social party purchase or the plan has been changed a lot (removed from demonstrations); iii) irregulated procedures or unqualified entities (under rectify). This part will make alert to the problem projects

(continued)

Third-grade indicators	Fourth-grade indicators	Calculation	Reason for selecting this indicator
	Gross investment of removed projects	Sum of the investment one province's projects that are removed form PPP management pool or national demonstrations, including those are rectified	Like the total number indicator, this part is to prevent from unfulfilled or false report on project capital
	Serious irregulated or illegal events	Sum of the number one province's irregulated or illegal projects that cause negative social impact seriously	Negative indicator. Punish those that re irregulated or illegal seriously. Now there is still no such project so we add this indicator to alert for risks

PPP regulated level scores and ranking are shown in Table 3.48 and Figure 3.43. The top three provinces are Hunan, Anhui and Inner Mongolia, with the score 87.54, 83.10 and 76.35 separately. The last three provinces are Beijing, Liaoning and Chongqing, with the score 47.80, 46.65 and 45.55 separately. Beijing and Chongqing's total number of provincial demonstrations and national honored cities/counties are relatively few, and their projects' percentage of those finished VFM and fiscal capacity evaluation is lower than average performance of nation level, so they performs badly in the regulated level part. As for Liaoning, its total number and investment of removed projects is relatively larger holding back its ranking.

Table 3.48　2017 PPP Regulated Level Scores and Rankings

Provinces	Score	Rank	Regions	Provinces	Score	Rank	Regions
Hunan	87.54	1	Central	Guangxi	59.83	17	South
Anhui	83.10	2	East	Fujian	59.48	18	East
Inner Mongolia	76.35	3	North	Yunnan	58.67	19	Southwest

(continued)

Provinces	Score	Rank	Regions	Provinces	Score	Rank	Regions
Jilin	71.26	4	Northeast	Jiangxi	56.35	20	East
Shandong	71.05	5	East	Gansu	54.65	21	Northwest
Shanxi	70.74	6	North	Shanghai	53.60	22	East
Zhejiang	70.15	7	East	Guizhou	53.48	23	Southwest
Henan	70.01	8	Central	Tibet	53.10	24	Southwest
Hubei	67.50	9	Central	Qinghai	53.06	25	Northwest
Jiangsu	65.81	10	East	Ningxia	52.44	26	Northwest
Guangdong	65.33	11	South	Heilongjiang	51.97	27	Northeast
Xinjiang	64.78	12	Northwest	Tianjin	49.15	28	North
Hebei	62.31	13	North	Beijing	47.80	29	North
Sichuan	61.93	14	Southwest	Liaoning	46.65	30	Northeast
Shaanxi	61.74	15	Northwest	Chongqing	45.55	31	Southwest
Hainan	60.95	16	South				

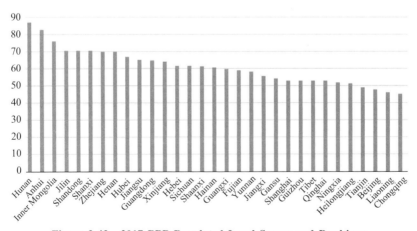

Figure 3.43 2017 PPP Regulated Level Scores and Rankings

PPP regulated level scores and ranking of 7 regions are shown in Table 3.49 and Figure 3.44.

Table 3.49 2017 PPP Regulated Level Scores and Rankings of 7 Regions

No.	Regions	Provinces involved in the calculation	Average score
1	Central China	Henan, Hubei, Hunan	75.01
2	East China	Shanghai, Jiangsu, Zhejiang, Anhui, Fujian, Jiangxi, Shandong	65.65
3	South China	Guangdong, Guangxi, Hainan	62.04
4	North China	Beijing, Tianjin, Shanxi, Hebei, Inner Mongolia	61.27
5	Northwest China	Shaanxi, Gansu, Qinghai, Ningxia, Xinjiang	57.34
6	Northeast China	Heilongjiang, Jilin, Liaoning	56.63
7	Southwest China	Sichuan, Guizhou, Yunnan, Chongqing, Tibet	54.55

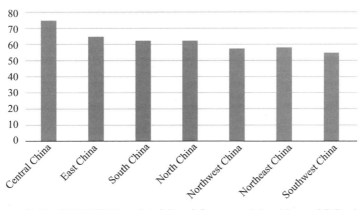

Figure 3.44 2017 PPP Regulated Level Scores and Rankings of 7 Regions

Central China ranks 1st. Its outstanding behave on National demonstration effect benefits a lot, ranking 1st on National, Provincial demonstration and honored prefectures term. Also it ranks 2nd on complete rate of VFM and fiscal capacity evaluation. Its shortcoming is that the amount of removed projects shows to be relatively high and ranks 7th, which might means that this region faces operation problem on small scale projects.

East China ranks 2nd. It's also due to the demonstration effect that it ranks 2nd and 3rd separately on the total number of National demonstrations and Nationally honored cities or counties. Also, among its projects, the complete rate of

VFM and fiscal capacity evaluation is relatively high, and the removed rate is low as well.

South China ranks 3rd. That's because its good compliance work, the complete rates of VFM and fiscal capacity evaluation both rank the 1st, also total number and investment of its removed projects are relatively small and get 1st ranking. But the National demonstration effect of projects in this area shows to be low, especially on provincial demonstrations and Nationally honored cities and counties, it only ranks 6th, which holds back its ranking and means that local governments in this region should improve the quality of projects.

North China ranks 4th. Most of its indicators are in the middle course, with the National demonstration related ones seems not that well and need to be improved.

Northwest China ranks 5th. Though rankings of the Nationally honored cities or counties and the removed projects are both in the top three, the relatively lower ranking on National demonstrations, especially the 7th place on complete rate of VFM and fiscal capacity evaluation, together hold back its ranking. This shows that the argument work on previous stage is imperfect and need to be improved.

Northeast China ranks 6th. Though there are not many removed projects, but the complete rate of VFM and fiscal capacity evaluation is relatively low. And it ranks only 7th on National demon strathons and Provincial demonstrations, showing that the model effect is relatively low and this region should consider more about project quality improvement.

Southwest China ranks 7th. This is mainly because its Nationally honored cities or counties is relatively few and ranks 7th. Also its total number and investment of removed projects ranks 6th and 7th separately. And on other indicators in this part it also behaves not that well, holding back the ranking.

5. The degree of PPP transparency

The degree of PPP transparency consists of four fourth grade indicators, namely PPP information disclosure rate, PPP market transparency index, PPP government website information disclosure, and PPP government website information quality. The data are from Rongbang Ruiming database, China PPP Market Transparency Report of 2017 and the website of each provincial finance department. These indicators measured whether the government PPP project management and operation work is open and transparent. And whether the relevant information is easy and accessible to enterprises and the public. Our project is aimed at promoting the standardization and transparency of PPP projects and improving policy communication, information disclosure and public supervision. The specific index system is shown in Table 3.50.

Table 3.50 The Degree of PPP Transparency Indicator System

Third-grade indicators	Fourth-grade indicators	Economic meaning	Reason for selecting this indicator
The degree of PPP transparency	PPP information disclosure rate	The total number of published documents for all projects as a percentage of the total number of public documents	Measure the level of disclosure of PPP project documents. Project information disclosure is a powerful guarantee for the smooth operation of PPP projects. The higher the level of information disclosure, the more complete the supervision of PPP projects, the lower the risk and the better the degree of development. Taking into account the availability of the data Rongbang Ruiming database, it is considered that there are 4 feasibility studies for the feasibility of each project in the provincial administrative region
	PPP transparency index	The extent to which PPP's responsible entities disclose information about PPP projects	Comprehensively measure the transparency of PPP projects. The index comes from the "China PPP Market Transparency Report of 2017". Based on the public content, time points and methods, the PPP center data is constructed based on the Ministry of Finance, reflecting the basic situation and implementation plan of the provincial administrativeregion to fully disclose the PPP project in time

(continued)

Third-grade indicators	Fourth-grade indicators	Economic meaning	Reason for selecting this indicator
	PPP government website information disclosure	If the Finance Department website have a PPP information disclosure column	Measure whether the government actively provides PPP policy information for enterprises, and timely publicize PPP work plans and work progress. This indicator helps governments and businesses communicate policy and project information in a timely manner and is subject to public scrutiny
	PPP government website information quality	Whether the PPP public information on the website of the Finance Department is full, updated, and sorted	Measuring whether government information disclosure work is in place, so that enterprises and the public can easily obtain more effective and timely policy and project information, and improve PPP work efficiency and work quality

Among them, the PPP information disclosure rate counts the ratio of the number of published documents to the total documents; the PPP transparency index cites the research results of the China PPP Market Transparency Report of 2017, which is based on the Ministry of Finance's PPP project management database and reserve database. According to the Ministry of Finance's request for information disclosure at different stages of the PPP project, it reflects the disclosure of operational information and project documents of PPP projects in various provincial administrative regions. The PPP government website information disclosure and PPP government website information quality indicators evaluate the information disclosure work of the provincial finance department, and promote the related work.

The PPP transparency degree score rankings are shown in Table 3.51 and Figure 3.45. Among them, the top three provincial administrative regions are Anhui Province, Jilin Province, and Hebei Province, with scores of 95.51, 92.10, and 91.42 respectively. The provincial administrative regions at the end of the three ranks are Gansu Province, Tibet Autonomous Region, and Chongqing Municipality, with scores of 21.33, 16.85, 5.75 respectively. Chongqing's information disclosure rate and transparency index scores are too low, and there is no PPP information disclosure platform, so the degree of PPP transparency is ranked last.

Table 3.51 PPP Transparency Scores and Rankings in 2017

Provinces	Score	Rank	Regions	Provinces	Score	Rank	Regions
Anhui	95.51	1	East	Jiangsu	72.13	17	East
Jilin	92.10	2	Northeast	Henan	70.40	18	Central
Hebei	91.42	3	North	Hainan	68.83	19	South
Fujian	89.50	4	East	Jiangxi	65.06	20	East
Inner Mongolia	84.26	5	North	Beijing	58.62	21	North
Shandong	83.09	6	East	Heilongjiang	56.84	22	Northeast
Ningxia	82.27	7	Northwest	Guizhou	50.47	23	Southwest
Yunnan	79.61	8	Southwest	Tianjin	44.49	24	North
Shaanxi	78.87	9	Northwest	Shanghai	38.33	25	East
Hubei	78.81	10	Central	Hunan	36.84	26	Central
Sichuan	78.14	11	Southwest	Guangxi	33.66	27	South
Shanxi	78.00	12	North	Liaoning	26.37	28	Northeast
Zhejiang	76.78	13	East	Gansu	21.33	29	Northwest
Xinjiang	74.19	14	Northwest	Tibet	16.85	30	Southwest
Qinghai	73.46	15	Northwest	Chongqing	5.75	31	Southwest
Guangdong	72.94	16	South				

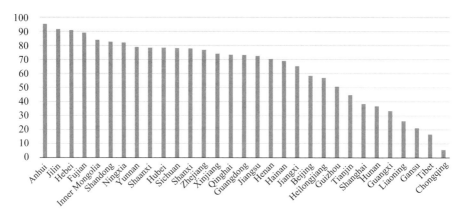

Figure 3.45　PPP Transparency Scores and Rankings in 2017

PPP Transparency scores and ranking of 7 regions are shown in Table 3.52 and Figure 3.46.

Table 3.52　PPP Transparency Scores and Rankings in 2017

No.	Regions	Provinces involved in the calculation	Average score
1	East China	Shanghai, Jiangsu, Zhejiang, Anhui, Fujian, Jiangxi, Shandong	74.34
2	North China	Beijing, Tianjin, Shanxi, Hebei, Inner Mongolia	71.36
3	Northeast China	Shaanxi, Gansu, Qinghai, Ningxia, Xinjiang	66.02
4	Central China	Henan, Hubei, Hunan	62.02
5	South China	Guangdong, Guangxi, Hainan	58.48
6	Northwest China	Heilongjiang, Jilin, Liaoning	58.44
7	Southeast China	Sichuan, Guizhou, Yunnan, Chongqing, Tibet	46.17

The degree of PPP transparency in East China ranked first, mainly due to the information disclosure rate and PPP market transparency index scores ranked first, indicating that the project related information and documents are in place, although the establishment of the PPP government website is not all set up.

The PPP transparency degree ranked No. 2 in North China, mainly due to the PPP government website information disclosure and PPP government website

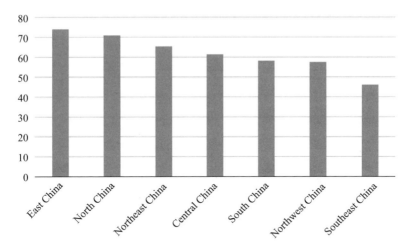

Figure 3.46　PPP Transparency Scores and Rankings in 2017

information quality score ranking are the first. All the government websites in the region have established a PPP information disclosure column, and classified the information. However, the PPP information disclosure rate of the region is low, and the PPP market transparency index has room for improvement, resulting in a lower ranking.

The Northwest China ranked third in the degree of PPP transparency, mainly due to the PPP government website information quality score ranked first. Although the PPP column has not been established in all regions, but the column information disclosure quality is better. Projects in the region have lower information disclosure rates and PPP market transparency indices.

Central China ranked 4th in PPP transparency, mainly due to higher market transparency index scores. However, the PPP information disclosure rate is relatively low, and since there are only three provinc in the region, the PPP column has not been established in all provincial websites, which has a greater impact on the score.

South China ranked 5th in the degree of PPP transparency. Although the project information disclosure rate score is ranked second, the market transparency, PPP government website information disclosure and PPP government website quality scores are all in the middle, and the overall ranking is slightly lower.

The Northeast China ranked sixth in the degree of PPP transparency. Although the PPP information disclosure rate and the PPP market transparency index are ranked third, the remaining projects are slightly weaker, especially the PPP government website has a lower quality of information disclosure, ranking seventh, which reduces the overall ranking.

The Southwest China ranked 7th in the degree of PPP transparency, mainly due to the PPP information disclosure rate, PPP market transparency index, and PPP government website information disclosure scores ranked seventh. The level of information disclosure in the region is divided into two levels. The provinces that are not perfect and open need to pay more attention to the work, starting from the specific projects and government affairs, and improving the transparency of PPP work.

6. PPP implementation

The implementation of PPP consists of six fourth grade indicators, namely, public satisfaction, construction progress compliance quality compliance, cost compliance, social capital or project company's annual operational performance, and interim report evaluation results. The specific index system composition is shown in Table 3.53.

Table 3.53 Composition of PPP Implementation Indicator System

Third-grade indicators	Fourth-grade indicators	Economic meaning	Reason for selecting this indicator
PPP implementation	Public satisfaction	Average score of all warehousing projects with public evaluation mechanisms	Measure the actual benefits of PPP projects providing public services. The Notice on Promoting the Guiding Opinions on Government and Social Capital Cooperation Models in the Public Service Field (Guo Ban Fa [2015] No. 42) pointed out that a comprehensive evaluation system involving the government and the public should be established. Incorporating a public evaluation mechanism into the project contract helps to assess whether the project actually provides public services to differentiate from government procurement

(continued)

Third-grade indicators	Fourth-grade indicators	Economic meaning	Reason for selecting this indicator
	Project construction progress compliance	The proportion of projects that were publicly reported in the PPP Center of the Ministry of Finance and progressed as scheduled accounted for the number of projects in the implementation phase	Measure whether the overall PPP project starts construction as scheduled. The Interim Measures for the Administration of Information Disclosure of the Comprehensive Information Platform of PPP of the Ministry of Finance (caijin[2017] No.1) requires the implementing agency or the project company to immediately disclose the progress of the project construction and the compliance review of the PPP project contract, and supervise the project on time and in accordance with the plan
	Quality compliance	The proportion of projects publicly reported by the Ministry of Finance PPP and meeting the quality standards as a percentage of the number of projects in the implementation phase	Measure whether the average project quality of the PPP project in the provincial administrative region is up to standard. The Ministry of Finance's PPP Interim Measures (caijin[2017] No.1) require the implementing agency or the project company to immediately disclose the conformity review of the project quality and the PPP project contract, and supervise the project to ensure the quality is completed
	Cost compliance	The proportion of projects that are publicly reported in the PPP center of the Ministry of Finance and meets the cost inspection standards as a percentage of the number of projects in the implementation phase	It is measured whether the average cost of the PPP project in the provincial administrative region is achieved as planned. The PPP Interim Measures of the Ministry of Finance (caijin[2017] No.1) requires the implementing agency or the project company to immediately disclose the conformity review of the project cost and the PPP project contract, and the supervision project is completed at the appropriate cost according to the contract

(continued)

Third-grade indicators	Fourth-grade indicators	Economic meaning	Reason for selecting this indicator
	Social capital or project company's annual operational performance	Return on social capital or project company assets disclosed in all implementation phase projects	Measure the operatingreturn of the PPP project in the provincial administrative region. The Ministry of Finance's "PPP Interim Measures" (caijin[2017] No.1) requires immediate disclosure of the social capital or project company's financial status and project operational performance. The inclusion of performance in the assessment can reflect the quality of PPP project operations, change the current status of PPP project construction, and guide PPP work to re-operate
	Interim report evaluation results	The proportion of the number of projects that have been publicly reviewed and approved in the PPP Center of the Ministry of Finance as a percentage of thenumber of projects in the implementation phase	Measure the average operating status of the PPP project company in the provincial administrative region. The Ministry of Finance's "PPP Interim Measures" (caijin[2017] No.1) requires immediate disclosure of the project company's performance monitoring report, mid-term evaluation report, major changes or termination of the project, project pricing andprevious price adjustments. The mid-term evaluation report can comprehensively reflect the overall operation of the project company

The above indicators are valuable for evaluating the performance of PPP, but the data is not available at the moment, so we listed them as recommended indicators. The implementation of PPP comprehensively measures the progress of the operation of PPP projects after project storage from the aspects of project construction and operation results, resource utilization efficiency, professional and social assessment, and is conducive to the project life cycle supervision and management. Realizing the essential characteristics of PPP project "operation" using project assets to provide public services to the public and to obtain compensation based on the quality and quantity of public services.

7. PPP handover

The PPP transfer situation consists of two fourth grade indicators, which are the test results of the project facility handover standards and the post-project evaluation results. The above indicators are valuable for evaluating the results of the PPP project handover stage, but the data is not available at the moment, so it is listed as a recommended indicator. The handover of the PPP project marks the end of the life cycle of the project PPP cooperation. The project company needs to transfer the project facilities and related rights to the government or other designated institutions under the contractual conditions and procedures. Although the PPP project has been operating in China for several years, there are still no projects entering the transition phase. With reference to foreign experience and research results, the value assessment of project facilities and the delivery of equity at the transition stage will be the key to the smooth progress of this phase. The PPP Center of the Ministry of Finance requires the handover of the project to open the project to meet the standard compliance test and the post-project evaluation results, so as to measure and assess the rationality of the value assessment and equity arrangement to ensure the smooth completion of the PPP project cooperation. The spacific index system composition is shown in Table 3.54.

Table 3.54 Composition of the PPP Handover Indicator System

Third-grade indicators	Fourth-grade indicators	Economic meaning	Reason for selecting this indicator
PPP handover	Project facilities handover test results	The proportion of all approved and publicly handed over projects to the total number of transferred projects	Measure whether the PPP project will eventually meet the handover criteria. Before the handover, the PPP project needs to evaluate the value of the project facilities when it is handed over. It needs to meet a number of standards such as rights and technology, and pass the performance test to meet the handover requirements. The compliance test of the handover standard will help to ensure the quality of the project assets and guarantee the rights and interests of the transferred parties

(continued)

Third-grade indicators	Fourth-grade indicators	Economic meaning	Reason for selecting this indicator
	Post-project evaluation results	Performance evaluation score after project handover for all transition phase projects	After the completion of the project handover, the financial department will organize relevant departments to perform performance evaluation on project output, cost-effectiveness, regulatory effectiveness, sustainability, and application of PPP mode, marking the official end of the life cycle of a PPP project. The evaluation results can be used as a comprehensive indicator to evaluate the overall results of the PPP project

3.3.3 PPP Risk & Revenue

PPP risk & revenue measures the internal and external benefits and potential risks of PPP projects during its life cycle, which are the factors determining the value of PPP projects. Only when the PPP project itself has sufficient value it is meaningful to adopt PPP mode for investment. In this way, the advantages of PPP mode are taken and expected goals are achieved. The internal benefits refer to the economic return brought by the project, while the external benefits refer to the social value that considers positive externality. And the project risks are those potential factors causing the project to fail. Reasonable internal and external benefits and low risks make PPP projects more profitable and attractive, representing higher quality of the project.

The indicator is composed of three third-grade indicators. They are PPP project revenue, PPP project risk and PPP external benefits. Furthermore, PPP project revenue is composed of four fourth-grade indicators, including return on total investment, return on capital, fair profit margin and VFM (Value for Money) index; PPP project risk is composed of two fourth-grade indicators, including total project risk cost ratio and risk isolation ratio; PPP external benefits is composed of six fourth-grade indicators. They are benefits on public service, benefits on pollution treatment & environment protection, benefits on tourism and culture development, number of library projects of poor counties, amount of investment of library projects of poor counties, coverage rate for poor counties. The PPP risk & revenue indicator framework and explanation are shown in Table 3.55 and Figure 3.47.

Table 3.55　Composition and Explanation of PPP Risk & Revenue

Second-grade	Third-grade	Fourth-grade	Calculation	Reason for selecting this indicator
PPP risk & revenue	PPP project revenue	Return on total investment	Average of return on total investment of PPP projects in this province	The indicator is based on the internal rate of return according to the cash flow model of total investment in *The Economic Evaluation Methods and Parameters for Construction Project* (3rd edition). It can reflect the comprehensive rate of return for all participants brought by PPP projects
		Return on capital	Average of return on capital of PPP projects in this province	The indicator is based on the internal rate of return according to the cash flow model of capital in *The Economic Evaluation Methods and Parameters for Construction Project* (3rd edition), taking financial leverage into account. It can reflect the rate of return for investors brought by PPP projects

(continued)

Second-grade	Third-grade	Fourth-grade	Calculation	Reason for selecting this indicator
		Fair profit margin	Average of fair profit margin of PPP projects in this province	Fair profit margin helps the government reasonably determine the operating subsidy based on construction cost, operating cost and profit level. In an ideal situation, it should be based on the medium & long-term loan interest rate of commercial banks, distinguish between user-fee and Availability-based PPPs and fully take into account risk factors. Also, it should avoid being too high or too low
		VFM index	Average of VFM index of PPP projects in this province	VFM is short for "Value for Money". VFM index reflects whether the PPP mode achieves value for money and maximizes the use of resources compared to the traditional mode
	PPP project risk	Total project risk cost ratio	Ratio of total risk cost to total investment; Then calculate the average of all PPP projects	The total project risk cost estimates the potential risk cost of a project after fully taking into account the probabilities and consequences of each major risk facor (confirmed in the risk identification and allocation process). This ratio reflects the relative cost of risks for a PPP project
		Risk isolation ratio	Proportion of PPP projects with SPV (Specific Purpose Vehicle)	SPV helps to realize limited recourse of PPP projects and serves as an important form of risk isolation. It plays an important part in controlling risks and improving revenue

(continued)

Second-grade	Third-grade	Fourth-grade	Calculation	Reason for selecting this indicator
PPP external benefits		Benefits on public services	Proportion of PPP projects in field of public services	Field of public services includes culture, sports, medical care, pension, education, tourism, etc. The indicator reflects the role that PPP mode plays in field of public services, encouraging the government to correct related externalities
		Benefits on pollution treatment & environment protection	Proportion of PPP projects in field of pollution treatment and environment protection	Field of pollution treatment and environment protection includes public transportation, water supply and drainage, ecological construction, water conservancy construction, renewable energy, forestry, tourism, etc. The indicator reflects the role that PPP mode plays in field of pollution treatment and environment protection, encouraging the government to correct related externalities
		Benefits on tourism and culture development	Proportion of PPP projects in field of culture and tourism	Field of tourism and culture includes tourism and culture industries. The indicator reflects the role that PPP mode plays in field of tourism and culture, encouraging the government to correct related externalities
		Number of library projects of poor counties	Quoted	The indicator generally measures how PPP mode performs in poor areas, aiming to stimulate the application of PPP mode in helping poor counties out of poverty

(continued)

Second-grade	Third-grade	Fourth-grade	Calculation	Reason for selecting this indicator
		Amount of investment of library projects of poor counties	Quoted	Same as above
		Coverage rate for poor counties	Proportion of poor counties with PPP library projects	The indicator measures the coverage of PPP projects in poor areas, aiming to stimulate the application of PPP mode in helping poor counties out of poverty. Also, it encourages poor counties to adopt PPP mode in order to improve infrastructure environment and develop the economy

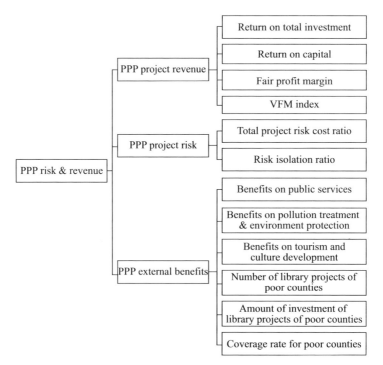

Figure 3.47 PPP Risk & Revenue Indicator Framework

Based on the collected data, PPP risk & revenue indicatos of 31 provinces are calculated. The magnitude and ranking of PPP risk & revenue are shown in Table 3.56 and Figure 3.48.

Table 3.56 Scores and Rankings of PPP Risk & Revenue in 2017

Provinces	Score	Rank	Regions	Provinces	Score	Rank	Regions
Guizhou	78.49	1	Southwest	Shanxi	48.13	17	North
Shandong	74.68	2	East	Jilin	44.35	18	Northeast
Henan	73.80	3	Central	Ningxia	44.20	19	Northwest
Inner Mongolia	69.91	4	North	Shanghai	43.67	20	East
Hunan	65.39	5	Central	Hainan	42.84	21	South
Xinjiang	64.89	6	Northwest	Tianjin	42.10	22	North
Yunnan	62.14	7	Southwest	Guangdong	41.95	23	South
Hubei	55.64	8	Central	Heilongjiang	40.96	24	Northeast
Hebei	55.46	9	North	Jiangxi	40.34	25	East
Sichuan	55.27	10	Southwest	Liaoning	39.61	26	Northeast
Zhejiang	55.05	11	East	Tibet	38.59	27	Southwest
Anhui	54.58	12	East	Gansu	32.82	28	Northwest
Jiangsu	54.18	13	East	Chongqing	32.44	29	Southwest
Fujian	51.21	14	East	Qinghai	31.08	30	Northwest
Guangxi	50.33	15	South	Beijing	30.46	31	North
Shaanxi	49.98	16	Northwest				

Guizhou ranks 1st. It's obvious that PPP project revenue, PPP project risk and PPP external benefits are all scored high, ranking 6th, 4th and 2nd separately, which show tremendous advantage, especially on developing PPP projects in poor counties. Its number and value of library projects of poor counties are top nationwide and coverage rate for poor counties is also at a high level.

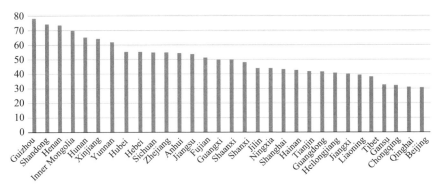

Figure 3.48　Scores and Rankings of PPP Risk & Revenue in 2017

Inner Mongolia ranks 4th. The main reason is that PPP external benefits ranks in a high place as 3rd. PPP project revenue which ranks 19th has a relatively neutral impact; But project risk incurs a negative impact, ranking 24th. The highlight of Inner Mongolia is the significant external PPP benefits, especially the great efforts on pollution treatment, environment protection and cultural and tourism development.

Xinjiang ranks 6th, basically owing to the excellent external PPP benefits which ranks 6th; PPP project risk ranks 18th; But project revenue is ranked in an inferior place as 24th. As with Guizhou and Inner Mongolia, it attaches importance to external benefits of PPP projects in which way the government can correct the externalities.

Chongqing ranks 29th, mainly due to the bad grades of all three sub-indicators. The project revenue, risk and external benefits rank 26th, 27th and 27th separately. The return on total investment and return on capital are at a relatively lower place. What's more, there is still no PPP project of poor counties registered in the management library of the Finance Department, which remains to be achieved in the future.

Beijing ranks 31st, which attributes to the fact that PPP project risk and PPP external benefits rank low as 31st and 28th separately. However, PPP project revenue which ranks 3rd is good. From the aspect of risks, the total project risk cost ratio is slightly high and needs to be controlled; As for external benefits, it can be observed that the application of PPP mode on public services and tourism and culture is rather limited.

Same as above, the average score of each geographic region is calculated and ranked for comparison and analysis. The result is shown in Table 3.57 and Figure 3.49.

Table 3.57　Scores and Rankings of PPP Risk & Revenue of 7 Regions in 2017

No.	Regions	Provinces involved in the calculation	Average score
1	Central China	Henan, Hubei, Hunan	64.94
2	East China	Shanghai, Jiangsu, Zhejiang, Anhui, Fujian, Jiangxi, Shandong	53.39
3	Southwest China	Sichuan, Guizhou, Yunnan, Chongqing, Tibet	53.39
4	North China	Beijing, Tianjin, Shanxi, Hebei, Inner Mongolia	49.21
5	South China	Guangdong, Guangxi, Hainan	45.04
6	Northwest China	Shaanxi, Gansu, Qinghai, Ningxia, Xinjiang	44.60
7	Northeast China	Heilongjiang, Jilin, Liaoning	41.64

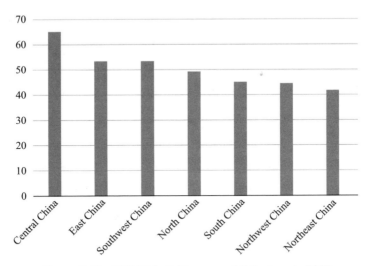

Figure 3.49　PPP Risk & Revenue of 7 Regions in 2017

PPP risk & revenue of Central China ranks 1st, basically owing to the fact that PPP external benefits rank the top. And PPP project revenue ranks in a medium place as 3rd. But PPP project risk which ranks 6th hinders.

PPP risk & revenue of East China ranks 2nd, basically because of PPP project revenue and risk rank in a high place as 1st and 2nd separately. PPP external benefits rank 3rd, which is in a medium place.

PPP risk & revenue of Southwest China ranks 3rd, mainly due to PPP project revenue and PPP external benefits ranking 2nd. PPP project risk which ranks 3rd has a relatively neutral impact.

PPP risk & revenue of North China ranks 4th. PPP project revenue ranks 5th; PPP project risk ranks 5th; PPP external benefits ranks 4th.

PPP risk & revenue of South China ranks 5th. PPP project risk shows a great advantage as ranking the top. However, PPP project revenue and PPP external benefits are ranked in an inferior place as 7th and 6th separately, incurring a negative impact.

PPP risk & revenue of Northwest China ranks 6th. The reason lies in the fact that PPP project revenue and risk are ranked in a relatively lower place as 6th and 7th. PPP external benefits rank 5th which has a relatively neutral effect.

PPP risk & revenue of Northeast China ranks 7th. The reason lies in the fact that PPP external benefits are ranked in a relatively lower place as 7th. Both PPP project revenue and risk rank 4th which has a relatively neutral effect.

3.3.4 PPP Development Potential

As the PPP mode means that the government cooperates with private capital to participate in public infrastructure construction, the PPP development potential reflects the unmet need for public infrastructure in a region. The greater this demand is, the more opportunities there are for PPP projects to be carried out in the future. Meanwhile the willingness of local governments to participate in PPP market in order to enhance public services is more significant, forming a stronger driving force for the promotion and development of the PPP mode. The indicator serves as a powerful predictor of the potential PPP market size of a region, pointing out where the PPP mode will have the brightest development prospect.

The PPP development potential indicator is composed of four third-grade indicators. They are infrastructure level, urbanization rate, infrastructure investment, reserve projects. Furthermore, the infrastructure level is composed of 17 fourth-grade indicators which reflect the unmet need for public infrastructure, including electricity consumption per capita, water supply per capita, public transport vehicles per 10 000 citizens, road network density, etc.; Urbanization rate itself is a basic indicator; Infrastructure investment is composed of three fourth-grade indicators, including the annual growth rate of infrastructure investment, amount of infrastructure investment per year and the ratio of infrastructure investment to GDP, which evaluate the current performance of infrastructure investment of a region; Reserve projects is composed of four fourth-grade indicators, including the number of reserve projects, the amount of investment of them, the corresponding growth rate of the number and the amount of investment. The PPP development potential indicator framework and explanation are shown in Figure 3.50 and Table 3.58.

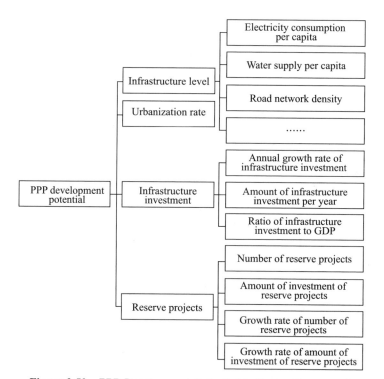

Figure 3.50 PPP Development Potential Indicator Framework

Table 3.58　Composition and Explanation of PPP Development Potential

Second-grade	Third-grade	Fourth-grade	Calculation	Reason for selecting this indicator
PPP devel-op-ment potential	Infrastructure level	Electricity consumption per capita	Total electricity consumption/regional population	These indicators measure the level of infrastructure of a region with negative relationship, reflecting the potential demand for the PPP mode in the future
		Water supply per capita	Total urban water supply/regional population	
		Road network density	Road mileage/area of the region	
		Drainage pipeline density	Total length of drainage pipe/area of the region	
		Sewage treatment capacity	Designed capacity of sewage treatment plants to treat sewage per day and night	
		Harmless treatment rate of domestic garbage	Amount of domestic garbage treated harmlessly/total amount of domestic garbage	
		City gas penetration rate	Ratio of gas users to total population	
		Internet penetration rate	Ratio of Internet users to total population	
		Number of elderly service beds per 10 000 people	Number of elderly service beds/regional population× 10 000	
		Public library building area per 10 000 people	Total area of public library buildings/regional population× 10 000	
		Public transport vehicles per 10 000 people	Number of public transport vehicles/regional population× 10 000	

(continued)

Second-grade	Third-grade	Fourth-grade	Calculation	Reason for selecting this indicator
		Number of primary and secondary schools per 10 000 students	Number of primary and secondary schools/number of students in primary and secondary schools×10 000	
		Number of health technicians per 10 000 people	Number of health technicians/regional population×10 000	
		Number of beds in medical institutions per 10 000 people	Number of beds in medical and health institutions/regional population×10 000	
		Number of public toilets per 10 000 people	Number of public toilets/regional population×10 000	
		Urban green coverage	Green area of built-up area/total area of built-up areas	
		Green area per capita	Total green area/regional population	
	Urbanization rate	Urbanization rate	Urban population/total population	The progress of urbanization will constantly generate great and diverse demand for infrastructure and public services, which means a promising prospect for PPP mode

(continued)

Second-grade	Third-grade	Fourth-grade	Calculation	Reason for selecting this indicator
	Infrastructure investment	Growth rate of infrastructure investment	Quoted	The higher the indicator is, the more rapidly the demand for infrastructure investment grows, providing a good condition for PPP development because infrastructure investment is an important form of PPP projects
		Amount of infrastructure investment	Quoted	The indicator directly measures the demand for infrastructure investment of a region as an important form of PPP projects
		Ratio of infrastructure investment to GDP	Amount of infrastructure investment/regional GDP	The indicator measures the importance and activity of infrastructure investment in the local economy. This is another aspect of infrastructure investment and the potential of PPP development
	Reserve projects	Number of reserve projects	Quoted	Reserve projects are on the stage of identification and have potentials to be formal projects. The scale of reserve projects reflects the future scale of PPP projects

(continued)

Second-grade	Third-grade	Fourth-grade	Calculation	Reason for selecting this indicator
		Amount of investment of reserve projects	Quoted	Measuring the growth trend of reserve projects
		Growth rate of number of reserve projects	Quoted	
		Growth rate of Amount of investment of reserve projects	Quoted	

Based on the collected data, PPP development potential indicators of 31 provinces are calculated. The magnitude and ranking of PPP development potential are shown in Table 3.59 and Figure 3.51.

Table 3.59　Scores and Rankings of PPP Development Potential in 2017

Provinces	Score	Rank	Regions	Provinces	Score	Rank	Regions
Guizhou	63.85	1	Southwest	Anhui	47.32	17	East
Xinjiang	59.15	2	Northwest	Fujian	47.07	18	East
Henan	58.61	3	Central	Shandong	46.70	19	East
Hubei	58.26	4	Central	Shanxi	43.27	20	North
Yunnan	57.98	5	Southwest	Guangdong	42.54	21	South
Tibet	57.34	6	Southwest	Jilin	41.67	22	Northeast
Sichuan	56.51	7	Southwest	Chongqing	41.63	23	Southwest
Guangxi	52.47	8	South	Ningxia	38.82	24	Northwest
Jiangxi	50.32	9	East	Inner Mongolia	38.30	25	North
Shaanxi	49.67	10	Northwest	Liaoning	37.61	26	Northeast
Hebei	49.53	11	North	Tianjin	37.38	27	North

(continued)

Provinces	Score	Rank	Regions	Provinces	Score	Rank	Regions
Hunan	48.88	12	Central	Jiangsu	37.06	28	East
Gansu	48.64	13	Northwest	Zhejiang	36.78	29	East
Heilongjiang	48.47	14	Northeast	Shanghai	25.76	30	East
Hainan	47.68	15	South	Beijing	23.83	31	North
Qinghai	47.59	16	Northwest				

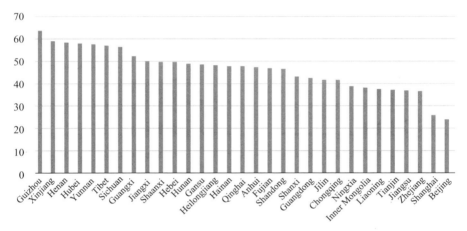

Figure 3.51   Scores and Rankings of PPP Development Potential in 2017

Guizhou ranks 1st, mainly owing to infrastructure level, infrastructure investment, urbanization rate and reserve projects ranking 6th, 4th, 2nd and 2nd separately. It should be noted that infrastructure level and urbanization rate are all negative indicators here, which means that the weaker the indicator is, the higher PPP development potential is and the greater demand for PPP projects there will be. Therefore, the low level of infrastructure and urbanization and large scale of reserve projects will stimulate the development of PPP mode in Guizhou.

Henan ranks 3rd. The main reason is that infrastructure level, infrastructure investment, urbanization rate, reserve projects all rank in a high place as 7th, 7th, 7th and 5th. Although lying in a relatively economically developed region, the province fails to reach a high level of infrastructure and has a high ratio of rural population. In addition, the great infrastructure investment and large scale of reserve projects also create more chances for PPP development.

Hubei ranks 4th, which can be attributed to the high ranking of infrastructure investment and reserve projects as 5th and 1st separately. Infrastructure level and urbanization rate both of which rank 19th have a relatively neutral impact. The province lies in a relatively developed region and benefits from nice infrastructure environment. But the large-scale infrastructure investment and rapid growth rate of reserve projects recently make it rank high in PPP development potential.

Ningxia ranks 24th, mainly due to the bad grades of infrastructure level, infrastructure investment, reserve projects which rank 26th, 24th and 23rd separately. Urbanization rate ranks in a medium place as 17th. Although lying in the remote northwestern region, the province gets a low score of infrastructure level (as a negative indicator). So, the demand for infrastructure investment is less.

Shanghai ranks 30th. The main reason is that infrastructure level, infrastructure investment and urbanization rate indicators are ranked in a low place as 30th, 28th and 31st separately. Reserve projects rank in a medium place as 16th. Developed areas such as Shanghai usually have sound infrastructure facilities and a lower ratio of infrastructure investment to GDP. The growth rate of infrastructure investment and reserve projects are also limited, leading to a smaller PPP development potential.

Same as above, the average score of each geographic region is calculated and ranked for comparison and analysis. The result is shown in Table 3.60 and Figure 3.52.

Table 3.60　Scores and Rankings of PPP Development Potential of 7 Regions in 2017

No.	Regions	Provinces involved in the calculation	Average score
1	Southwest China	Sichuan, Guizhou, Yunnan, Chongqing, Tibet	55.46
2	Central China	Henan, Hubei, Hunan	55.25
3	Northwest China	Shaanxi, Gansu, Qinghai, Ningxia, Xinjiang	48.77
4	South China	Guangdong, Guangxi, Hainan	47.56

(continued)

No.	Regions	Provinces involved in the calculation	Average score
5	Northeast China	Heilongjiang, Jilin, Liaoning	42.58
6	East China	Shanghai, Jiangsu, Zhejiang, Anhui, Fujian, Jiangxi, Shandong	41.57
7	North China	Beijing, Tianjin, Shanxi, Hebei, Inner Mongolia	38.46

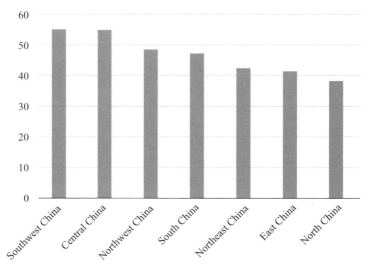

Figure 3.52　PPP Development Potential of 7 Regions in 2017

PPP development potential of Southwest China ranks 1st, basically owing to the fact that infrastructure level, infrastructure investment, urbanization rate and reserve projects all rank the top as 1st, 2nd, 1st and 2nd separately.

PPP development potential of Central China ranks 2nd, basically because of infrastructure investment and reserve projects rank in a high place as 1st. Both of infrastructure level and urbanization rate rank 3rd, which is in a medium place.

PPP development potential of Northwest China ranks 3rd. mainly due to urbanization rate ranking 2nd. Infrastructure level, infrastructure investment, reserve projects which rank 5th, 4th and 4th separately have a relatively neutral impact.

PPP development potential of South China ranks 4th. Infrastructure level gets a good score and ranks 2nd. Infrastructure investment and urbanization rate rank in a medium place as 3rd and 4th. But its reserve projects which rank 7th hinder.

PPP development potential of Northeast China ranks 5th. Infrastructure level and urbanization rate rank in a medium place as 4th and 5th separately. But infrastructure investment and reserve projects are ranked in an inferior place as 7th and 6th, incurring a negative impact.

PPP development potential of East China ranks 6th. The reason lies in the fact that both of infrastructure level and urbanization rate are ranked in a relatively lower place as 6th. And both of Infrastructure investment and reserve projects rank 5th which have a relatively neutral effect.

PPP development potential of North China ranks 7th, which can be attributed to the low rankings of infrastructure level, infrastructure investment and urbanization rate as 7th, 6th and 7th separately. Reserve projects rank in a medium place as 3rd.

Chapter 4 Policy Suggestions

4.1 Government Guarantee Area

4.1.1 Promote the Development of PPP in the Central and Northern Regions from both Macro and Micro Aspects.

On July 23, 2018, Premier Li Keqiang pointed out at the State Council Executive Meeting that it is necessary to guarantee the funding needs of projects under construction. We must urge local governments to revitalize fiscal stock funds, and guide financial institutions to ensure the financing needs of financial platform companies in accordance with the principle of marketization, and avoid the halt of funds supply or unfinished for the necessary projects under construction. In the process of building PPP projects, the financial funds from the government are important source of funds and guarantees for the project. Therefore, the abundance of financial funds in various provinces has an important impact on the development of local PPP projects.

According to the calculation results of the PPP government fiscal support index, the data of the central and northern regions lag significantly behind the southeastern region, indicating that the economic development level and fiscal capacity of the central and northern regions are relatively backward. This is the same as the measurement of GDP in 2017. It can be seen that the lower level of economic development and government fiscal revenue is very unfavorable for the development of local PPP projects and the coordinated development of national PPP projects.

The relevant data in the Operation Index in this book indicates that the degree of regional economic development is basically positively correlated with the operating rate and implementation rate of local PPP projects.

'PPP' is the abbreviation of 'Public Private Partnership'. If the government's fiscal capacity does not allow the government to give local enterprises sufficient support in terms of funds, it will be very unfavorable for the government to establish long-term relationship and stable cooperation with the social capital. Due to insufficient government fiscal funds and low expenditure limits, the funds provided to PPP projects will be reduced accordingly. This results in a shortage of funds for project construction and the possibility of troubles in turnover will be greatly increased, and the projects will be more vulnerable to capital chain breaks and project failures.

From a micro perspective, the default rate and arrears rate of PPP projects will increase with the pressure of government financial, which is not conducive to the improvement of local government's reputation and the development of local PPP projects. The capital adequacy and goodwill of the partner (government) will usually be considered before social capital enters. Therefore, it is recommended that governments in economically backward regions formulate PPP projects based on their own development. For example, the government can help poor areas to develop poverty alleviation plans and provide appropriate financial support to help them implement them.

From a macro perspective, it is possible to appropriately increase central transfer payments or cut tax. Fund the construction of public infrastructure in the relevant provinces and implement education and medical service guarantees is also needed. In terms of financial investment, we can strengthen the deepening reform of the local financial market system, set investment incentives, encourage and introduce foreign capital, and give preferential tax and policy preferences to leading enterprises in the target region. In terms of business and industry, it is necessary to cultivate and support characteristic economic and key enterprises, increase support for local advantageous industries, and support high-tech industry development. The market environment of backward provinces should be changed in a targeted manner from multiple dimensions to enhance their financial capacity. Reduce debt levels, improve fiscal self-sufficiency, and provide good fiscal security for local PPP development is also important.

4.1.2 Establish and Improve PPP-related Laws and Regulations to Improve the Level of Nomocracy.

In 2017, China strengthened the construction of laws and regulations related to PPP. In response to problems in the development of local PPP projects, various provinces have issued corresponding regulatory requirements and guidance. However, while the total amount of laws and regulations has increased, the overall level is still not high, and the difference in the level of nomocracy in various regions is a more prominent problem.

In East China and South China, the system of government construction is relatively complete, the decision-making process is highly transparent, and there is a strong awareness to ensure the development of PPP projects in the local area through law, which provides a good demonstration role for other regions. Areas with relatively backward development of nomocracy urgently need to change their concepts, strengthen legislation and enforcement against PPP projects, and actively formulate policies and measures to achieve "overtaking".

The synergy and driving action between cities cannot be ignored. The areas adjacent to geographical areas have more similarities and greater comparability. Relatively backward provinces should select reference objects to conduct multi-dimensional comparison, and actively explore the development road of PPP. They should develop and introduce effective laws and regulations according to local conditions. Exert regional synergy in order to improve the balance of regional development.

4.1.3 Local Governments need to Further Improve the Matching between Fund Size and Project Size, Improve the Internal Structure Design of the Fund, Prevent and Control Risks in order to Promote Balanced Development between Regions.

In 2016, with the approval of the State Council, the Ministry of Finance and the multi-party social capital established Chinese PPP Fund with a registered capital of 180 billion yuan, which is intended to provide financial support for the development of PPP projects around the country. At the same time, local governments are also actively studying the establishment of PPP guidance funds to improve the availability of funds for the landing and development of local PPP projects. The two comprehensively reflect the government's financial protection of PPP projects. In 2017, China PPP Funds have been launched in various places, making project decisions and providing financing assistance. More governments have set up local guidance funds at the provincial level, and the government's financial protection has been greatly improved.

However, the overall scale of PPP fund is not large enough. In face of huge number and scale of projects, a large amount of social capital is strongly required to ensure steady operation. The scale of funds varies greatly across different regions and the mismatch between funds and projects still exists. At the same time, these funds fail to isolate or control internal risks very well. Their securities and supporting capacities still need to be enhanced.

On one hand, the local government needs to match funds' scale with projects' scale further. On the other hand, the internal structure of PPP funds needs to be improved and the risk isolation along with internal control should be strengthened. The Ministry of Finance ought to make overall planning and arrangement in order to give support to PPP projects in accordance with varying development conditions across regions and reduce default risk in those project-concentrated regions. Achieving regional balance of PPP's development is also a necessity.

4.1.4 Further Normalize Working Procedures, Enhance Working Efficiency, Improve the Transparency and Credibility of the Government.

The degree to which the government is trusted by the public has a fundamental impact on the development of PPP. Governments' credibility is closely related to the implementation of public functions and the realization of public goals. Except for northeast China, in 2017 local governments in all regions across China performed well in the aspect of credibility, the quantitative scores of which are close to each other and can basically reach a good level.

When it comes to specific measures, three aspects are worth considering. Firstly, the government should perform its functions more reasonably and effectively. Standardizing working process and enhancing working efficiency are also indispensable. Secondly, the transparency of the government needs to be improved. Local governments are supposed to take public appeal into account more often when choosing the scope and frequency of information disclosure. Thirdly, conduct field visits to areas with good credibility in order to get acknowledge of local conditions and sum up experience.

PPP is a kind of cooperation between the government and social capital. The credibility of the government directly affects social capital's recognition and willingness to invest. A trusted government can achieve its goals in a more orderly and efficient way. At the same time, the public's sense of gain can be fulfilled as well.

4.2 Private Participation Area

4.2.1 Reduce Financing Costs and Increase the Overall Participation Rate of Social Capital.

As the cleaning up and rectification of Ministry of Finance's PPP management library comes to an end and Political Bureau of the CPC Central

Committee's meeting has decided to strengthen infrastructure construction, banks and other financial institutions have begun to increase investment in infrastructure construction field and some enterprises feel the remission of PPP's financing problem to some extent. However, when it comes to lowering threshold for social capital and improving social capital's participation rate, we still have a long way to go.

In policy terms, the central government's attitude to local governments' debt becomes much more cautious. More efforts have been made to reduce local governments' debt as well as recessive debt. PPP projects which are related to government debt or recessive debt are required to dissolve the debt within a time limit, which means a more significant role of social capital in the field of infrastructure construction. Therefore, the proportion of social capital in PPP projects will gradually increase. Correspondingly, social capital will take on more responsibilities and the financing pressure will gradually increase. Meanwhile, however, the monetary and credit environment has undergone a structural change. The "new rules on capital management" requires that the leverage ratio of financial system be reduced and shadow banking business, which flooded in the past, ought to be changed. The tightening of market funds will lead to an increase in financial cost, thus exerting pressure on social capital that is willing to participate in PPP projects.

Therefore, in the context of increasing financing cost, it is necessary to reduce the lending rate of PPP projects offered by banks and other financial institutions through policy guidance so as to reduce the financing pressure of enterprises that participate in PPP projects. Responsibilities ought to be clarified and the transparency of the projects needs improving. While strictly controlling the leverage ratio of local governments, it is also necessary to prevent local governments from transferring debts to enterprises and prevent the phenomenon of "real debt with shares". While implementing the "new rules on capital management" to prevent systemic financial risks, it is necessary to ensure market liquidity and eliminate financial institutions' reluctance to provide enterprises with sufficient liquidity.

4.2.2 Increase Participation Rate of Private Enterprises & Hong Kong, Macao and Taiwan Enterprises & Foreign-funded Enterprises.

The biggest difficulty that social capital encounters is financing. In the context of the Ministry of Finance's cleaning up PPP management library, financial institutions are rather cautious and the approval rate of private enterprises' financing demand is extremely low. In the bond market, however, the polarization is also obvious. Investors prefer state-owned enterprises to private enterprises. The insufficient subscription of private enterprises' bond is common and those with high credit rating are no exception. According to the 2017 annual report offered by the national PPP comprehensive information platform, in most provinces or municipalities private enterprises account for less than 50%, with the exception of only a few. Therefore, only through improving financing conditions and creating a fair market environment for private enterprises can the participation rate of private enterprises be effectively enhanced.

In terms of specific measures, first of all it is necessary to create a fair and just bidding environment. The phenomenon of "running through the back door" and regional discrimination should be eliminated. Meanwhile, unfair treatment of private enterprises needs to be reduced. Only through these measures can we ensure that enterprises winning the bid are those of competence and experience. Secondly, create a relatively relaxed business environment for PPP participating enterprises and reduce taxes and fees accurately. Guide social capital to participate in PPP projects, promote the benign cycle of PPP model, and enhance social capital's operation experience. Third, reduce the capital burden of enterprises. Financial institutions should be guided to lower the financing threshold for PPP participating enterprises. It is also important to ensure that enterprises have sufficient liquidity for the construction of multiple projects.

In addition, the enthusiasm of Hong Kong, Macao, Taiwan and foreign-funded enterprises also needs to be enhanced. According to the 2017 annual report offered by the national PPP comprehensive information platform, the proportion of Hong Kong, Macao, Taiwan and foreign investors is less than 10% in most provinces or municipalities, some of which attracts no theseinvestors at all. Compared with private enterprises, foreign-funded enterprises have relatively loose financing conditions, but they are not enthusiastic about investing PPP projects. Their understanding of PPP projects are not comprehensive and deep communication with local government is insufficient. As a result, they have doubts about the sustainability, return on investment and risks of PPP projects, which result in low PPP participation rate. Therefore, it is necessary to strengthen the communication between the government and Hong Kong, Macao, Taiwan and foreign-funded enterprises so as to relieve their concerns about PPP projects and guide them to realize the value of PPP. Only in this way can the enthusiasm of Hong Kong, Macao, Taiwan and foreign enterprises be aroused.

4.2.3 Establish Laws or Regulations regarding the Mechanism of Social Capital's Withdrawal and Improve the Construction of PPP Market in China.

The standardized withdrawal mode of social capital is conducive to improving the social capital's trust in PPP projects and benefits the development of PPP market. In recent years, China has launched PPP projects on a large scale and a large number of them have come into operation. Among these projects, however, only a few have expired and social capital has successfully withdrawn. Therefore, China strongly needs universal normative laws or regulations regarding social capital's withdrawal. The modes of withdrawal includes transfer after maturity, share repurchase, after-sale lease, IPO listing, asset securitization, PPP exchange and so on. The flexibility of withdrawal mode will greatly influence social capital's willingness to enter PPP market and is one of the indicators to measure the perfection of PPP market as well.

4.3 Project Operation Area

4.3.1 Optimize Resource Allocation

Optimize industrial resource allocation. In 2017, PPP projects within the top three industries account for a high proportion of total projects in each province, most of which range from 60% to 80%, and the highest one reaches 90%. PPP projects are concentrated in the fields of municipal engineering, transportation, ecological construction & environmental protection and urban comprehensive development. The main reason is that operation mode in these fields is relatively mature and China's demand for infrastructure is still high. Local government's relatively tight fiscal space also contributes to this. However, excessive concentration of resources in the same field is likely to lead to excessive competition and unbalanced development. In addition to GDP, local governments are supposed to improve urban and rural construction. In particular, they need to provide better public services and improve the lives of urban residents, which is related to as many as 18 fields where PPP can be applied. The state council has issued several documents advocating the application of PPP in agriculture, medical care, old-age care, culture, tourism and other fields as well.

Encourage diversification of PPP projects, explore ways to convert existing projects into PPP mode and develop PPP projects in new fields so as to provide cooperative channels for social capital to extensively invest in infrastructure and public utilities, ensure capital gains and achieve coordinated development. In order to expand the industry coverage of PPP, negative list management can be implemented to reduce restrictions on social capital and create equal opportunities. When valuating demonstration projects, it is necessary to consider whether the project explores new fields or employ new models according to local situations and whether the project belongs to the field supported by industrial policies. In order to allocate resources efficiently, industrial balance assessment in the annual conclusion of financial affordability demonstration is indispensable, so as to coordinate resources, improve work efficiency and adjust expenditure for next year.

Optimize regional resource allocation. In 2017, the average regional concentration ratio of PPP projects across China is 48%. There is a great difference between varying provinces, with the highest ones ranging from 70% to 80% and the lowest ones ranging from 20% to 30%. PPP can be applied in infrastructure, public services, environment protection and poverty alleviation. Therefore, overall planning for the financial resources should be made so as to help identify and develop high-quality projects. Information exchange channels across different levels of administrative areas counts as well, which facilitates social capital's access to a variety of information, promotes balanced development of regional economy and prevents regional difference from enlarging.

4.3.2 Strengthen Standardized Administration

The main measures to strengthen standardized administration are as follows.

1. Strict threshold for Ministry of Finance's PPP management library. In 2017, total investment of all the projects in the Ministry of Finance's PPP management library increases by 32%, and the total number of projects increased by 38%. While all the provinces or municipalities are promoting PPP projects into Ministry of Finance's PPP management library, some problems, such as shoddy quality, are exposed as well. The average landing rate of those projects in Ministry of Finance's PPP management library is only 40%, and the proportion of projects that have been publicly evaluated for value and demonstrated for financial affordability are just over half. Ministry of Finance's PPP management library is under dynamic management, and entering the management library itself is not an administrative licensing. However, from the perspective of social capital and financial institutions, entering Ministry of Finance's PPP management library or even being listed as model projects means the affirmation of project quality.

Therefore, on one hand, quality of projects in the Ministry of Finance's PPP management library should be strictly controlled. According to "Notice on Regulating Public-Private Partnership (PPP) project library integrated information management platform" ([2017] No.92) of the ministry of finance, PPP projects with three types of problems (not appropriate for PPP mode; insufficient preparation in advance; lack of performance payment) is strictly prohibited from entering project management library. It is necessary to enhance the standard of value-for-money evaluation and financial affordability demonstration, which includes attaching importance to quantitative analysis and calculation of projects, ensuring the feasibility of engineering design and financing arrangement and paying attention to the authenticity and rationality of projects. On the other hand, the government is required to clearly explain to the partner in negotiation or contract that entering PPP management library does not represent any financial commitment from the government, nor does it mean that there is no risk in the project. Listing PPP projects as model projects is aimed at put the demonstration benefits of PPP projects into practice and the nature of PPP projects cannot be changed.

2. Press ahead with clearing and rectification. By 2017, 174 projects have been cleared from Ministry of Finance's PPP management library or demonstration library, with a total investment of more than 600 billion yuan. The main reason for the removal from Ministry of Finance's project management library is that PPP mode is no longer used, and the main reason for the removal from Ministry of Finance's demonstration libraries is that these projects have not yet come into operation. Guided by "Notice on Regulating Public-Private Partnership (PPP) project library integrated information management platform" ([2017] No.92) of the ministry of finance, the rectification work is still in progress. PPP projects in the project management library should conform to the PPP implementation standard at full life cycle. Standards and measures are supposed to be established for the normalized and institutionalized quality review, supervision and rectification. Importance ought to be attached to the operation review of PPP projects. Remove those projects which fail to pass the operation review and integrate review performance into the government performance evaluation in order to make the cost of being removed greater than that of entering the project management library, which urges the government to carry out careful evaluation of PPP projects before application. Speed up the landing of PPP projects and ensure the quality of PPP projects via long-term institutional constraints. At the same time, it is necessary to follow up

the work after clearing and rectification. Ensure continued implementation of the agreement between the government and social capital after projects' being removed from Ministry of Finance's PPP management library. Deal with the problem of changing or even rescinding contract and clarify the responsibility allocation. Follow up the rectification projects in time and urge the rectification to be in place within the period.

3. Promote credit management. After the establishment of a fair and reasonable contract, the government shall perform duties in accordance with the contract. At present, whether the government can create conditions for the integration of resources is the most concerned issue of social capital. Due to the lack of credit or default records of the government, the cost of governments' default is not high and the change of government's leaders has a great impact on whether the contract can be continued. Therefore, the credit risk of the government is high and social capital tends to lose a lot after the default. Similarly, the default of social capital and financial institutions will directly lead to the suspension of construction, the rupture of capital chain and the project abortion. Therefore, an official credit system should be established to integrate all parties' credit information and make this system public, which can reduce information asymmetry of all parties and enhance social capital's willingness to participate. At the same time, improve the liability compensation mechanism after the breach of the contract in order to reduce the losses of the other participants.

4. Strengthening information disclosure. According to the requirements of the ministry of finance, projects in Ministry of Finance's PPP management library needs to disclose basic information and a number of documents, but the disclosure rate (feasibility report, implementation plan annex, procurement document, PPP contract) is less than 25% on average, and the disclosure rate of value-for-money evaluation and financial affordability demonstration is just over 50%. Therefore, firstly, local governments should be urged to timely submit or make up for the missing information. Secondly, clarification of main content of the PPP project over the entire life cycle is indispensable. To be specific, center around the realization of value-for-money evaluation to make the disclosure list, work out

various measures for sharing, dispute disposal during entire life cycle (preparation, bidding & purchasing, construction, operation, transfer and so on). Thirdly, the submission of quantitative data, early stage quantitative analysis of the project and the project operation quality assessment should be promoted. Forthly, local governments should strengthen local PPP information platform construction and timely release key information, such as local regulatory documents, PPP projects' progress, etc. Governments ought to make sure that information disclosure is organized, timely and accessible. Frequent feedback is necessary to prevent empty platform and lack of management. Ensure full information available and make the information platform serve the public, social capital, financial institutions. Public supervision is also indispensable. Finally, due to the public nature of PPP, its information disclosure can be combined with the openness of other public affair information by local government.

4.3.3 Guarantee the Income of PPP Projects & Prevent from the Risk of Insufficient Return

The risk of insufficient return refers to the risk that after finishing the project, the payment can't realize the expected return or even can't cover the initial investment. Although VFM (value of money) is one of the important targets that PPP projects intend to achieve, a too lowreturn will surely make the projects unattractive enough. This will discourage private capital from taking part in, and even make the project unavailable economically, which lead the project to fail.

Take Hangzhou Bay Bridge as an example. This PPP project takes the BOT mode and guarantees the private enterprises, who take part in as private capital, a right to charge the toll for 30 years. However, just at the opening, the bridge's actual traffic volume is proved to be more than 30% less than expectation. Even after operating for more than four years, the actual volume still can't reach the expectation. Since the toll is the only source of earnings of this project, the investment is probably hard to be covered. Besides, later on, more bridges and tunnels are completed around, which disperse the passengers and reduce the payment flow of the project. This increase the risk of insufficient return of this project, which may lead to recall the project in advance.

Hence we can see that the sufficient payment and stable cash flow take decisive roles on the success of the project. If the payment or cash flow can't be guaranteed, the financing of the project will also be affected, then increase its pressure on additional investment and cost of financing. This could be sowing the seeds of abortion of the project.

According to relative statistics, from 2014 up to now, among the projects that have reported their returns, there have been more than 120 cases where the return on investment was lower than the 5-year benchmark interest rate, accounting for about 6.1% of the total investment scale. Thus, to guarantee the feasible profit of PPP projects should be taken into serious consideration by the policy maker.

For this reason, first of all, the government should set reasonable bidding and return conditions, use technics to prevent from irrational and illegal bidding, thus to prevent from racing to the bottom or winning the bid with an unreasonable low price. To achieve this, it is necessary to choose return rate indicators that are clearly defined, accurate and suitable, to prove the fairness and comparability of decision-making and evaluation. While when estimating the profit of the projects, the government supervision should make the private sector use scientific and systematic methods to get reasonable and objective results, so as to avoid over-optimism or underestimation. Secondly, some local governments are reluctant to apply PPP mode to projects with high returns. This should be adjusted, to guide the local governments to treat the private capital fairly and let them share the return, only then will the quality of PPP projects will get guaranteed.

Besides, it is important to remind that to guarantee reasonable profits doesn't mean to promise exact or fixed returns. We should always obey the principal that the local government can't promise fixed returns, and the risk of the projects must be shared fairly between public and private capital. The reasonable profits that private partners can get depend on how well they finance, construct and operate the project, which can be restricted by KPI and recourse after default.

4.3.4 Establish Risk Identification and Allocation Mechanism & Enhance the Prevention and Control of Potential Risks

Risks of PPP projects comes from a variety of resources. The reason mainly lies in: too many different participants; complex disposition of responsibilities; too long construction periods; a lot of uncertainties when carried out actually. So it is common to see that the projects will face some difficulties and risks in actual. Thus, to make the project to be ran successfully, going through with the risk identification and allocation work in advance turns out to be important.

Firstly, the local governments should raise their awareness of risk management. The PPP sector in local governments should carry out risk management through the whole life cycle of PPP projects. Also, a unified, centralized PPP management information system is well needed to be established, which will classified the projects by their properties, periods, participants and so on and manage them in an organized way. This will also help to identify common risks and specific risks. Meanwhile, the local governments should introduce specialist on risk managements into PPP sector to help to identify and prevent from the risks efficiently.

Secondly, it's important to establish effective risk sharing mechanism and ensure its flexibility. The government should clearly claim PPP's risk sharing principal, establish effective risk sharing mechanism, to balance the risk that different parties take to fit the shares and duties they take. The risk allocation should hold on to "the most appropriate" principal, which means that based on different kinds of risks of PPP projects, let the party who can control and deal with the risks most appropriately to take this risk. Therefore, the local governments should let the public sectors take the risks come from their area, let the private sectors take the risks come from theirs, while let the public and private partnership share the common risk. Who takes what should be decided based on the kinds, levels of risks and a reasonable proportion.

In the process of implementation, an effective supervision mechanism should also be established. All the PPP sectors should improve their communication to clarify the target and content of supervision, to clarify who supervise whom, so as to standardize the supervision process and integrate the supervision methods, then they can work together to form a unified, thorough supervision system.

Finally, we should enhance the structure of deal which can separate projects' risks from investors' risks, so as to prevent private business risks from affecting PPP projects. No matter in China or internationally, most PPP takes the mode that set up an SPV (Special Purpose Vehicle) to carry out the project. SPV can effectively enhance the independence of PPP projects and reduce the shock from risks from private capital, which means that when the private side, because of any reason, is not able to continue its PPP project, this project can quickly be handled or taken over, with creating a relatively good legal basement to take new investors in. Otherwise, the project will be stacked into an awkward situation.

Chapter 5 Application for PKU · China PPP Index

5.1 PPP Index: Evaluate the Development of PPP among Provinces to Provide Reference for Investors

PPP index, built up from three aspects as government support, social participation and projects operation, thoroughly evaluate the development status and development prospects of PPP projects among provinces. Therefore, when the private capital consider to invest on PPP, the ranking PPP index yields can provide useful reference for them. Under the investment demand, by taking the overall indicators, investors will tend to invest in provinces that rank at more front.

Nowadays PPP in China is under the status that develop fast even wildly. Though now there are still some disorders in the market, such as unsteady policies, lack of contract spirit and unclear return mechanisms, with the more importance Chinese government attachs to PPP and the continuous publish of legal and policies, the PPP in China will become more standardized. With the improve of PPP, this mode will hold a larger market share and play a more important role in infrastructure construction by government. Thus, the local governments should attach importance to the perfection of PPP development environment. The PPP index can be used by provinces rank lower to find their drawbacks and make improvements. Only in this way can they attract outside investment to take part in local PPP projects.

5.2 Government Guarantee Index: Assess Government Fiscal capacity

The Government Guarantee Index can evaluate not only provinces' capability when financing PPP projects by government, but also the overall fiscal capacity among governments in different provinces. This part of index thoroughly consider the indicators which can assess the government fiscal status and available capital balance, like fiscal revenue, debt balance, fiscal self-sufficiency ratio and so on. In some ways, this reflects the level of one zone's economy development, financial capital sufficiency, then can measure the fitness to invest in this area.

Besides, when assessing governments' fiscal capacity on other projects, the framework this part of index provides is also useful to be referred. It can adopt other indicators in.

5.3 Private Participation Index

5.3.1 Assess Private Capital's Activeness to Drive the Local Governments to Raise the Ratio of Private Capital in PPP

PPP, partnership between public and private, it emphasize the role the private side plays in public infrastructure construction, which to improve the efficiency of projects operation and reduce the pressure of government finance. 'Business participation' (PPP Business Diversity) assesses participation level of private, foreign and Hong Kong, Macao and Taiwan enterprises, to examine the actual usage of private capital. For a long time, the local governments do have preference for state-owned enterprises when inviting bid for PPP. With the same quote and capital, the private enterprises are still inferior to those state-owned, which will prevent from pure private capital from participating in PPP projects and crack down their activeness. Therefore, 'PPP Enterprise Participation' will judge the degree private enterprises take part in PPP projects by calculating the ratio of numbers of private, foreign, Hong Kong, Macao and Taiwan enterprises to that of the total, to create incentives for local governments to adopt and attract private capital.

Moreover, this index can motivate the local governments to raise the ratio of private capital to the number of enterprises that join PPP and to the amount of investment, which will make better use of the efficiency and experience of private capital.

5.3.2 Assess Nongovernmental Capital's Activeness to Drive the Local Governments to Raise the Ratio of Nongovernmental Capital

'PPP Business participation' (PPP Social capital) assesses the overall potential of nongovernmental capital among provinces. This index examines the scale and ratio of nongovernmental capital among provinces through indicators like investment scale of social capital, investment ratio of social capital to the total, local enterprises IPO ratio and so on. PPP projects needs wide participation of nongovernmental capital, thus their investment capacity and scale are all reasonable indicators to assess how much the enterprises are involved in PPP.

Besides, this indicator can get incentives to governments among provinces to let them take actions, to introduce the social side with comprehensive capacity in, raise the ratio of their shares and promote them to fit in the projects more deeply. Thus the local nongovernmental capital will be well used in construction of PPP projects, to make the construction and operation more efficiency and keep its sustainable growth.

5.4　Project Operation Index

5.4.1　Evaluate the Potential of PPP among Provinces

PKU China PPP Index's Secondary Index, PPP Development Potential, is to evaluate PPP's potential market in the future, which mainly depends on one zone's infrastructure construction, degree of urbanization, construction investment scale and project storage scale. This secondary index can be used to analyze different sectors' contribution to PPP development potential, and to find out their relative strengths and weaknesses. For example, Beijing's PPP Development Potential score is 23.83, ranking the 31st. That is because Beijing's infrastructure construction is relatively complete, which means its increasing space and investment's growth space are comparatively small. Besides this, Beijing holds fewer projects reservation. Beijing performs weak on PPP's development potential with these specific causes.

5.4.2 Applied to Evaluate the Overall Benefits of Regional PPP Projects

The second-level Indicator "PPP risk & revenue" of PKU · China PPP Index System evaluate the overall benefits of regional PPP projects in terms of PPP project return, PPP project risk and PPP external benefits, which can be applied to analyze benefits and risks of PPP projects from various aspects. What's more, it can be used to analysis advantage and disadvantage.

For example, Beijing's 'PPP risk & revenue' scores 30.46, ranking 31st. The advantage of Beijing lies in its higher level of return of PPP projects (3rd). But it has relatively great risk exposure of PPP projects (31st) and few external benefits (28th), making the general situation of PPP projects in Beijing still backward.

Appendix: Calculation of PKU · China PPP Index

1. Determination of Indicators of PKU · China PPP Index

PKU · China PPP Index emphasizes systematicness, objectivity, scientificalness, operability and comparability. It adopts an evaluation system combining both subjective and objective methods, analyzing the development of PPP markets in each province comprehensively. Based on macroeconomic theories, the expert method and Analytic Hierarchy Process method, this book analyzes the PPP market in each province in detail.

The index strives to achieve the following four objectives: The first is to measure the level of local government guarantee and hope that the local government can provide better protection for the operation of PPP projects; The second is to reflect the overall operational status of the PPP market, to guide the entry of private funds, to provide reference for institutional investors; The third is to standardize the behavior of private participants participating in the PPP market, so that the PPP market operates in a healthy and orderly manner; The fourth is to assess the development opportunities of different provinces through the indicator of PPP development protential.

PKU · China PPP Index is an objective indicator system. The three first-grade indicators including government guarantee index, private participation index and project operation index measure the PPP development in each province from three dimensions. The indicator system consists of 3 first-grade indicators, 14 second-grade indicators, 40 third-grade indicators and 123 fourth-grade indicators. Considering accuracy, comprehensiveness and availability of data, each grade of indicators is synthesized step by step with weighting calculation.

2. Procedure of Constructing PKU · China PPP Index

The first step is the design of PKU · China PPP index system. The indicators all derive from authoritative organizations such as the Ministry of Finance of the People's Republic of China, the National Bureau of Statistics, and the official websites of the provincial governments. The number of indicators is appropriate and the data is completely objective, ensuring the perfectness of PKU · China PPP index system.

The second step is data acquisition and processing. Raw data is collected from following sources: Data released by the Ministry of Finance and other government departments, such as 2017 Annual Report (Ministry of Finance) from Project Management Library on the National PPP Integrated Information Platform; the statistical bulletin of the National Economic and Social Development of different provinces; the implementation of the budgets of the provinces in 2017, and the draft budget for 2018; Rongbang Ruiming database; Wind database; other channels.

PKU · China PPP Indicators fully consider the data sources' stability, continuity, normalization and uniformity of calibration, making the data comparable and easy to calculate. At the same time, it emphasizes the scientific processing of data, supplemented by the weight system for calculation, avoiding the ambiguity and non-retroactivity of the indicators. It insures that the analysis is objective and the procedure can be replicated.

The third step is data verification. Through expert and professors' repeated argumentation and multi-dimensional comparison and monitoring of data, the relevant indicators is processed synchronously and standardized.

The fourth step is the modeling and calculation index. Combining with the previous theoretical research and the corresponding data, China PPP index model can be established. Then the results of 2017 annual index are calculated.

The PKU · China PPP index system has passed expert argumentation. The indicators are complementary and less correlation, avoiding both overlapping and missing features. They complement each other and comprehensively cover all aspects of PPP market development. They are representative and comparable, and indicators with sharp difference are in different categories. The weight system of PKU · China PPP Index is authoritative and scientific since a large amount of suggestions by professors are considered.

3. Raw Data Processing

The processing of raw data includes positive-correlation correction and standardization. Since the raw data of different indicators are different in dimension which makes indicators incomparable, the construction of indicators needs to eliminate the dimensional difference. This can be realized though data standardization so that the numerical value can reflect the level of index accurately. Specifically, the book applies initialization transformation to achieve this.

The fourth grade indicators contain various types of indicators such as scale, quantity, and ratio which differ in units and meanings. It is necessary to conduct de-scale operations to standardize them. In this process, the standardization of the fourth grade indicators is carried out by relativization method based on the change range of the indicators.

Let the maximum value of the k-th indicator be M, the minimum value be m (where $k = 1, 2, \ldots, n$), and the original data be X_k. According to the positive-correlation and negative-correlation characteristics of the index, the initialization of the indicators is as follows:

When the indicator X_k is a positive-correlation indicator, the value after initialization transformation is $x_k = \dfrac{X_k - m}{M - m}$;

When the indicator X_k is a negative-correlation indicator, the value after initialization transformation is $x_k = \dfrac{M - X_k}{M - m}$;

Through the above transformation, the dimensionless indicators are obtained.

4. Calculation of PKU · China PPP Index

On the basis of the establishment of the indicator system, the weights of each indicator are determined, and the sub-indicators are linearly weighted according to the weights level by level, leading to the aggregated PKU · China PPP index. The setting of index weights plays an important role in the final result of PKU · China PPP Index. At present, there are two major types of weight setting methods: objective weighting method and subjective weighting method. The objectiveweighting method relies on the raw data of each indicator and calculates the index weight of the original data under certain statistical standards. This method is completely independent of human subjective judgment and therefore has strong objectivity, but the shortcoming is that it ignores the economic significance analysis of the indicators. From the perspective of methodology, this method relies entirely on historical data, which essentially reflects the historical and post-viewing information value and cannot conform to the forward-looking characteristics of PPP development. Therefore, in order to better guide the promotion of PPP development, this book mainly adopts the expert method which endows weights subjectively, supplemented by the indicator quantity method and the analytic hierarchy process to determine the final index weights. Specifically, under the expert method, experts are invited to participate in seminars and express opinions on determining weights with corresponding reasons provided. Then the weight system is constructed after overall consideration. The analytic hierarchy method is shown in Table 1.1. It determines the relative weight between indictors by pairwise comparison at first, which represent relative importance between different indicators, then gives the weight of each indicator eventually in a comprehensive way.

Analytic Hierarchy Method

Indicator Comparison	Weight Comparison
Equally important	Equal
More important	Larger
Most important	Maximum

Postscript

The Peking University China PPP Index Report is first launched by the Peking University PPP Research Center. Based on the research and evaluation of the development of China's PPP market, this book constructs the PKU · China PPP index from the perspectives of government guarantee, private participation and project operation, in order to reflect the development of PPP in various provinces in China comprehensively and accurately. At the same time, we provide some relevant thinking and policy recommendations to promote the development of China's PPP market, and hope to make some contribution to help bulid a healthy, stable and rapid China's PPP market.

The PKU · China PPP Index and its report can be successfully launched. In the first place, we need to thank the China Public Private Partnerships Center. China Public Private Partnerships Center provided a large number of PPP-related data, which provides a solid data foundation for the calculation of the index. Beijing Rongbang Ruiming Investment Management Co., Ltd. also provided partial data support for the calculation of PKU · China PPP index.

We have received much precious support from different experts in the process of writing the PKU · China PPP Index Research Report. They have provided many constructive professional suggestions. I appreciate it very much for your support from deep of my heart. In particular, I would like to thank: Jiao Xiaoping (China Public Private Partnerships Center), Sun Qixiang (Peking University PPP Research Center), Han Bin (China Public Private Partnerships Center), Deng Bing (Peking University PPP Research Center), Xie Fei (China

PPP Center), Xia Yingzhe (China PPP Center), Zhao Fuqing (China PPP Center), Zhang Ge (China PPP Center), Li Boya (Peking University PPP Research Center), Zhang Han (Beijing Fortune Consulting Co., Ltd.), Peng Song (Beijing Rongbang Ruiming Investment Management Co., Ltd.), Sun Jinyu (Strategic Research Institute of Oriental Garden Co., Ltd.) Sun Mengfan (China Life Investment Holdings Co., Ltd.) and Ren Bo (CITIC Trust Co., Ltd.).

The head of the research group is Professor Wang Yiming, the head of the Department of Finance at Peking University School of Economics. Other members of the group include: Wang Lifu, Dong Jingyan, Liang Yue, Liu Weiqi, Shao Ruicheng, Zhang Qiqi, Zhu Tong and Song Yanna.

PKU · China PPP index is a summary and evaluation of China PPP's achievements since 2014. It also contains recommendations and expectations for future PPP development. Due to the limited time and energy of the members of the research group, coupled with the difficulties in information disclosure and data acquisition, there are still some inadequacies in the PKU China PPP index. We hope that readers can criticize and propose precious suggestions to help us gradually revise and improve PPP index.

PKU PPP Index Research Group